Teaching
Mathematics
Meaningfully

Teaching Mathematics Meaningfully

Solutions for Reaching Struggling Learners

by

David H. Allsopp, Ph.D.
University of South Florida
Tampa, Florida

Maggie M. Kyger, Ph.D.
James Madison University
Harrisonburg, Virginia

and

LouAnn H. Lovin, Ph.D.
James Madison University
Harrisonburg, Virginia

PAUL H. BROOKES PUBLISHING CO.®

Baltimore • London • Sydney

Paul H. Brookes Publishing Co.
Post Office Box 10624
Baltimore, Maryland 21285-0624

www.brookespublishing.com

Typeset by Barton Matheson Willse & Worthington, Baltimore, Maryland.
Manufactured in the United States of America by
George H. Buchanan Printing, Bridgeport, New Jersey.

Library of Congress Cataloging-in-Publication Data

Allsopp, David, Ph.D.
    Teaching mathematics meaningfully : solutions for reaching struggling learners /
by David H. Allsopp, Maggie M. Kyger, and LouAnn H. Lovin.
        p.   cm.
    Includes bibliographical references and index.
    ISBN-13: 978-1-55766-866-0 (pbk.)
    ISBN-10: 1-55766-866-3 (pbk.)
    1. Mathematics—Study and teaching (Elementary)   2. Mathematics—Study and
teaching (Middle school)   3. Mathematics—Study and teaching (Secondary)
4. Attention-deficit-disordered youth—Education.   5. Learning disabled teenagers—
Education.   I. Kyger, Maggie M.   II. Lovin, LouAnn H.   III. Title.

QA13.A44 2007
371.9'0447—dc22   2007001640

British Library Cataloguing in Publication data are available from the British Library.

Contents

About the Authors

David H. Allsopp, Ph.D., Associate Professor of Special Education, College of Education, University of South Florida, 4202 East Fowler Avenue, Tampa, Florida 33620

Prior to his work at the University of South Florida, Dr. Allsopp was a middle school special education teacher. He holds a doctorate in special education with a minor in leadership from the University of Florida. Dr. Allsopp's research and writing interests include effective instructional methods for struggling learners emphasizing mathematics instruction, effective practices for helping students achieve social and behavioral success, and the application of technology in the preparation and professional development of special education teachers. Dr. Allsopp served as co-author with Esther Minskoff, Ph.D., of *Academic Success Strategies for Adolescents with Learning Disabilities and ADHD* (Paul H. Brookes Publishing Co., 2003).

Maggie M. Kyger, Ph.D., Associate Professor and Chair, Department of Exceptional Education, MSC 6908, James Madison University, Harrisonburg, Virginia 22807

Dr. Kyger, who earned her doctorate from the University of Virginia, is a former special education teacher whose current research activities include effective instruction for students with special needs, teacher candidate preparation, and collaboration and co-teaching models. She has also worked as a consultant and professional development trainer in the areas of positive behavioral support and effective academic strategies for students with attention and learning problems. Dr. Kyger co-directs Learning Leaders, a mentoring program for young children with learning and attentional problems, at the Alvin Baird Center in Harrisonburg.

LouAnn H. Lovin, Ph.D., Associate Professor and Chair, Department of Middle, Secondary, and Mathematics Education, College of Education, MSC 6912, James Madison University, Harrisonburg, Virginia 22807

Dr. Lovin, a former classroom teacher, earned her doctorate in mathematics education from the University of Georgia. She teaches mathematics methods and mathematics content courses for prospective prekindergarten through eighth-grade teachers as well as practicing classroom teachers. Dr. Lovin specializes in research on teacher knowledge; in particular she explores the nature of the mathematical knowledge needed for teaching mathematics in meaningful ways. She coauthored the *Teaching Student-Centered Mathematics* series for Grades K–3, 3–5, and 5–8, with John A. Van de Walle (Allyn & Bacon, 2005).

Acknowledgments

We would like to thank all of the students, teachers, parents, and researchers who have been instrumental in helping us to better understand the needs of struggling learners in mathematics. Although we could not possibly list everyone, there are two individuals who we would especially like to acknowledge: Cecil Mercer, noted special educator, whose initial research and writing in the area of mathematics informed the field on how the application of effective practices in special education can be effectively applied to mathematics; and John A. Van de Walle, whose work in mathematics education has been so influential in helping teachers and teacher educators better understand student-centered mathematics instruction. Finally, we would like to thank all of the teachers we have worked with who have helped us learn how the methods described in this book can be effectively applied in classrooms.

I

How This Book Can Help Teachers and Their Students

+	⟋⟋	÷	4x	×	7³

1

Introduction

Welcome to *Teaching Mathematics Meaningfully: Solutions for Reaching Struggling Learners.* This chapter explains the purpose of the book and for whom the book is written, the type of students this information hopes to serve, the book's organization, and how the book can be used to meet the needs of teachers in a variety of educational settings. In addition, this chapter introduces a professional development web site that was co-developed by the authors to enhance the understanding and ease of use of the information described in this book.

PURPOSE

The purpose of this book is to help teachers of struggling learners to understand mathematics in meaningful ways. *Meaning* is the seminal theme of this book. Creating access for struggling learners to the meaning of mathematics is the focus of the strategies described herein. To create such access, teachers must be effective *decision makers.* To help struggling learners become mathematical problem solvers, teachers must be problem solvers themselves. This book is organized to provide teachers and those who want to become teachers with an informed yet practical process for doing this very important job.

Two primary bodies of literature and practice—special education and mathematics education—inform the book's content. The authors of this book represent these two disciplines of special education and mathematics education. Collaboration between these two disciplines is essential for this book to achieve its purpose. Both the content and the pedagogy must be represented and integrated in an informed and accurate way if the content of K–12 mathematics is to be made accessible to struggling learners.

AUDIENCE FOR THE BOOK

This book is written for any educator or educator in training who wants to enhance his or her ability to teach mathematics effectively to struggling learners. Special educators, elementary educators, middle and high school mathematics educators, preservice and in-service teachers alike can all benefit from this book.

The emphasis of this book is on *how* to teach mathematics to struggling learners. Although an understanding of and a value for teaching the big ideas of mathematics in general is a critical component of the instructional framework presented in this book and is covered in Section II, it is assumed that readers have at least a basic understanding of the mathematics curriculum (i.e., mathematics concepts) that they are responsible for teaching. If they do not, then it is assumed that they have access to additional resources for learning about the mathematics curriculum. Van de Walle and Lovin (2006a; 2006b; 2006c) are excellent resource books that can help teachers enhance their mathematical content knowledge as well as their pedagogical content knowledge (e.g., how children conceive of mathematical ideas versus how adults do, which kinds of representations are helpful or problematic in helping students understand particular mathematical concepts).

WHO ARE STRUGGLING LEARNERS?

The phrase *struggling learners* can mean different things to different people. For the purpose of this book, struggling learners include 1) students with identified disabilities that affect learning, particularly students with cognition-based disabilities (e.g., learning disabilities, attention-deficit/hyperactivity disorder (ADHD), mild to moderate developmental disabilities, and traumatic brain injury); and 2) students who experience significant difficulties with learning in school but who are not identified as having a disability, traditionally identified in the literature as *students at risk for school failure.* Students from diverse cultures and students who are English language learners also may benefit from many of the strategies that are described in this book. However, the research base that supports the information in this book, in large part, does not address these specific groups of students directly.

HOW THE BOOK IS ORGANIZED

The book is organized into four sections and two appendices. Section I, How This Book Can Help Teachers and Their Students, provides an overview of the book's purpose and organization (this chapter) and provides a conceptual framework that integrates four universal features of effective mathematics instruction for struggling learners (Chapter 2). This conceptual framework provides a structure for the remaining three sections. Sections II through IV describe how educators can design and implement the *universal features* framework and thereby provide effective mathematics instruction for struggling learners.

Section II, Understanding and Teaching the Big Ideas in Mathematics, introduces five mathematical big ideas (content) and five big ideas about mathematical processes (Chapter 3). Section II explains why it is important for educators to understand why and how the big ideas enhance mathematical success for struggling learners and why educators must value teaching the big ideas (Chapter 4).

Section III, Barriers and Gateways to Meaningful Mathematics Instruction, describes common learning characteristics of struggling learners and how these characteristics create barriers for learning mathematics (Chapter 5). In addition, Chapter 6 describes how various curriculum delivery methods create additional barriers for these students. Chapter 7 summarizes basic information about how struggling learners learn and how this information applies to mathematics. Chapter 7 also provides tips for helping students move successfully from initial understanding of a new mathematical concept to generalizing the concept to other contexts and adapting knowledge to other concepts. General teaching techniques that facilitate learning for struggling learners also are discussed.

Section IV, Assessment and Teaching Strategies for Making Mathematics Meaningful, describes mathematics instructional practices and strategies that address the barriers described in Section III and helps struggling learners understand the meaning of mathematics. Chapters 8 through 10 describe and provide examples of research-supported strategies for continuous assessment that informs mathematics instruction, strategies for promoting initial understanding of new mathematical concepts, and strategies for promoting proficiency in using mathematics and for generalizing mathematical understanding to multiple contexts. Chapter 11 illustrates how educators can incorporate the strategies that are described in Chapters 8 through 10 when they plan differentiated instruction for a variety of environments (e.g., inclusive/co-teaching classrooms, resources environments, full-time special education environments, home). Chapter 12 summarizes how to adapt several common technology tools that are used for mathematics instruction for struggling learners and how to integrate several technology applications to enhance mathematics outcomes for these students.

Appendices A and B include examples of forms and plans that supplement the implementation of the universal features framework. Purchasers of *Teaching Mathematics Meaningfully: Solutions for Struggling Learners* are granted permission to photocopy and/or print out these forms from the book. None of the forms may be reproduced to generate revenue for any program or individual. Photocopies and/or printouts may only be made from an original book.

HOW TO USE THIS BOOK

This book has been structured around four *anchors,* or universal features, to provide meaningful mathematics instruction for students with learning difficulties: 1) understanding and teaching the big ideas in mathematics and the big ideas for doing mathematics, 2) understanding learning characteristics of and barriers for struggling learners, 3) continuously assessing learning and making informed instructional decisions, and 4) making mathematics accessible through responsive teaching (see Figure 1.1 for an illustration of the four universal features of meaningful mathematics instruction). If instruction is anchored using these four universal features, then a beginning framework is set for teaching mathematics successfully to struggling learners. Once the concepts of these universal features are grasped, they can be applied in any educational environment. Guidance, in the form of teaching plans that integrate these anchors and that address multiple educational contexts and student needs, is provided in Chapter 11 and the Appendices. Moreover, MathVIDS, an award-winning web site, is available to assist teachers in learning further about effective mathematics instruction for struggling learners. Among other features, MathVIDS provides digital video models of exemplary teachers modeling in their own classrooms many of the strategies that are described in this book.

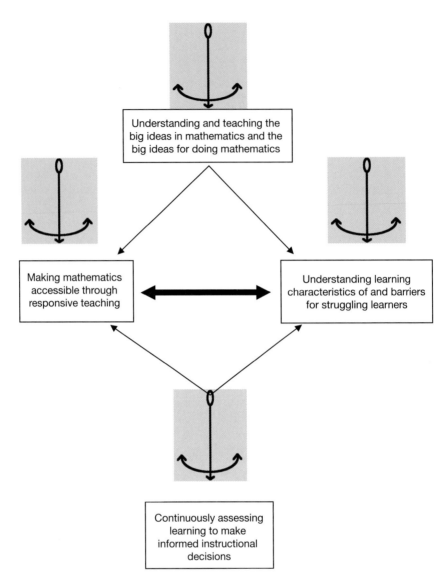

Figure 1.1.   Four universal features of meaningful mathematics instruction for struggling learners.

HOW TO USE MATHVIDS

MathVIDS (Mathematics Video Instructional Development Source, 2001) is a web site that was co-developed by two of the authors, Dr. David Allsopp and Dr. Maggie Kyger, and Dr. Richard Ingram, the Computing Coordinator for the College of Education at James Madison University in Harrisonburg, Virginia, to assist teachers who teach mathematics to struggling learners. MathVIDS was funded through the United States Department of Education and the Virginia Department of Education. This web site has several important components and features to enhance learning for educators who use the site for professional development. Two major components include multimedia descriptions of 14

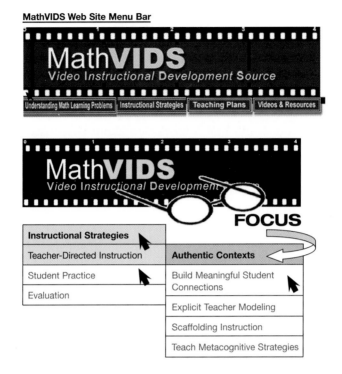

Figure 1.2. MathVIDS Focus graphic description.

research-supported mathematics instructional practices for struggling learners. A central feature is the use of digital video of real teachers in real classrooms modeling the use of the strategies. Audio and text elaboration accompany the video clips to help viewers pinpoint those specific practices that the model teachers use and that particularly help struggling learners. Another major feature of the web site is teaching plans for key mathematical concepts that are found in the K–5 curriculum and that show how to integrate the 14 research-supported instructional strategies. Digital video also accompanies these teaching plans, and the plans are downloadable for printing. Other components and features of the web site include examples of metacognitive learning strategies for particular types of mathematical concepts, descriptions of assessment strategies and information on why struggling learners have difficulty learning mathematics. You can access the MathVIDS web site at coe.jmu.edu/mathvidsr.

Figure 1.2 shows the MathVIDS Focus graphic. This MathVIDS Focus graphic will appear in the text when there is information available on the MathVIDS web site to support particular information that you are learning about in the book. Below the MathVIDS Focus logo is a representation of the drop-down navigation menu that you will find on the web site. Cursor icons ( ) show how to navigate to the place on the web site that relates to the instructional practice, strategy, idea, or example that supports the section of the book you are currently reading. For example, to find information about the teacher-directed instructional strategy "teaching within authentic contexts," you would place your cursor over and click the Instructional Strategies button on the top menu bar of the MathVIDS web site. When you select a button on the menu bar, a drop-down menu will appear directly below that button. In this case, the words *Teacher-Directed Instruction, Student Practice,* and *Evaluation* appear. When you scroll the cursor over each of these drop-down buttons, a cascading drop-down menu will appear directly to the side of that button. For *Teacher-Directed Instruction,* all of the instructional strategies that correspond to this area appear. To get to the desired strategy, simply click on the appropriate button. For example, Figure 1.2 shows that if you click on Authentic Contexts, then you would find information about that instructional strategy. Each button you select is shaded. Lighter shaded buttons show where to start, whereas the darker shaded button shows the link to the pertinent information. The text for buttons that are not relevant for navigation is light gray in color.

Video of real teachers in real classrooms modeling effective mathematics instruction for struggling learners is a prominent feature of the MathVIDS web site. For particular instructional practices that are described in Chapters 8 through 10, the MathVIDS Video Focus graphic will appear to alert the reader to video models of these practices. Each video highlights the important instructional features that are emphasized in this book for each instructional practice. Figure 1.3 shows an example of a MathVIDS Video Focus graphic for the assessment practice Mathematics Dynamic Assessment.

VIDEO FOCUS
Dynamic Assessment

See a middle school teacher implementing this strategy at the MathVIDS website: *Dynamic Assessment* web page.

Figure 1.3. MathVIDS Video Focus graphic example: dynamic assessment.

We hope that educators find the organization of the book helpful for furthering their professional development in effectively teaching mathematics for struggling learners. In addition, we hope that readers find the MathVIDS website a helpful enhancement to the information presented in this book. We wish you good fortune on your journey toward achieving improved mathematics learning outcomes for struggling learners in K–12 schools.

2

Universal Features of Meaningful Mathematics Instruction for Struggling Learners

S truggling learners must have three important needs met in order to achieve success in the K–12 mathematics curriculum: 1) teachers who are committed to ensuring that they learn mathematics; 2) teachers who have a conceptual framework for why struggling learners have difficulties learning mathematics; and 3) instruction that addresses their learning needs, thereby allowing them to understand mathematics.

In Chapter 1, four universal features of meaningful mathematics instruction for struggling learners were introduced: 1) understanding and teaching big ideas in mathematics and the big ideas for doing mathematics, 2) understanding learning characteristics of and barriers for struggling learners, 3) continuously assessing learning and making informed instructional decisions, and 4) making mathematics accessible through responsive teaching. As Figure 2.1 (which is repeated from Figure 1.1 in Chapter 1) suggests, each of these four anchors for meaningful and effective mathematics instruction for struggling learners is connected integrally to each other. The double-ended arrow between the responsive teaching anchor and the learning characteristics/barriers anchor shows the reciprocal relationship between these two universal features. For example, for teachers to respond to students' learning needs, they need to understand how to implement effective instructional practices (responsive teaching). Conversely, teachers must understand how barriers to learning have an impact on what and how students learn (learning barriers) so that they can select instructional practices that are responsive to students' needs. However, teaching mathematics does not happen in a vacuum. Teachers must understand the big ideas of mathematics, including content big ideas (the *what* of mathematics) and process big ideas (*how* mathematics is done). Such understanding supports responsive teaching by informing teachers about what they need to teach (content big ideas) and the multiple ways in which their students can do mathematics (process big ideas). By understanding the mathematics curriculum, teachers

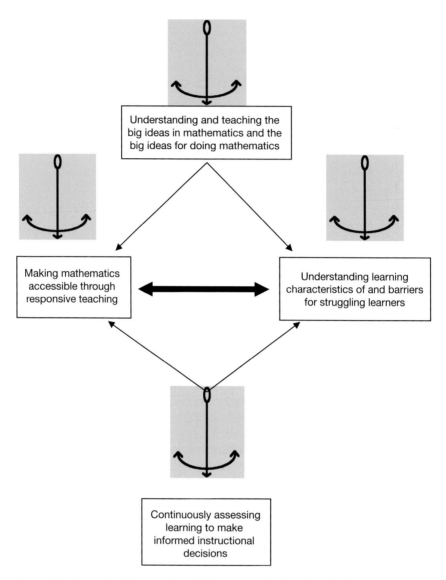

Figure 2.1. The model of the four universal features of meaningful mathematics instruction for struggling learners showing interrelatedness of responsive teaching, big ideas of mathematics, learning characteristics of struggling learners and barriers to their learning, and the importance of continuous assessment.

are equipped to make good decisions that are based on the learning needs of their students. The arrows that flow from the big ideas anchor to the responsive teaching anchor and the learning characteristics/barriers anchor show these relationships. Similar to the big ideas anchor, the continuous assessment anchor informs the responsive teaching anchor and the learning needs/barriers anchor. Responsive instruction is informed by student performance data collected continually that show whether students are learning so that timely instructional decisions can be made. In turn, this informs teachers about the extent to which particular instructional practices meet the learning needs of their students. The arrows that flow from the continuous assessment anchor to the responsive teaching anchor and the learning characteristics/barriers anchor depict these relationships.

UNIVERSAL FEATURES

Understanding and Teaching the Big Ideas in Mathematics and the Big Ideas for Doing Mathematics

The K–12 mathematics curriculum can be organized according to five content strands. These can be thought of as the *what* of the mathematics curriculum: 1) number and operations, 2) algebra, 3) geometry, 4) measurement, and 5) data analysis and probability (National Council of Teachers of Mathematics [NCTM], 2000). Each of these content strands has unique features and ideas that allow for their categorization into separate areas of mathematics. Unfortunately, this separation frequently is carried to an extreme: Some people think of mathematics as separate bodies of ideas that consist of isolated rules and procedures that often simply must be memorized. This perspective of mathematics offers a very narrow and false view of what mathematics really is about. It is true that mathematics is composed of different areas, such as algebra and geometry, but these areas actually are connected to each other in numerous ways. When seeking ways in which the areas of mathematics are related, one can see how mathematics really is a connected body of ideas that does make sense.

Teachers must understand the connections among concepts within each strand as well as those between strands, especially as they relate to the particular K–12 curriculum that they teach. For example, in measurement, the notion of unit is paramount, whether you are talking about inches or square feet. The notion of the unit or the whole also is important when working with number and operations in part–whole fractions and proportions. Students' understanding of the notion of unit and its role in mathematics can make generalization to other areas easier. Moreover, teachers must prioritize the task of helping their students make these connections so that students can achieve success with the K–12 mathematics curriculum.

In the development of a more comprehensive view of mathematics, these five processes of *doing* mathematics also should be considered: 1) problem solving, 2) reasoning and proof, 3) connections, 4) communication, and 5) representation (NCTM, 2000). The NCTM maintains that the processes of *doing* mathematics "highlight ways of acquiring and using content knowledge" (NCTM, 2000, p. 29). All students, including struggling learners, should and can engage in mathematics using these processes. Although some students with significant cognitive disabilities may be stronger in certain ways of doing mathematics than in others, generally all struggling learners can do mathematics in ways that are consistent with each of these process standards. All too often, struggling learners are provided with instruction that emphasizes singular ways of doing mathematics (e.g., computations) because the thought is that they cannot do mathematics in ways that require greater levels of higher order thinking (e.g., reasoning, problem solving). Such practice is based on false assumptions about what struggling learners can do. It also is a practice that contradicts the current literature base (e.g., Cawley, 2002; Cawley, Parmer, Yan, & Miller, 1998; Chard & Gersten, 1999).

This book places an emphasis on the big ideas that are related to how students *do* mathematics because *how* students learn mathematics is tied intricately to *what* they ultimately learn and understand. Understanding something means more than "you have it or you don't." Understanding exists on a continuum. At one end of the continuum exists an understanding in which the ideas are not very well connected to other ideas. This type of understanding, called instrumental understanding (Skemp, 1978), is often the result of ideas that have been memorized and "learned" without meaning. Ideas understood in this manner have a higher likelihood of being forgotten. If a person is provided with opportunities to actively seek and make connections between ideas, he or she can develop a deeper, more connected network of ideas that results in a type of understanding called relational understanding (Skemp, 1978). This type of understanding consists of a meaningful network of concepts and procedures that, over an active lifetime of learning, only becomes more densely connected and useable. One is very likely to never have a complete, full understanding of a particular idea because as one learns about new ideas, new connections to existing ideas can be made. That is what makes lifelong learning so important and exciting. Clearly, our goal for all students is that they develop a relational understanding of mathematical ideas. This type of understanding is best developed by instruction that engages students in the processes of *doing* mathematics (using mathematical understandings in meaningful ways to develop deeper, more connected mathematical knowledge) in contrast to instruction that emphasizes the learning of isolated mathematical concepts and skills.

Understanding Learning Characteristics of and Barriers for Struggling Learners

The key to helping struggling learners achieve success with the K–12 curriculum is to understand *why* they have difficulty learning mathematics. This book focuses on two major areas of barriers for struggling learners in mathematics. One area involves a common core of learning characteristics, one or more of which struggling learners may possess. These learning characteristics, discussed in Chapter 5, include attention and memory difficulties, learned helplessness, passive approaches to learning, processing and metacognitive deficits, low levels of academic achievement, and math anxiety.

The second major area that can create barriers for struggling learners has to do with how the mathematical curriculum is delivered. These curriculum-delivery-related issues, discussed in Chapter 6, include spiraling curriculum, mastery learning, algorithm-driven instruction, cyclical reforms, and use (or non-use) of effective teaching strategies.

Chapter 7 describes six stages of learning for struggling learners. These stages provide educators with a foundation for perceiving how assessment and instruction relate to *how* students learn. As educators better understand why struggling learners have difficulty learning mathematics, they become better equipped to understand how teaching methods have an impact on students' learning. In turn, this empowers teachers to make better instructional decisions about how they teach their students.

Continuously Assessing Learning to Make Informed Instructional Decisions

Continuous assessment of learning simply means that educators should evaluate what students know and can do before, during, and after instruction. Before teaching any mathematical concept, teachers should evaluate students' knowledge and experiences related to the concept. This includes evaluating their prerequisite knowledge and skills and their experiences and interests that might relate to the target concept. Chapter 8 describes how assessment can be done to gain a clear picture of students' knowledge about a target concept and prerequisite skills that are associated with the concept. This picture of learning includes students' level of competency in understanding mathematical concepts and performing mathematical skills; their level of understanding (concrete, representational, or abstract); whether they can choose an example of a concept or skill (i.e., receptive understanding) or show their understanding without being provided choices (i.e., expressive understanding); and whether they have procedural knowledge, conceptual knowledge, or both. If students are not proficient in the knowledge and skills that are necessary for understanding the target concept, then they will have difficulty being successful. If students do possess the prerequisite knowledge and skills that are needed to understand the target concept, then knowing their experiences and interests that relate to the concept can help teachers to develop meaningful learning contexts within which to teach the target concept. Chapter 8 describes the Mathematics Interest Inventory, a tool for learning about students' interests and experiences outside mathematics per se that is used to integrate students' interests and experiences in meaningful ways as teachers plan, assess, and teach their students.

During instruction, it is vital that teachers determine whether students understand the target concept and are able to use it proficiently, two skills integral to the success of struggling learners. Students may understand a target concept at different levels from one another and use it at different levels of proficiency. For example, some children, when adding, do not readily "count up" (e.g., when given two numbers, a student counts up from one of the numbers, adding the second number) but will "count all" (e.g., when given two numbers, the student begins counting up from zero until all numbers are added). Students in the latter example seem to understand adding and have some level of proficiency, but they lack sophistication in their thinking and approach. Evaluating student understanding *during* instruction allows educators to monitor the success of instruction so that changes can be made immediately. This prevents the loss of valuable instructional time and helps teachers to avoid surprises such as waiting until the class moves on to the next concept or unit before realizing—too late—that some students did not understand it.

After instruction, evaluating where students are in terms of their learning of the target concept provides teachers with a foundation for planning further instruction. In some cases, students might demonstrate sufficient understanding to move to the next target concept. In other cases, they may demonstrate the need for additional instruction or response opportunities to become proficient (i.e., they can demonstrate understanding of the concept or can perform the skill with a high level of accuracy and at a satisfactory rate).

By determining this information after instruction occurs and before the next lesson is planned, teachers have a format for planning subsequent instruction so that it best meets the learning needs of the students. Chapter 8 describes a fluid process for continuously assessing students in practical yet informative ways to guide instructional decision making.

Making Mathematics Accessible Through Responsive Teaching

A primary purpose of this book is to help educators make the learning of mathematics accessible to struggling learners. *Access* is an important concept in successful mathematics instruction for these students. Because of the learning barriers that these students face, educators must be creative in their thinking about how to provide them with meaningful mathematics learning experiences. In the context of teaching struggling learners, access is defined as the methods, practices, or procedures that the teacher plans and implements that directly address the learning characteristics of these students, thereby increasing the likelihood that students have a clear understanding of the mathematics concept. When students can process the concept in ways that make sense to them or in ways that are accessible given their own learning abilities and needs, they are more likely to understand the concept.

SUPPORT FOR THE FOUR UNIVERSAL FEATURES

The four universal features for making mathematics meaningful for struggling learners, including an understanding of and instruction in both content and process big ideas, an understanding of learning characteristics of and barriers for struggling learners, continuous assessment of learning and instructional decision making, and an ability to make mathematics accessible, are not all-encompassing. However, they provide educators with an informed framework for effectively teaching mathematics. Each universal feature represents an important element of effective instruction in mathematics for struggling learners and is supported by literature in both special education and mathematics education fields.

Support in Content and Understanding

The concept of teaching the big ideas in mathematics for struggling learners has been a topic of discussion in the literature (e.g., Cawley et al., 1998; Carnine, Dixon, & Silbert, 1998; NCTM, 2000; Parmar & Cawley, 1991; Educational Resources Information Center/Office of Special Education Programs (ERIC/OSEP) Special Project, 2002). For example, Cawley and colleagues (1998) emphasized the importance of moving beyond basic skills instruction for struggling learners. They advocated concentrating on how students *reason* about the mathematics that they do and on helping students build connections between and among mathematical concepts. Carnine and colleagues (1998) advocated for teaching big ideas that cut across the mathematics curriculum (e.g., use of arrays or area models for multiplication of whole numbers) as a method for helping struggling learners apply the same idea to other mathematical ideas (e.g., multiplication of fractions, decimals and polynomials).

Mathematics educators long have espoused the need to teach the big ideas, not only the big ideas that compose the *what* of K–12 mathematics but also the big ideas for *doing* mathematics. The NCTM clearly identifies both content standards (the *what* of K–12 mathematics) and process standards (the *doing* of mathematics; NCTM, 2000). Several mathematics educators have advocated the integration of these standards with the need to apply them on the basis of the individual strengths and weaknesses of struggling learners (e.g., Baroody, 1987; Van de Walle, 2005). For example, Baroody (1987) contended that traditional ways of teaching mathematics (i.e., skills-only approach) does not meet these students' developmental or psychological needs, resulting in a lack of understanding and significant gaps in the students' mathematical knowledge. In essence, focusing also on the big ideas instead of solely on individual skills and concepts provides opportunities for students to construct connections between various skills and concepts.

Support for Understanding Barriers

Special education has long held as major tenets both the importance of understanding the learning characteristics of struggling learners and the importance of applying that understanding to teaching these students (Minskoff, 1998). Similarly, mathematics education long has advocated for developmentally appropriate instruction whereby teachers use their knowledge of child development to provide mathematics instruction that is consistent with students' developing cognitive abilities (Carpenter, Fennema, Franke, Levi, & Empson, 1999; Kami, 2000). Without the knowledge of how children learn mathematics, educators tend to teach in ways that can be detrimental to students' learning of mathematics in meaningful ways (e.g., Kami, 2000). Related to struggling learners specifically, much has been discovered regarding why these students have difficulty comprehending mathematics. As a result of characteristics that derive from disability, language differences, and cultural diversity, barriers occur for these students and make it difficult for them to make meaning of mathematics. Two primary types of barriers are reported in the literature: barriers that result from the learning characteristics of struggling learners and barriers that result from the interaction of these learning characteristics and how the mathematics curriculum is taught (e.g., Allsopp, Lovin, Green, & Savage-Davis, 2003; Baroody, 1987; Cawley et al., 1998; Cawley, Parmar, Foley, Solomon, & Roy, 2001; Gagnan & Maccini, 2001; Mercer, Harris, & Miller, 1993; Mercer, Jordan, & Miller, 1996; Miller & Mercer, 1997).

Support for Continuous Assessment

In addition, the use of continuous assessment of students' understanding to make informed instructional decisions in mathematics long has been advocated in the literature. Assessment procedures such as curriculum-based assessment and curriculum-based measurement result in teachers' greater awareness of both their students' learning needs and their students' day-to-day progress in meeting learning goals and objectives (e.g., Allinder, Bolling, Oats, & Gagnon, 2000; Miller & Mercer, 1993; Shafer, 1998; Woodward & Howard, 1994). The NCTM maintains that assessment should be an integral part of instruction, providing not only the teacher but also the student with information about the student's learning. With this information, teachers will be better able to modify their instruction and students will be better able to modify their activity, all with the ultimate goal of students coming to a deeper understanding of the concepts being studied. A review by Black and Williams (1998) of more than 250 studies strongly supports the notion that students' learning is improved considerably when teachers consistently use formative assessment to guide their instruction.

Support for Providing Access

The literature that supports the final universal feature of providing access to successful mathematical learning experiences for struggling learners through effective teaching practices builds on the literature support for the first three universal features. As the literature evolves, there is greater awareness that mathematics instruction should be more than direct teaching of basic skills and that struggling learners can learn mathematics at much deeper levels of understanding than previously believed. This is especially true when instructional practices that are characterized by different levels of teacher support are implemented (Mercer, Lane, Jordan, Allsopp, & Eisele, 1996). This continuum of instructional choices for struggling learners is implemented most successfully when conscious thought is applied to *what* students are ready to learn, how they will be asked to *do* it, how it relates to their *knowledge,* and the *barriers* that might make learning difficult for them. When such responsive teaching is applied to teaching struggling learners, success is more likely to occur. Fortunately, a growing body of literature documents mathematics instructional practices that respond to the needs of struggling learners (e.g., Baxter, Woodward, & Olson, 2005; Bottge, Heinrichs, Metha, & Hung, 2002; Cawley et al., 1998; Lock, 1996; Kroesbergen & van Luit, 2002, 2003; Maccini & Gagnon, 2000; Mercer, Jordan, et al., 1996; Miller, Butler, & Lee, 1998; Owen & Fuchs, 2002; Vaughn, Gersten, & Chard, 2000).

The model for effectively teaching mathematics for struggling learners described in this chapter can be used to help educators conceptualize, plan, and evaluate their own mathematics instruction. As the reader learns more about how each universal feature can be implemented, it will be helpful to refer back to the universal features model periodically and reflect on how the particular methods described "fit" with the model and his or her own teaching. This model can also serve as a structure for evaluating the extent to which an adopted curriculum addresses the mathematics learning needs of struggling learners.

II

Understanding and Teaching the Big Ideas in Mathematics

3

The Big Ideas in Mathematics and Why They Are Important

It's one thing not to see the forest for the trees, but then to go on to deny the reality of the forest is a more serious matter.

—Paul Weiss

Number sense is something that all students should develop. It is so important for mathematical work that it often is identified as one of the content strands in state standards. Number sense can be difficult to pinpoint, however. A group of teachers gave the following definitions for number sense: counting, skip counting, place value, one-to-one correspondence, ordering numbers, comparing numbers, patterns, counting money, telling time, and mental math. From a broader perspective, number sense can be thought of as a flexible understanding of numbers and their relationships to other numbers. The teachers' definitions could be considered to be some of the pieces (ideas and skills) that are needed to develop this broader notion of number sense. One could think of the teachers' ideas as the trees of the forest—ideas that teachers try to help students develop and understand so that they can develop the larger concept, or the big idea: the forest.

THE BIG IDEAS AND WHY THEY ARE IMPORTANT

In planning and instruction, teachers must be careful to see the forest *and* the trees. Here's why. Number sense is a broad idea that encompasses a range of concepts and skills. One idea or one skill does not equate to number sense. However, sometimes teachers are so focused on the trees (the smaller pieces) that they forget to step back and consider the forest in which they are working. By keeping in mind this notion of what the smaller concepts and skills are building, teachers can develop a more purposeful and unifying direction for instruction by looking for and finding ways in which seemingly unconnected ideas and skills are related. Focusing on individual skills and concepts without understanding how these individual skills and concepts develop the bigger idea can result in holes in students' knowledge. It also leads to the belief that

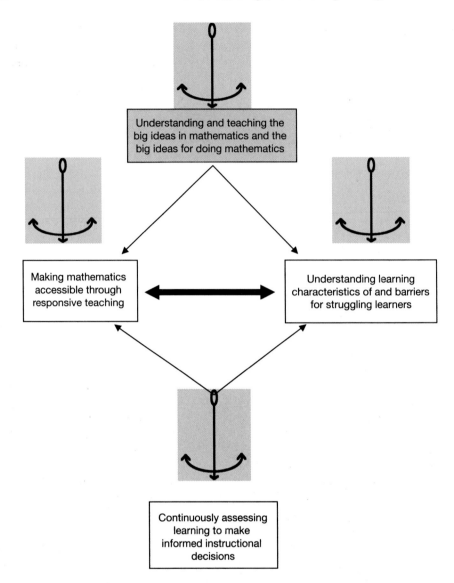

Figure 3.1.   Big ideas anchor highlighting the importance of teaching big ideas *in* mathematics and the big ideas for *doing* mathematics.

mathematics consists of isolated bits and pieces of information and procedures. In addition, if teachers are able to identify the big idea, then teaching
and learning the numerous skills and concepts within that big idea can be less
overwhelming because teachers, as well as their students, can see how it all
fits together.

Let's look again at the Universal Features Model introduced in Chapter 1.
This chapter addresses the first anchor of this model of meaningful mathematics instruction for struggling learners (see Figure 3.1). This chapter is about the
big ideas in mathematics: those broader ideas that are more than skills. The big
ideas in mathematics can provide teachers with direction and a framework for

teaching if they become aware of them. Certain big ideas in mathematics, such as number sense, are typically identified as organizing themes in the mathematics curriculum in the United States. The National Council of Teachers of Mathematics (NCTM; 2000) identified these themes, or content strands, as

- Number and operations (which includes number sense)

- Algebra

- Geometry

- Measurement

- Data analysis and probability

These themes form a comprehensive foundation of the mathematics that all students should learn. In addition to these content-oriented big ideas, some big ideas or processes have been identified for *doing* mathematics (i.e., "ways of acquiring and using content knowledge" [NCTM, 2000, p. 29]):

- Problem solving

- Reasoning and proof

- Connections

- Communication

- Representation

These content strands and processes are not disjointed; they overlap and are related.

Number and Operations

One might list the skills that are related to operations as the standard procedures for addition, subtraction, multiplication, and division of various numbers. However, the notion of operations encompasses much more than these standard procedures for computation. The big ideas that are related to operations focus on the meaning of the operations as well as the relationships between the operations (i.e., operation sense). For example, in learning about division, students can consider how division is related to subtraction (i.e., division can be thought of as repeated subtraction). Furthermore, when students learn the standard procedure for long division, the teacher can help them to understand that this procedure is based on the repeated subtraction meaning of division. When helping students develop the skills for computation, teachers must keep in mind the big ideas of developing number sense as well as operation sense. In actuality, well-developed number sense forms a founation for operation sense and computational fluency, defined by NCTM as "having and using efficient and accurate methods for computing" (2000, p. 32). In other words, students can begin to develop an understanding of computation while developing an understanding of number. For example, students can be asked to think of different ways to represent the number 7 with counters. One student might show one set of five counters and another set of two counters. Another student might choose to show six counters in one set and

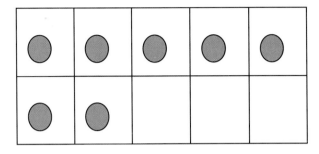

Figure 3.2. Ten frame showing the number 7. Ten frames can help students look for and visualize relationships between numbers. The number 7 can be thought of as a row of 5 objects and a row of 2 objects (as shown) or as 3 less than 10.

another set with only one counter. Yet another student might split seven counters into a set of three and a set of four. Using a 10 frame, as in Figure 3.2, students can begin to develop relationships between numbers and the benchmark numbers of 5 and 10. By using a 10 frame such as the one provided in Figure 3.2, students can describe how many more counters they would need to make 10 or how many the bottom row of counters needs to make a group of five. The ideas of addition and subtraction are implicit in these students' activity and can be capitalized on when students are ready.

A person who has a well-developed sense of number readily looks for ways to pull apart numbers to create easy and efficient ways to perform a computation, similar to how proficient readers use phonemic awareness/phonological awareness to decode text to read for meaning. Moreover, understanding how operations relate to each other can be helpful in finding efficient and accurate computational methods. A person who has a well-developed sense of number and operations is not bound to only one way to perform a computation but uses the numbers involved to find a quick method of computation. Consider how knowing the relationship between multiplication and addition and having a good understanding of place value are helpful in using these ways to compute 28×16: A person could multiply 30 by 16 to get 480 and then subtract 32 (two 16s) $(30 \times 16 = 480 - 32)$, or subtract 30 from 480 and then take away 2 more, both of which result in 448 $(480 - 30 - 2)$. Alternatively, to multiply 28 by 16, the person may think it easier to separate 28 into 20 and 8 first and then multiply 20×16 to get 320 (just think $2 \times 16 \times 10$). To compute 8×16, the person could separate the 16 into 10 and 6, then compute $8 \times 10 = 80$ and $8 \times 6 = 48$. Finally, the person could add 320 to 80 to get 400, + 48 to get 448.

Refer to the recommendations made by the NCTM in the *Principles and Standards for School Mathematics* for a summary of the guiding ideas that are related to number and operations: Instructional programs from prekindergarten through Grade 12 should enable all students to

- Understand numbers, ways of representing numbers, relationships among numbers, and number systems

- Understand meanings of operations and how they relate to one another

- Compute fluently and make reasonable estimates (NCTM, 2000, p. 32)

Algebra

Many people, when they think of algebra, think of the manipulation of numbers and symbols or the graphing of equations conducted in a rote manner. However, there is more to algebra than just symbol manipulation or procedures for graphing. Algebra is actually a problem-solving tool that uses numbers and symbols to represent real-life phenomena. Becoming competent in algebra (not just symbol manipulation) gives a person more power to solve problems that they encounter in day-to-day life. By modeling these phenomena through the use of symbols and equations, people are able to make more informed decisions about the situation. In short, algebra allows complex ideas to be expressed concisely, which can make the analysis of the ideas easier.

The NCTM recommends that with respect to algebra, instructional programs from prekindergarten through Grade 12 enable all students to

- Understand patterns, relations, and functions

- Represent and analyze mathematical situations and structures using algebraic symbols

- Use mathematical models to represent and understand quantitative relationships

- Analyze change in various contexts (2000, p. 37)

Ideally, algebra should find its way into K–12 curricula in the form of pattern seeking and generating, looking for relationships between quantities, and using various representations (e.g., concrete or pictorial representation, language, graphic, table or numeric, symbolic) to better understand a variety of mathematical situations. Investigations with numbers can lead to the development of their properties, which are the attributes that any number or set of numbers possess: odd/even, positive/negative, commutative, associative, and so forth. These properties can be a basis for subsequent work with symbols and algebraic expressions, creating explicit connections between concepts within algebra and number and operations. For example, as students become aware of the commutative property of addition, they can express that property for any real numbers represented by a and b as $a + b = b + a$ (e.g., $3 + 2 = 2 + 3$). The use of variables allows expression of both this property and numbers in general terms, a powerful tool of algebra. Furthermore, students can begin to form an understanding of mathematical modeling by considering how situations can be described using mathematics.

Viewing algebra in a broader sense can make it more apparent why algebraic competence is important. The methods and ideas of algebra are applicable across many areas of mathematics and the sciences and what may seem to be nonmathematical work. In technological fields, such as engineering and medicine, algebraic competence is an obvious necessity because workers have to look for and anticipate patterns in situations, and they either have to model phenomena mathematically or interpret and use models effectively. Traditionally, nontechnological fields such as psychology and the social sciences require a person to be able to examine situations through data and statistical analysis, which incorporates the notion of mathematical modeling—that is, how numbers represent or illustrate a particular phenomenon. When the application and analysis parts of algebra are emphasized, it becomes evident that algebra actually is a unifying component across all mathematics.

Geometry

Geometry, like number and operations and algebra, is a broad area that encompasses a range of concepts and skills. Geometry can be thought of as being organized around four big ideas: 1) shapes, 2) location (where in space objects are located and how this location is communicated), 3) transformations (how shapes can be moved), and 4) visualization. The following are foundational components of geometric thinking that all students should be able to do:

- Analyze characteristics and properties of two- and three-dimensional geometric shapes and develop mathematical arguments about geometric relationships

- Specify locations and describe spatial relationships using coordinate geometry and other representational systems

- Apply transformations and use symmetry to analyze mathematical situations

- Use visualization, spatial reasoning, and geometric modeling to solve problems (NCTM, 2000, p. 41)

This list goes beyond merely identifying particular two- and three-dimensional shapes. Students can learn about the world around them by using these unifying ideas of geometry to describe and analyze structures in real-life contexts. For example, students can use the notion of transformations and symmetry in the study of art and architecture. Geometry also complements and supports the study of other areas of mathematics by providing a different way to represent and think about ideas. For example, area models often are used to represent multiplication of numbers, the coordinate plane is used to represent algebraic equations, and spatial representations such as the 10 frame are used to represent number.

Measurement

Measurement can be defined as "the assignment of a numerical value to an attribute of an object" (NCTM, 2000, p. 44). For example, when one says that a football field is 100 yards in length, a numeric value is assigned to the length of the field where the game of football is played. One might order a 12-ounce drink to quench thirst. The numeric value, 12 ounces, represents the attribute volume of liquid in the cup. These two examples show how number is embedded within measurement. When one thinks about measurement, what naturally may come to mind are units of measure, such as inches, feet, quarts, and squared centimeters. Consequently, learning about units of measure can become the focus of instruction. However, students first must understand the attribute that they are being asked to measure (e.g., length, area, volume, time, angles). In the football field example, the attribute is linear in nature (i.e., length); in the drink example, the attribute is volume. When students understand the attribute, they can begin to understand how the units of measure actually provide meaningful information. The NCTM suggests that measurement instruction from prekindergarten through Grade 12 enable all students to

- Understand measurable attributes of objects and the units, systems, and processes of measurement

- Apply appropriate techniques, tools, and formulas to determine measurements (NCTM, 2000, p. 44)

Once students understand various attributes of objects that can be measured and then what it means to measure, they can begin to learn about units of measure and the tools (e.g., rulers, compasses, clocks) that are used to make measurements. Because measurement is so pervasive throughout all areas of mathematics as well as other disciplines (e.g., science, social studies, art) and daily life, teaching and learning measurement should involve minds-on, hands-on experiments so that students develop a strong, conceptual basis. Moving too quickly to memorization of formulas and unit conversions tends to thwart this conceptual development.

Data Analysis and Probability

Data analysis and probability can be elusive to students, especially when taught in a procedural manner. As in measurement, moving too quickly to memorization of formulas can impede true understanding of the concepts of data analysis and probability. As recommended by the NCTM, instructional programs from prekindergarten through grade 12 should enable all students to

- Formulate questions that can be addressed with data and collect, organize, and display relevant data to answer them

- Select and use appropriate statistical methods to analyze data

- Develop and evaluate inferences and predictions that are based on data

- Understand and apply basic concepts of probability (NCTM, 2000, p. 48)

Both of these areas of mathematics actually have a great deal in common, and identifying these connections should be an emphasis in instruction. Data analysis and probability both focus on data and can be understood most meaningfully through data collection and examination of data. In addition, the notion of sample size affects work in both areas. In data analysis, sample size affects how closely the statistic converges toward the population parameter; in probability, the number of trials affects how closely empirical probability converges toward theoretical probability. Most important, learning about data analysis and probability should arise from meaningful contexts for students so that when something seems counterintuitive, students have a context to which to refer to make sense of the situation.

BIG IDEAS: THE *HOW* (DOING) OF MATHEMATICS

Throughout the discussion about the content standards, a sense of the presence of many of the process standards, such as problem solving, reasoning and proof, connections, communication, and representation, should be felt. As with the content standards, the process standards are interrelated and not easily teased apart from each other or from the content standards. Whereas the content standards are the *what* of mathematics, the process standards are the *how* of mathematics, how one *does* mathematics. However, the *how* of mathematics is intricately connected to the *what* of mathematics. *How* someone learns the mathematical content has an impact on *what* he or she ultimately learns. If all that students "learn" in mathematics are mathematical procedures that are presented to them by the teacher in a chalk-talk manner (i.e., monologue lecture), then they tend to perceive that mathematics is simply a set of rules and procedures that may or may not make sense. Their resulting knowledge base will undoubtedly be full of holes. However, if students *learn* mathematics in a problem-solving manner in which an emphasis is placed on reasoning and making connections, then students can come to understand mathematical ideas in more in-depth ways.

The goal is to help students become independent, critical thinkers who understand the purposes for mathematics and the ways in which mathematics can be applied meaningfully. Because learning mathematics *through* these processes is how the best mathematical learning takes place, both the teacher *and* the student should be engaged in these mathematical processes; the processes are not the sole domain of the teacher. Thus, teachers must purposefully provide opportunities for students to engage in these processes as they learn mathematics.

Problem Solving

Problem solving should be a regular part of classroom instruction to help students become critical thinkers and independent learners. One of the most important roles of the teacher is to pose genuine problems to students as opposed to routine exercises. If students immediately have a way to solve a given problem, then the task is likely to be a routine exercise, not a genuine problem. A genuine problem is one in which the solution is not obvious at first. With genuine problems, students have to become detectives, looking for information that may be helpful in determining a solution. Sometimes a path taken does not end with a successful solution, but it may provide some insights about another path to take toward a successful solution. It is through this process of problem solving that connections between ideas arise and that learning takes place. *It is the teacher's role to help make these connections and significant ideas in students' work explicit to all students.* According to *Principles and Standards for School Mathematics,* "Without the ability to solve problems, the usefulness and power of mathematical ideas, knowledge, and skills are severely limited" (NCTM, 2000, p. 182). This is not to say that there is not a time and a place for routine exercises, such as practicing a procedure for calculating the mean for data sets or solving quadratic equations using the quadratic formula, but routine exercises should not occupy a majority of instructional time and should occur only after students understand the mathematical ideas (e.g., mean, quadratic equations and their solutions) in a conceptual manner.

In this process, students should learn about and share multiple ways to solve routine exercises and genuine problems alike. The processes of looking for and making sense of multiple strategies help students build a repertoire of strategies, make connections between mathematical ideas, and learn to be to be risk takers because students realize that there can be more than one way to approach a task.

Many teachers believe that students have to have the basics (e.g., facts, procedures) before students can engage in problem solving, so that problem solving can become more like an appendage or afterthought than a way of learning mathematics. NCTM advocates teaching and learning mathematics *through* problem solving. The "basics" should be developed through focusing on problem solving, authentic contexts, and underlying concepts so that students can use ideas that are closer to their ways of thinking, which increases the likelihood of their being successful. Different strategies and even the standard algorithms for computation can be developed in this manner.

Consider the following task for having students think about adding multidigit numbers prior to their being taught the standard algorithm. (A lesson describing how this approach might be used with struggling learners is described in Chapter 11.)

There were 37 Boy Scouts and 61 Girl Scouts at the park on Saturday. How many scouts were at the park on Saturday?

Carpenter, Fennema, Franke, Levi, and Empson (1999) have identified three stages through which children move when working with combining numbers. Children first have to directly model all of the numbers in the situation and count them all. They may use concrete materials to do so, or they may use their fingers if the numbers are small enough. Eventually, through experience in working with problems and listening to how other students have approached the task *while the teacher highlights significant ideas in students' approaches,* children begin to develop more efficient ways to count such as counting on (described earlier in the chapter). No longer do they *need* to model every number, but they can now operate on a given number and count up from there. At the third level, students use number relationships they have learned through this type of problem solving, such as knowing that 8 is 2 away from 10, so 8 + 5 is 8 + 2 and then 3 more. Students begin to look for ways to pull numbers apart to make combining the numbers easier, thus reinforcing number sense and place value. Children, when allowed to add numbers in ways that make sense to them, start with the larger place value. So for this task, students at this level would add 30 + 60 and then add the 7 + 1 to the 90. This approach also dovetails very nicely with estimation because we start with the most significant digit in the number to estimate. Teachers have used students' approaches to then develop the standard algorithm. The standard algorithm should not be the first strategy children experience in combining or separating numbers because it does not make sense to them (i.e., it is too abstract for them even with concrete materials) and is not conceptually based on place value or number sense. Think about the language used with the standard algorithm. What is the "3" called in "37"? This procedure is digit-oriented, so the underlying concepts of place value and number sense are masked from the student. Using students' ideas to move toward the standard algorithm helps students make sense of this procedure. Consequently, they can use the procedure more accurately. And, in the process, they have learned a variety of strategies and continued to build their understanding of place value and number sense.

Obviously, students must understand earlier concepts. But when teachers think of these concepts with a big idea perspective, they can more easily move away from this notion of having students drill and memorize the basics before moving to higher level tasks. These basics should be developed in a conceptual manner just as much as higher level concepts.

Ideas for helping struggling learners to develop effective problem solving strategies are described in Chapter 9.

Communication

As students learn mathematics, communication between students and between teacher and students should be encouraged. Communication can occur in multiple forms (e.g., written and verbal language, pictures and diagrams) and can be used by a student or teacher to communicate ideas. Communicating ideas should be a common activity for students in mathematics classes. As students solve problems, they can be encouraged to share their approaches. Students also can be encouraged to look for alternative ways to solve the problems and then compare across strategies to see the similarities and differences between the strategies.

Both students and teachers can benefit in several ways from students communicating about their mathematical work. Asking students to explain their reasoning provides opportunities for students to think through their ideas and to learn to articulate, but it also provides opportunities for a teacher to make more explicit for all students the significant ideas in students' contributions. Communication provides the teacher with opportunities to gather information about students' understanding as they explain their reasoning. Sharing a variety of approaches makes it explicit to participants that students are using strategies to solve tasks and that there can be different methods for arriving at solutions.

Students may not always be used to or comfortable with explaining their answers. Unless such explanation is common and built into the process, a student may assume that a teacher's request for such explanation means their answer is incorrect, which has traditionally been the practice in many schools and classrooms. When teachers are explicit and consistent with students about using this process to make sense of how they are thinking—and when teachers ask students to explain their reasoning even when their answers are correct—students can begin to realize that mathematics is more than just right and wrong answers. To encourage this type of exchange, the teacher may find it necessary to model the type of explanation in a "think aloud" manner. This process can be very helpful to struggling learners, in particular, because these students typically are not aware that problem-solving strategies exist and therefore do not use them. By observing other students using strategies and the teacher explicitly pointing these strategies out and encouraging communication about their use, struggling students are provided with a naturally occurring modeling mechanism in class.

So, an essential role of the teacher is to capitalize on students' ideas that may not be apparent to other students. Through the sharing of ideas, the teacher is afforded opportunities to make significant ideas in students' work explicit for the entire class. For example, suppose that students are drawing pictures to make sense of the following task:

> Tommy and Ray made the same amount of money for years. However, last year, Tommy got a raise of 10%. Ray got a pay cut of 10%. This year, Ray got a 10% raise, and Tommy got a 10% cut. Do Tommy and Ray now make the same amount of money? Why or why not?

In solving this problem, some students realize that the whole changed from one year to the next, whereas many other students do not recognize this significant idea. By having students share their different approaches, including their reasoning, the class can compare and contrast their ideas to determine whether the reasoning used is mathematically valid and why or why not. It is important that teachers ensure that such comparisons be made explicit (i.e., clear) so that struggling learners can process and understand them. Examples of explicit modeling techniques that teachers can employ to achieve this goal are described in Chapter 9.

Reasoning and Proof

The focus in a traditional mathematics class tends to be on the answer only. It should be apparent at this point, however, that when one considers the *processes of doing* mathematics, the focus becomes more than the answer. NCTM advocates widening the focus to also include the reasoning and strategies behind arriving at an answer (see Figure 3.3). The reasoning used by teachers and students should always be connected to concepts to ensure that students are developing connections between mathematical ideas and not merely memorizing meaningless pieces of information that have a tendency to be forgotten.

Consider a classroom in which all that is listened for is a correct answer. Suppose students are comparing fractions, such as $\frac{2}{3}$ and $\frac{3}{4}$. In this type of setting, when a student responds that $\frac{2}{3} < \frac{3}{4}$ the expectation is that the student will be told that he or she is right. However, what if the student were asked to explain *how they know* $\frac{2}{3} < \frac{3}{4}$ and the student responds, "Well, I know that $2 < 3$ and $3 < 4$, so $\frac{2}{3}$ must be less than $\frac{3}{4}$." This should raise a red flag for the teacher that this student has some misconceptions and can actually provide some insight into what to focus on first in addressing this misconception. Focusing on only the answer can have obvious pitfalls. Consequently, teachers need to broaden what they are listening for. As Figure 3.3 indicates, in a sense-making classroom, answers are also part of the picture. The difference can be found in what else happens in the learning environment.

It often is through examining strategies that students come to identify more efficient ways of approaching various tasks, a process of reasoning. Not only do students build a repertoire of strategies but also they begin to look for different and more efficient ways to operate. Because they are using another process, reasoning, and proof, as they work through problems, they operate meaningfully in multiple ways, not simply the way in which they initially learned. Also, because students are expected to make sense of mathematics,

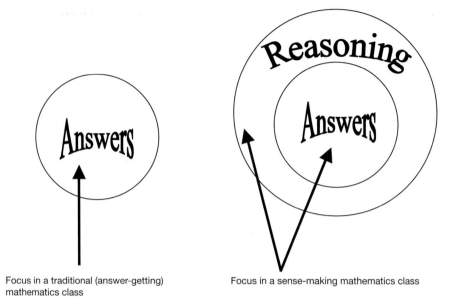

Focus in a traditional (answer-getting)   Focus in a sense-making mathematics class
mathematics class

Figure 3.3.   Focus of mathematics instruction: Answer-getting versus sense-making classrooms.

they routinely should be asked to explain their reasoning (in either written or verbal form) and to provide proof, at an appropriate level, that their approach is mathematically valid. Focusing on reasoning *and* answers convinces students that mathematics can make sense. Multiple examples of approaches for helping struggling learners to communicate their mathematical reasoning in ways that support their learning needs are described in Chapters 8 and 9.

Representation

According to *Principles and Standards for School Mathematics*, "The term *representation* refers both to process and to product—in other words, to the act of capturing a mathematical concept or relationship in some form and to the form itself" (NCTM, 2000, p. 67). Representation supports communication and reasoning by allowing students to express their thinking in a variety of formats. Representations can be in the form of diagrams, drawings, conventional as well as nonconventional symbols, graphs, and so forth. The benefit of using representations is captured by the adage, "A picture is worth a thousand words." In keeping with the idea of using different approaches to problems, representations can afford different ways to explain a solution and can provide insight into connections between ideas. Teachers should avoid teaching representations as ends in themselves. Representations should arise as needed and should support the work at hand in meaningful ways.

Representations can serve two purposes, as a way to 1) reason about and think through a problem and 2) communicate one's thinking. Some students have to start with a picture or representation to determine an answer. Other students may not need the picture or the representation to *get* the answer, but may use it to help them articulate their reasoning. For example, suppose students are asked to solve the following problem:

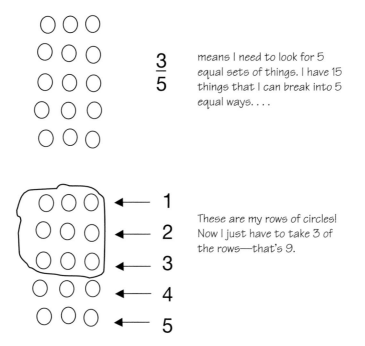

Figure 3.4.   A student uses a representation to make sense of and solve a problem.

Kerry hit ⅗ of her 15 basketball jump shots. How many jump shots did she make?

One student may start with a picture such as in Figure 3.4. By drawing and thinking about what ⅗ means, the student is able to find the answer, 9. Another student may have learned only the procedure to multiply the numbers, but does not understand why, and in fact, has to be reminded to multiply with "problems like this." He or she may be able to arrive at the number 9 as the answer, but only after the teacher has told the student the operation he or she needs to use. When students have "learned" a procedure without meaning (i.e., connecting it to concepts), it can be helpful to have them attempt to use a picture to understand what is happening in the procedure so that it makes more sense to them.

Representations support students as they reason and communicate about mathematics. They also provide teachers with another window into a student's understanding and possible misconceptions. For example, what does the student's drawing in Figure 3.5 tell the teacher about this student's understanding of comparing fractions?

Teaching students to draw solutions and create representations of their mathematical understandings is emphasized in Chapters 8 through 11.

Connections

Helping students make connections between ideas can help them to gain a better and more lasting understanding of mathematics. Connections can be

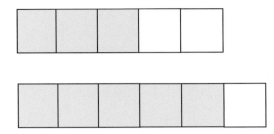

Figure 3.5.   Student's drawing to show $\frac{3}{5} < \frac{5}{6}$.

made between ideas within mathematics as well as between mathematical
ideas and ideas outside mathematics. When considering mathematics as a co-
herent whole (i.e., the forest) instead of separate, isolated pieces (i.e., the trees),
looking for and making connections seem natural. By emphasizing connections
through tasks and questions, teachers can nurture a disposition to look for and
use connections to solve problems. Connections help students learn mathematics, but connections also help students appreciate the utility of mathematics because they can see how it translates to contexts outside mathematics—
even problem solving in everyday life! Helping struggling learners to see and
make mathematical connections is an important goal in mathematics instruction. Approaches for ensuring that students make meaningful connections are
described later in this book, particularly in Chapter 9.

Bridging Between a Child's
and an Adult's View of Mathematics

Research in mathematics education has provided teachers with new knowledge about how children think about mathematics differently from most adults
(e.g., Carpenter et al., 1999; Lamon, 1996; Kami, 1985; Kami, 1989; Ross, 1989;
van Hiele, 1986). If teachers find holes in their content knowledge or pedagogical content knowledge, several resources are available that can further this
area of teachers' professional development (e.g., Lamon, 1999; Sullivan & Lilburn, 2002; Van de Walle & Lovin, 2006a, 2006b, 2006c). NCTM offers several
excellent resource materials for teachers, the latest of which is the Navigations
Series. (Teachers can find information about the Navigations Series as well as
other NCTM resources at www.nctm.org.) This series targets each of the content strands (Algebra, Geometry, Probability and Data Analyis, Number and
Number Sense, and Measurement) as well as the process standards (Problem
Solving, Reasoning and Proof, Connections, Communication, and Representation) from the "big idea" perspective and provides explanations of how students tend to reason about the mathematics. So when teachers find themselves
staring into the faces of students who are afraid to take a risk, when they are
aware of how students think developmentally about mathematics, they are
better able to suggest strategies that are closer to where their students are in
their thinking than an adult's way of thinking about the mathematical idea.
When teachers grow professionally in this way, it can help them tremendously
as they work with struggling learners to find success with mathematics.

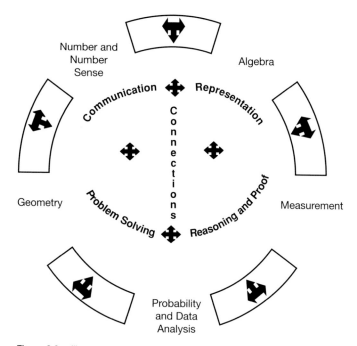

Figure 3.6. Illustration of the reflexive relationship between the content and process big ideas in mathematics.

TEACHING BY SEEING THE FOREST AND THE TREES

Figure 3.6 shows the relationship between the important parts of the mathematics forest: the content big ideas, the *what* of mathematics; and the process big ideas, the *how/doing* of mathematics. We've placed the mathematical processes in the middle of the diagram because it is through these processes that students learn mathematics. The mathematical ideas are developed through students' activities as they engage in the five mathematical processes. It is important that teachers understand that this development does not naturally occur for struggling learners. Thus, teachers must purposefully provide opportunities for students to engage in these processes and just as important, to look for and capitalize on the significant ideas that emerge to make these explicit to all students.

As students come to understand and appreciate the expectation of making sense of mathematics and as they build a repertoire of strategies, they can begin to develop confidence in their ability to *do* mathematics. As a consequence of these experiences, students are not stymied when presented with a genuine problem. The problem may be novel, but the notions of problem solving, reasoning and proof, connections, communication, and representation are familiar enough to give them confidence to proceed.

Teachers have to ask themselves continually, "What are the big ideas toward which we are working? Why do we want students to learn this skill or that concept?" When teachers question themselves in this way, the focus moves from learning isolated ideas to forming relationships between ideas, which makes learning more meaningful because it becomes grounded in what they already know. Teachers begin to see ideas from different perspectives and to see ways to get to ideas that may not have been realized before. When teachers make looking for the forest (i.e., the big ideas) a priority in instruction, they develop a more purposeful and unified direction for instruction and, more important, for students' learning.

In the age of standards-based, high-stakes testing, it is even more important that struggling learners and their teachers value the forest and the relationships among its trees. Making judicial use of instruction time is vital. By understanding the mathematical forest and its structure, teachers can make good decisions about which mathematical trees to help students climb, thereby helping them to use the view from the top to see the forest and all that it entails for themselves.

4

The Importance of Valuing Mathematics and Mathematics Instruction for Struggling Learners

To be an effective mathematics teacher for struggling learners, a teacher must value mathematics as an important area of learning for these students. *A teacher must value mathematics as a subject that is essential to school and life success for students with learning difficulties and value teaching of mathematics as an important instructional area for professional development.* Two purposes of this chapter are to engage thinking about these two premises and to provide opportunities for readers to reflect on their current value system related to mathematics instruction for struggling learners. A third purpose is to set the stage for further professional development in effective mathematics instruction for struggling learners.

WHY VALUING MATHEMATICS AND MATHEMATICS INSTRUCTION IS IMPORTANT

At initial glance, the italicized statement in the preceding paragraph may seem obvious. However, on closer examination, this issue goes much deeper. Traditionally, high value has not been placed on mathematics instruction for struggling learners. Mathematics education for struggling learners has received little emphasis in the research literature in comparison with areas such as reading and language arts. Consequently, less is known in the field about teaching mathematics effectively for struggling learners than is known about effective teaching practices in other subject areas, such as reading and language arts. This has resulted in a comparatively weak research foundation for guiding educators and curriculum developers in terms of what to do to help these students learn mathematics.

Teacher preparation also has played a role in this situation. Special education preservice teachers typically receive little direct preparation in mathematics education. For example, Florida requires only 3 hours of coursework in mathematics education for certification in special education. In comparison, Florida requires 12 hours of reading education coursework (Florida Department of Education State Board of Education Administrative Rules). Although it is difficult to argue with placing a high level of emphasis on reading methods (literacy) instruction for teachers in preparation, the comparable lack of emphasis on mathematics should be a concern. Mathematics, like literacy, is a primary method of communicating thoughts and ideas in our world. Mathematics is "spoken" in many areas of everyday life and is a very necessary language to possess in order to function productively in life. Without an appropriate level of competency in mathematics, students will find it difficult to manage many important aspects of their lives such as budgeting, purchasing, practicing household tasks involving measurement including cooking and dispensing cleaning supplies and pesticides, planning for retirement, and so forth. One just needs to consider the important role that monetary credit plays in our lives today and the ramifications of mishandling one's credit to understand the importance of mathematical competence.

Many teachers in special education are not even aware of the learning standards that have been established by the NCTM (Maccini & Gagnon, 2002). Compounding this dichotomy between what teachers know and what they need to know is that in many other states such as Florida, certification is designed to cover grades kindergarten *through* 12, meaning that aspiring special education teachers are expected to be proficient in teaching the full K–12 mathematics curriculum. Although states are beginning to respond to this lack of mathematics preparation for special education teachers as a result of the highly qualified teacher mandate of the No Child Left Behind Act of 2001 (PL 107-110), the language of what *highly qualified* means seems to emphasize content expertise over pedagogical expertise. For example, consider the following language from the United States Department of Education about what constitutes highly qualified:

> Newly hired teachers in these covered LEAs [local education agencies] will have 3 years from the date of hire to become highly qualified in each core academic subject that they teach. In order to use this flexibility, covered [LEA's] will need to 1) ensure that all teachers in core academic subjects are highly qualified in at least one core academic subject they teach; 2) provide high-quality professional development that increases the teachers' content knowledge in the additional subjects they teach; and 3) provide mentoring or a program of intensive supervision that consists of structured guidance and regular, ongoing support so that they become highly qualified in the additional core academic subject(s) they teach (EdGov, 2004, p. 1).

The almost exclusive emphasis on content expertise rather than teaching methods (i.e., mathematics education coursework) and pedagogical content knowledge (how the content and learner interact) for determination of "highly qualified" dramatically contrasts with the research base that clearly demonstrates that student outcomes are greater when they have teachers who received training in educational methods (i.e., how to teach effectively), particularly those teachers who majored in education (e.g., Begle, 1979; Darling-Hammond, 2000; Monk, 1994).

Moreover, because of the small literature base, very few textbooks that focus on how to teach mathematics effectively for students with learning difficulties have been written, so even if pedagogy were a focus of the highly qualified requirements, there is little support for assisting teacher preparation programs to prepare teachers to teach mathematics effectively to these students.

The natural result of these factors—a limited research base and the limited emphasis on mathematics instruction in teacher preparation—is that educators are likely to place less value on mathematics instruction for struggling learners. Mathematics instruction for these students can be of secondary concern when decisions are made about which curriculum to adopt, how much instructional time should be allotted to content areas, and what should be emphasized for ongoing professional development. It is not difficult to understand, then, why educators may not value mathematics instruction for struggling learners to the degree that instruction in other areas is valued.

The value that is placed on mathematics instruction for struggling learners is within each educator's control. However, to some degree, the value that educators place on mathematics instruction can be affected by their own experiences with learning mathematics. If these experiences were positive, then one might be more likely to value mathematics more than those individuals whose experiences were negative. Therefore, how a teacher learned mathematics him- or herself can have an impact on the extent to which that teacher values mathematics instruction for struggling learners and how that educator teaches. If an educator learned mathematics through experiences that emphasized mostly abstract thinking and procedures, then it is likely that the educator will teach similarly, unless teacher preparation or professional development helped the teacher to understand other ways of teaching and learning mathematics. To learn mathematics, struggling learners need much more than instruction that is abstract in nature and that relies heavily on learning mathematical procedures. If a teacher's instruction is abstract in nature, then his or her teaching of mathematics to struggling learners likely has resulted in limited success. It follows that, in combination, previous negative experiences with learning mathematics and a limited understanding of how to teach mathematics effectively for struggling learners is a formula for placing limited value on mathematics instruction for these students. It is human nature for one not to value something that he or she finds difficult to do well or that results in little, if any, positive reinforcement (e.g., the satisfaction gained from observing students succeed).

HOW TO ENHANCE THE VALUE THAT TEACHERS PLACE ON MATHEMATICS INSTRUCTION FOR STRUGGLING LEARNERS

To value mathematics instruction for struggling learners, one must see the value that mathematics has for their lives. A meaningful approach is to think about it in relation to the students whom one currently teaches or the students whom one will be teaching. It is the individual needs, strengths, and circumstances of students that provide the palette for thinking about how their understanding of mathematics can have a positive impact on their lives. Activity 4.1 provides a framework for thinking about this important value. Use Figure 4.1 to consider the importance of mathematics in students' lives (see Appendix A for a blank version).

Activity 4.1
The Importance of Mathematics to Life

Take a few minutes to review Figure 4.1, and then brainstorm a list of different ways in which success in K–12 mathematics can benefit the lives of students with learning difficulties. Once you have done that, write each idea under the relevant category in Figure 4.1.

Activity 4.1 is a starting point for expanding one's thinking about the importance of mathematics for struggling learners. Many more ideas to be added to this categorized list can be gleaned by continuing to read this book and by involving yourself in continuing professional development. Another by-product of this reflective activity is that it provides teachers with a tangible strategy for helping their students to visualize the ways in which mathematics is important in their lives. As discussed in Chapter 5, struggling learners often lack metacognitive awareness; that is, they do not make connections among what they are learning, how they are learning, and how it relates to their personal lives. By helping students make the important connections between the mathematics that they learn and how it is useful to their lives, teachers help them to visualize the value of mathematics. In addition to this activity, Chapter 8 contains an informal assessment activity that will help teachers connect students' interests and experiences specifically to the particular mathematics concepts that they are learning in class.

Although an important aspect of becoming a better teacher for struggling learners is to value mathematics as an important subject for learning, another

Life skills		Graduation/ diploma	Success in other subject areas	Other
Current	Future			
Cashier: Making and counting change	Purchasing a car Calculating interest	Algebra 1	Civics/ Economics	College entrance requirements/ SAT and ACT

Figure 4.1. Brainstorming chart showing several examples of how mathematics is important in the lives of struggling learners.

aspect to this discussion must be addressed. Not only must teachers value the importance of mathematics in the lives of struggling learners but also they must value *providing effective mathematics instruction* for these students. Teachers must value engaging in professional development that helps them to develop solid mathematical knowledge for teaching (e.g., the connections between mathematical ideas, the conceptual meaning underlying procedures, how students make sense of mathematical ideas, and how that can be different from an adult's perspective) and to understand better the needs of struggling learners, how these needs relate to learning mathematics, and how to implement effective instructional practices that meet students' needs. For some, this may mean thinking differently about how they typically have taught mathematics. For others, this may mean changing how they think mathematics should be taught, on the basis of their previous learning experiences. For others, still, it may mean having higher expectations for struggling learners when it comes to learning mathematics and having higher expectations for themselves when it comes to ensuring that those expectations are met. For all teachers, it means embracing, in action, the value that it is the responsibility of educators to become better mathematics teachers for struggling learners. Activity 4.2 provides questions for a teacher to reflect on how to know the extent to which he or she values the teaching of mathematics to students with learning difficulties.

Activity 4.2

Write "yes" or "no" to each of the questions below. This activity can be completed as a group or cooperative learning activity or on an individual basis. Even a preservice teacher who is not currently in a field placement can think of students in past field placements or students who have been observed in the past, either as a student or as a volunteer.

1. Have you ever assumed that it was another teacher's responsibility to address the mathematics learning needs of any struggling learner whom you have taught?
2. Have you ever believed that you should not be expected to teach a struggling learner, including a student with identified learning difficulties?
3. Have you ever passed a student who is a struggling learner or given him or her a higher grade on an assignment than his or her performance reflected because you believed that it was the right thing to do or because you believed that he or she would never be able really to learn what was expected?
4. Have you ever used a less qualified person (e.g., paraprofessional, adult volunteer, student peer) to provide primary instruction for a student because you believed that all he or she really needed was one-to-one attention (rather than differentiated instruction by a qualified teacher on the basis of the student's individual learning needs)?
5. Have you ever moved on to teaching the next concept in your curriculum guide even though you knew that students did not learn what was just covered?

6.   Have you ever taken part in a "moan-and-groan" conversation with a colleague or colleagues in which the central topic was a struggling learner and how it was somebody else's fault for the student's problems (e.g., parent, another teacher, the context in which they live)?

7.   Have you ever lamented about having to go to a professional development activity or to take a class on mathematics, mathematics instruction, or teaching students with learning difficulties?

If you answered "yes" to any one of these questions, then it is likely that you need to enhance the value that you place on the teaching of mathematics for struggling learners. These questions come from the authors' own experiences as teachers, and they have engaged in most, if not all, of the actions suggested by each question. Having these experiences and reflecting on them over time—why the authors might have engaged in them and what impact they had on their effectiveness as teachers—allowed an examination of the value that was placed on teaching struggling learners effectively.

Even when one realizes that the value of teaching mathematics needs to be enhanced, it still may not change that at the root of the situation is the level of discomfort for teaching mathematics to struggling learners. See another reflective activity (Activity 4.3) in this chapter to self-examine further the extent to which you value mathematics instruction for struggling learners.

Activity 4.3 is intended to provide readers with some insight into potential reasons why they might not truly value the importance of teaching mathematics to struggling learners. If the activity was completed with a group, then it may provide insight into some other possible barriers that keep teachers, as a group, from placing high value on their role in teaching mathematics to struggling learners. If engaged in this professional development journey alone, consider asking a colleague to complete the activity and reflect on the implications of the responses together.

PREPAREDNESS TO TEACH MATHEMATICS TO STUDENTS WITH LEARNING DIFFICULTIES SELF-ASSESSMENT

The question, "How prepared am I to teach mathematics to struggling learners?" is one that must be examined critically if the goal is to teach mathematics *effectively* to these students. The degree to which one is prepared to be an effective mathematics teacher for struggling learners depends on one's professional development in several key areas:

1.   One's beliefs about the ability of struggling learners to learn mathematics

2.   One's knowledge of mathematics, the various processes for doing mathematics, and how the learner makes sense of the mathematical content

Activity 4.3
Valuing Mathematics Instruction

1. On a piece of paper, draw a line down the middle so that there are two columns. Approximately two thirds of the way down, draw a horizontal line across the paper so that it intersects the vertical line that you just drew (you should have an upside down "t" on your paper).

2. Label the first column, "Students to Whom I Really Enjoy Teaching Mathematics." Label the second column, "Students to Whom I Really Do Not Enjoy Teaching Mathematics."

3. In each column, describe the students (major characteristics that stand out to you) and why you do or do not like to teach them mathematics.

4. Compare your responses with others in your group or class. Discuss any insight or observations made.

5. At the bottom of each column (under the horizontal line), write and circle the number (on a scale from 1 to 10) that you think best represents that group of students' likelihood for success in learning mathematics for the year. In a few words, describe your reason for rating each group of students as you did.

6. Read both descriptions and ask yourself whether the reasons that you wrote for both groups of students are internal to the students (something about the students themselves) or external to the students (something in the students' environment). Reflect on the extent to which the reasons listed for the students for whom you do not like to teach mathematics relate to your role as teacher.

7. Discuss the following with your group or class:
   a. On the basis of group members' answers, what insights does the group have related to the responsibility that all teachers have for valuing mathematics instruction for students to whom they do not like to teach mathematics.
   b. Where does each group member see him- or herself in terms of valuing mathematics instruction for struggling learners?

3. One's understanding of why struggling learners have difficulty learning mathematics

4. One's understanding of and ability to implement effective mathematics instructional strategies that address the learning needs of struggling learners

The goal of this assessment is to assist teachers in identifying professional development needs and developing a plan for how to use this book to address identified needs and improve effectiveness in teaching mathematics for struggling learners. To accomplish these goals, a teacher must participate in self-reflection in an active way. One way to do this is to do Activity 4.4.

Activity 4.4
Self-Reflection Inventory

First, turn to the Teacher Self-Reflection Inventory in Appendix A and reflect critically on your own level of growth in each of the four key professional development areas. Then, profile the identified needs that you think most need to be developed. Finally, develop an individual professional development plan using the structure provided and remaining chapters. To do this, you will need to respond *honestly* to some questions that address each professional development area, reflect on your responses, and calculate where you are on a continuum of low need to high need for each professional development area. It is recommended that you then spend some time thinking about the results (your professional development "picture") so that you can develop an efficient plan for furthering your ability to become an effective teacher of mathematics to struggling learners.

Once you have prioritized your personal professional development needs, take some time to review the chapters in this book. Decide which chapters or sections within a chapter will best help you to develop yourself further in each professional development area. By doing this, you will have familiarized yourself with what is addressed in the remaining chapters of the book and reminded yourself of information in previous chapters that you might want to revisit. This will help you to individualize better your reading and study, whether you are taking a course, completing in-service, or doing your own professional development. The remaining chapters in this book provide information that will help teachers to overcome some or all of the barriers between current values and optimal values of mathematics and mathematics instruction for struggling learners. Because this book does not focus on the development of mathematical understanding for teachers or general mathematics education methods, readers who have professional development needs in these areas should consult additional resources that address these areas in particular. For example, Van de Walle and Lovin (2006a; 2006b; 2006c) as well as resources from NCTM such as the Navigations series are valuable resources for this purpose.

III

Barriers and Gateways to Meaningful Mathematics Instruction

5

Common Learning Characteristics that Make Mathematics Difficult for Struggling Learners

The big ideas in mathematics encompass both foundational knowledge and mathematical thinking/problem-solving processes. As outlined in previous chapters, struggling learners often have difficulty with learning mathematics. Therefore, it is incumbent on teachers to explore how these students' learning difficulties affect their success with mathematics. Although each student possesses unique, individual attributes and characteristics, several common learning difficulties can and do have a negative impact on mathematical learning. This chapter highlights eight learning characteristics that have a negative impact on the learning of mathematics for struggling learners. Each learning characteristic is described, including specific examples of how the learning characteristic affects students' mathematical understanding. This chapter, in conjunction with Chapters 6 and 7, addresses the second anchor of the Universal Features Model of meaningful mathematics instruction for struggling learners (see Figure 5.1).

EIGHT COMMON CHARACTERISTICS OF STUDENTS WHO STRUGGLE WITH LEARNING MATHEMATICS

Students who have learning difficulties that affect their ability to do well in mathematics come from a variety of backgrounds and experiences. Although each of these students is individual and unique, they share some common learning characteristics. By understanding the impact that these learning characteristics have on learning, teachers can plan and teach more effectively. Struggling learners may experience the negative learning impact of a number of characteristics that are the result of a disability, lack of previous successful experiences in mathematics, and ineffective teaching practices (Chard & Gersten, 1999; Geary, 1993; Ginsburg, 1997; Mercer, Jordan, et al., 1996; Mercer, Lane, et al, 1996; Miller & Mercer, 1997). The following eight characteristics

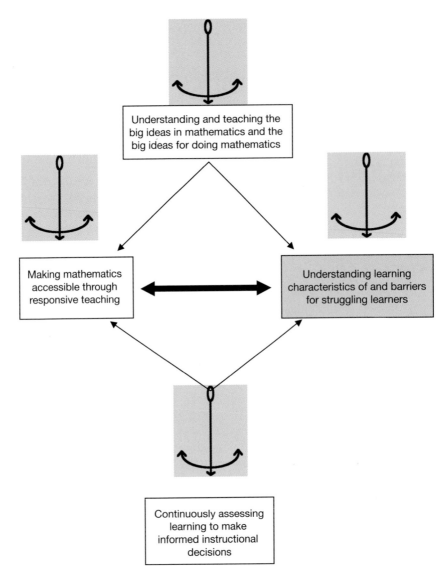

Figure 5.1.   Universal Features Model: Learning characteristics/barriers anchor.

reflect both characteristics that teachers most likely will encounter with students and characteristics that have high potential for having a negative impact on how students learn mathematics:

1. *Learned helplessness:* Students who experience continuous failure in mathematics expect to fail, resulting both in reticence to try something new and reliance on others to help them.

2. *Passive learning:* Struggling learners often are not active learners. They do not actively look for and make connections between what they already know and what they are presently learning. When presented with a problem-

solving situation, they do not implement strategies or activate previous knowledge to solve the problem.

3. *Memory difficulties:* Students with memory difficulties have difficulty with retaining and retrieving information, particularly related to basic addition, subtraction, multiplication, and division facts and multistep sequencing and problem solving.

4. *Attention difficulties:* Learning and doing mathematics requires a great deal of attention, especially when multiple steps are involved in the problem-solving process. During instruction, students who have attention difficulties often miss important pieces of information. When doing mathematics, students may also miss a step due to distractibility, thereby reaching an incorrect solution.

5. *Cognitive/metacognitive thinking deficits:* Metacognition has to do with students' abilities to monitor their learning, which involves 1) evaluating whether they are learning, 2) implementing strategies when needed, 3) knowing whether a strategy is successful, and 4) making changes when needed. These are essential skills for any problem-solving situation. Students with metacognitive deficits do not use these essential metacognitive thinking skills. Because problem solving is an integral part of mathematics, students who are not metacognitively adept will have great difficulty being successful with mathematics.

6. *Processing deficits:* Students with processing deficits have difficulty accurately perceiving what they see, hear, and/or feel. Many students with learning disabilities possess processing deficits. Their vision and hearing are intact, but their central nervous system processes information differently, leading to misperceptions regarding what they learn. For example, a student with a visual processing deficit may see a mathematics equation accurately, but the visual information that he or she inputs may get distorted when the brain processes it; therefore, what the student sees is not actually what he or she perceives. Other students may require more time to process information that they hear. To them, the teacher seems to talk too fast, when, in actuality, their central nervous system processes at a slower rate.

7. *Low level of academic achievement:* Students who experience failure in mathematics often have holes in their knowledge base. Struggling learners often have these holes for a variety of reasons. For example, students with a visual or auditory processing deficit require a longer time to process visual and auditory information than typical learners. Because of this they often do not have enough time or opportunity to master the foundational concepts and skills that make learning more complex mathematics possible.

8. *Math anxiety:* Struggling learners often approach mathematics with trepidation. Because learning and doing mathematics are difficult for them, "math time" often is an anxiety-ridden experience predisposing them to "shut down" when confronted with learning something new.

How the Eight Characteristics
Affect Learning of Mathematics

This section describes how each learning characteristic affects the learning of mathematics in general terms and the impact on learning as it relates to the five big ideas in mathematics and the five processes for learning and doing mathematics described in Chapter 3.

Learned Helplessness   Struggling learners frequently exhibit learned helplessness when they approach mathematical tasks and activities. These are the students whose hands are raised before you finish giving directions, who ask frequent questions, and who require a lot of prompting and reinforcement to complete mathematical tasks.

Why would a fifth-grade student want to have the teacher help him with each step of the problem? Why would a second-grade student start crying when asked to explain her answer? Why would a 10th-grade student refuse to do homework even when it means receiving a failing grade? Although such behaviors can stem from many reasons, likely causes of such behaviors as they relate to approaching mathematical tasks and activities are students' past experiences and negative attributions that are associated with these experiences. Previous mathematics learning experiences for struggling learners typically have not been successful ones. When mathematics instruction has been solely focused on right and wrong answers, even students as young as 5 years can quickly become intimidated when their answers and methods do not match the teacher's (adult's) way of thinking about the problem, especially when the teacher's method does not make sense to them. Past experiences such as these have taught these students that "I cannot succeed" or that "It does not matter how much effort I put forth because I will never get it right."

Consider this example from a hypothetical classroom. The students are working on the following task and have been asked to use concrete objects or draw pictures.

Brianna wants to purchase 15 Valentine's Day cards. She wants $\frac{2}{3}$ of the 15 cards to have a heart on them. How many cards will have hearts?

Many of the students either draw or use objects to illustrate that they have grouped the objects into groups of three and then colored or pulled two of the three objects to find $\frac{2}{3}$ of 15 (Figure 5.2). However, one student chooses to look at the entire 15 objects at once and looks for a way to break it up into three equal groups. Using his knowledge of multiplication, he thinks to try 3 groups of 5 (Figure 5.3). His representation looks different from Figure 5.2 because his groups are in groups of fives, not threes. What does the teacher do? In traditional settings that focus on only one way (usually the teacher's way) of solving a task, this student's strategy will likely not be considered or accepted. This repeated kind of reaction to a strategy or a solution that is different from what the teacher expects helps to create learned helplessness because students' often valid way of doing the mathematics is not acknowledged or allowed and the adult way of doing the problem is always followed, even if it does not make

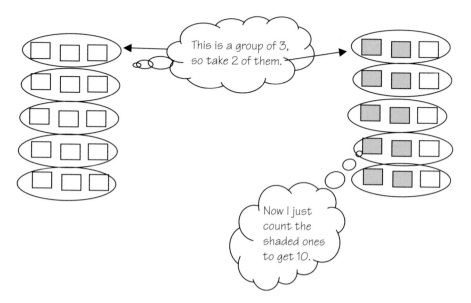

Figure 5.2. Student representation for ⅔ of 15 Valentine cards.

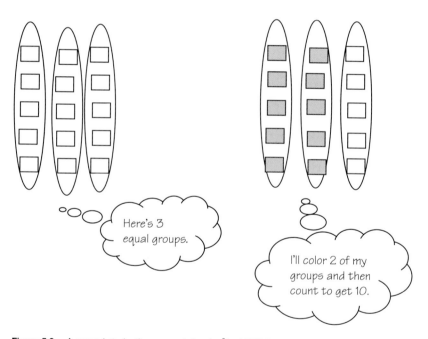

Figure 5.3. A second student's representation for ⅔ of 15 Valentine cards.

sense to the learner. Eventually, students shut down because they become convinced that they cannot do it. When a student uses an unexpected strategy or arrives at an unexpected solution, the best question a teacher can ask is if the solution is a mathematically valid way to solve this task. By going back to what the number ⅔ tells us, we can reason that we take our whole and break it into 3 equal parts and then take 2 of those equal parts to find the answer. Each student's approach did just this. The difference is that each student used a different whole. In the first solution, the whole was each group of 3. In the second solution, the whole was the 15 cards. It is the teacher's role to determine if a student's strategy and solution are mathematically valid and then to help make explicit for all students how it is indeed just another way to look at the task. Helping students consider how the wholes change helps develop flexibility in their thinking, but it also reinforces a central idea of fractions in particular: the significance of the whole. Moreover, the focus on reasoning circumvents the rejection of students' ways of thinking, giving them reason to believe that mathematics can make sense and that they can do it.

Unfortunately, if students continue to experience low rates of success, they begin to attribute their failure to internal factors—factors over which they have no control. Their internal self-talk includes such generalized negative statements as, "I can't do math," "I'm not smart enough," "I don't think that way," and, "Math is not my subject." Correspondingly, they attribute any success that they have to external factors ("I got lucky," "My teacher likes me and gave me the grade," and, "I passed because I used my new pencil"). Such thinking leads students to attribute their successes to external factors and their failures to internal factors, neither of which they can control. As they continue to experience difficulty, their attributes become entrenched, and they develop learned helplessness: "I can't do this by myself," "I'll never be successful unless someone helps me," "There is no point in trying to understand this," and, "I can't do it."

Students with learned helplessness often resist trying new strategies in problem-solving situations. They do not want to be wrong, so they will revert back to traditional or former ways of reasoning and problem solving, even if these ways do not make sense to them. Such behavior has a negative impact on their ability to build conceptual knowledge and generalize to new situations. Examples of instructional strategies that can assist students in overcoming learned helplessness include breaking down tasks into more manageable segments, providing visual organizers that cue students to important aspects of a concept, and continuously monitoring student progress so that instruction can be changed quickly if it is not successful. It is important to note here that these instructional strategies are not "doing the thinking" for the students, but are a way to provide structure to the task so that it is manageable for the students in their current state of learned helplessness. These strategies and others are described in more detail in Chapters 9 and 10.

Passive Learning   Given the difficulties that struggling learners experience with negative attributions and learned helplessness, they often develop a passive approach to mathematics. Afraid to engage actively in activities that might lead to more failure, they shy away from exploration and experimentation. They do not want to "discover" the answer, because, given their past experiences, they do not believe that they can. For these students, mathematics is a series of disconnected, rote actions that result in right or wrong answers. They do not actively look for and make connections between what they already know and what they are presently learning. When presented with a problem-solving situation, they do not implement strategies or activate previous knowledge to solve the problem.

For example, if a student knows that $4 \times 6 = 24$ but he has not yet developed automaticity with 4×7, 4×8, or 4×9, then one strategy to use is to add on (e.g., add 4 to 24 to get 28). However, a student who has learning difficulties and is reluctant to engage actively in mathematical problem solving often will not experiment with the add-on strategy to find new answers. He or she might use the strategy if taught it very explicitly but rarely will do so independently without prompting. The student must also know that multiplication is repeated addition to understand that adding on is a viable option. As students get older and mathematical concepts become more complex, this reluctance to take risks and try something new becomes a huge barrier to developing more sophisticated problem-solving skills, which can hinder their full understanding of these more complex mathematical ideas.

Passive learning can seriously impair students' ability to develop algebraic thinking because they often shy away from discovery and trial and error. Consequently, students who are passive learners will have difficulty making connections between number and operation sense concepts and algorithmic procedures. As an example, students who approach the problem 45×3 do so passively, thinking that the problem is too difficult to solve because of the size of the number, 45, and because they have to multiply. However, if they used what they already know about addition, then they could use the repeated addition strategy and find the solution ($45 + 45 + 45 = 135$). Or they could use place value to think about 45 as 40 and 5, find 40×3 and then 5×3, and then add $120 + 15$.

Embedding mathematical instruction in relevant authentic contexts and encouraging students to develop and consider several strategies to complete a task will help these students make important connections and develop flexibility in their thinking. It also will be helpful to provide an explicit way (e.g., a strategy journal for mathematics) for students to actually see their progress in developing and using alternative strategies for mathematical problem solving. The strategies discussed in Chapters 9 and 10 provide more information about ways to address passive learning.

Memory Difficulties   When working with struggling learners who have memory difficulties, it often is a case of "here today, gone tomorrow." Students with memory difficulties have a particularly difficult time remembering basic arithmetic fundamentals such as addition, subtraction, multiplication, and division facts. Memory deficits also play a significant role when students are solving multistep problems and when problem-solving situations require the use of step-wise problem-solving strategies. Moreover, students with memory difficulties may experience problems with moving from concrete to abstract understandings of important mathematical areas such as numbers and number sense. When confronted with multistep problems and/or time limits, they will have difficulty remembering all of the steps or the sequence of the steps or completing the task within a specific time frame, especially if the steps do not make sense to them. Memory is linked so closely to language and our ability to communicate that students with memory difficulties may have difficulty communicating their mathematical understandings if not provided with visual, auditory, kinesthetic, or tactile cuing and supports that are explicitly tied to concepts.

A common misconception about the memory difficulties of struggling learners is that the problem is an information storage problem only—that somehow, these students just cannot store certain kinds of information in memory. This belief probably arises because one day a student can do a math task but cannot the next day. Teachers then reteach the skill only to have the same experience repeated. This type of thing leads to people's questioning of students' motivation and their interest and sometimes their cognitive ability. However, this inconsistent performance has much more to do with how meaningfully students have stored information in their memory and the extent to which they possess efficient strategies for retrieving that information. For example, consider a student who is learning about numerators and denominators. He or she may have memorized that the numerator is the top number in a fraction and that the denominator is the bottom number because this is how the information was presented. When asked to identify the numerator and the denominator in a fraction at another time, however, he or she easily may mix up the two. There are several possible reasons for this, one being that the student did not have a meaningful way to store the information in his or her memory. Associating a name with an abstract symbol based on its position in space does not hold a lot of meaning for students. If, however, the numerator was demonstrated using concrete materials (e.g., two pieces of pizza from a pizza with four total slices) and associated with a meaningful context (e.g., sharing equal sections of pizza with a friend at the local pizza place), then it is more likely that the association would be meaningful. When the student goes to retrieve from memory the concept of a numerator, he or she will be more likely to do so more efficiently and accurately, because now he or she possesses a more meaningful association in memory.

It is important to differentiate between students who have difficulty remembering because they have trouble acquiring an understanding of a concept and those who acquire understanding but have difficulty retrieving the information from memory. Difficulty with acquiring understanding most likely is related to ineffective use of learning strategies (e.g., rehearsal and retention strategies, metacognitive strategies such as self-talk, connecting to existing knowledge) or ineffective instruction (e.g., lack of context, limited use of multisensory instruction). For these students, remembering what they learned is difficult because they have never really learned it. Difficulty with *retrieval* is more closely linked to problems with organization and association (i.e., linking to existing knowledge). Students who have difficulty with retrieval may not have developed efficient memory retrieval strategies. Providing students with visual organizers and multiple opportunities to represent problems and regularly integrating mnemonics into instruction can help ameliorate the effects of memory deficits. Chapters 9 and 10 outline these and other strategies in more detail. In particular, strategy instruction that incorporates mnemonics is described as an instructional practice that helps students with memory difficulties.

Attention Difficulties   Students with attention difficulties often miss important mathematical information as it is being discussed or as they engage in problem solving. Contrary to the popular opinion that students with attention deficits cannot attend, students with true attention deficits actually attend to too much! For these students, a multitude of sensory stimulation catches their attention. Because of this, they have trouble filtering out all of the information that their senses and brain are processing. Rather than not focusing on anything, these students are focusing on everything! Such hyperattention can occur both during teacher-led instruction and when students are engaged in mathematical learning activities that do not involve teacher-led instruction (e.g., independent problem solving, cooperative learning groups).

This heightened level of attention can negatively affect students' conceptual understandings of mathematics because it prevents them from ignoring stimuli that are not important to the learning task at hand, which then results in their missing important information related to the learning task. To build mathematical understanding and connections, students need to be able to compare similar and dissimilar figures, procedures, and processes using discrimination skills that require attention to important details. Mathematical thinking can become very restricted for students with attention difficulties, who are limited by their inability to filter out extraneous stimuli. They are less likely to accomplish comprehensive comparisons between and among similar and dissimilar concepts, inhibiting their ability to build mathematical connections.

Attention difficulties can have two very distinct outcomes related to mathematics. The first is that during instruction, students who have attention difficulties often miss important pieces of information. Without these important pieces of information, students have difficulty trying to implement the strategies or procedures that have just been discussed. For example, when learning the standard long division procedure, students may miss the *subtract* step in the *divide, multiply, subtract, bring down* long division process. Without subtracting in the proper place, the student will be unable to solve long division problems accurately. A better approach to use would be to teach procedures connected to concepts so that if students have somehow missed pieces of information, they can derive the next step because the procedure makes more sense and it is not something that is just memorized (see explicit trading method for long division in Chapter 9). Students with attention difficulties often rely on keywords that appear in the last question or sentence of a word problem to determine the correct operation. These students will focus only on the keyword, thereby missing other, important information. Attention difficulties also can affect problem solving, particularly in situations that require students to visualize the unique features of the problem while simultaneously visualizing the relationship among them so that they can develop a hypothesis to solve the problem. For example, using a graphing calculator, students can examine the effects of changing the coefficients in the quadratic equation $y = ax^2 + bx + c$. Students with attention difficulties attend to every slight modification in the graph rather than isolating how the graph changes in general.

A second outcome that occurs with students who have attention difficulties is that they may be unable to focus on the important features that make a mathematical concept distinct. For example, when these students are learning about geometric shapes, they may attend to features that are not relevant to defining the shapes. Instead of counting the number of sides to distinguish triangles from rectangles, the student may focus on size or color. When working with exponents and coefficients, such as x^2 and $2x$, they may attend only to the fact that there is a 2 involved and treat both expressions the same. They fail to distinguish that one expression involves an exponent and the other expression involves a coefficient.

Using visual, auditory, tactile (touch), and kinesthetic (movement) cues to highlight the relevant features of a concept is a helpful teaching technique for addressing attention difficulties. In addition, teaching students to use self-cuing strategies (i.e., strategies that prompt students to use a relevant cuing device to highlight important aspects of a problem) can be helpful. These as well as other strategies are discussed further in Chapters 9 and 10.

Cognitive/Metacognitive Thinking Deficits   Mathematics truly is a form of communication. To communicate effectively, one has to be aware of the audience, develop and deliver the message, and then monitor the communication to ascertain whether the message has been received as it was meant to be. Did I say what I meant to say? Was I clear? Is there a misunderstanding? If so, what is it and how can it be addressed? In oral language communication, this is the concept of conversational repair: the ability to detect and repair breakdowns in communication (Reed, 2005). When developing mathematical understanding, students also must be able to monitor and, as necessary, repair the communication effectively. They must be able to decide what is being said with mathematical numbers, symbols, and shapes and whether they understand the message; and, on the basis of their understanding, develop a response. Obviously, students need a strong sense of numbers, patterns and functions, geometric concepts, measurement, data analysis, and probability to communicate mathematically. However, students also need to be able to monitor how and what they communicate. They need to be aware of their use of problem solving, reasoning, and representation processes to monitor their understanding of the mathematics that they are communicating and fix misunderstandings when they occur.

For struggling learners to engage in these essential metacognitive skills, they need to be taught explicitly how to be metacognitive learners (Butler, Beckingham, & Novak-Lauscher, 2005; Deshler & Schumaker, 1986; Hughes & Maccini, 2000; Montague, Morgan, & Warger, 2000). Metacognitive strategy instruction involves teaching strategies to 1) recognize big ideas among details, 2) identify how information is structured, 3) see relationships between different sets of information, and 4) self-monitor learning. When students with metacognitive deficits use strategies to problem solve, they often use them inefficiently. Students must be provided with opportunities to learn about strategies. They also must be provided with multiple opportunities to use them and to generalize their use across a variety of contexts. Teachers who model using metacognition, who teach students problem-solving strategies, who reinforce students' use of these strategies, and who teach students to organize themselves so that they can access strategies will help students who have metacognitive deficits to become metacognitive learners. Chapters 9 and 10 discuss in greater detail how to teach strategies effectively and provide practice opportunities for students to strengthen mathematical metacognition.

Processing Deficits   Teaching mathematics is a complex task that involves multiple avenues of input as well as output. For many students with learning difficulties, some modes of input will be less optimal than others. Students with processing deficits are likely to misperceive information that is presented to their primary processing deficit. For example, if a teacher is con-

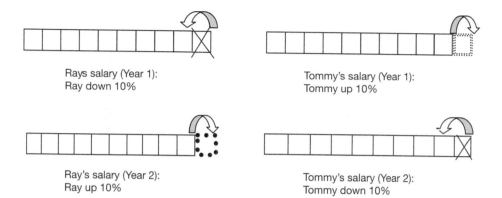

Figure 5.4.   A visually represented solution that may be confusing for students with a visual processing deficit.

ducting a discussion about how students used different ways to represent the number 7 with counters, then a student with an auditory processing problem may miss many of the key points of the discussion. A processing deficit does not mean that a student has acuity difficulties. In other words, as mentioned earlier, their eyesight or hearing is not impaired. The information gets mixed up as their brain processes what they accurately see or hear. Therefore, the student may hear each word, but because of a central nervous system dysfunction, his or her ability to process the separate speech sounds, to make connections between the sounds and known vocabulary, and/or to visualize the oral explanation may be seriously impaired.

The impact of visual processing deficits can be illustrated by a problem from Chapter 3: *Tommy and Ray made the same amount of money for years. However, last year, Tommy got a raise of 10%. Ray got a pay cut of 10%. This year, Ray got a 10% raise, and Tommy got a 10% cut. Do Tommy and Ray now make the same amount of money? Why or why not?* In this example, it was suggested that the teacher invite students to show different representations to find the solution to the problem. A student might draw a possible solution for the problem as in Figure 5.4.

To a student with a visual processing deficit, this visually represented solution may be very confusing. He or she may well see each line and each figure, but the central nervous system dysfunction that interrupts his or her visual processing may interfere with ready integration of visual symbols. It may take time for a student to perceive that the lines actually relate to each other to form a unique shape (arrow) or that there is a difference in direction or position.

Processing deficits can involve multiple input and output pathways (e.g., visual–motor, auditory–motor, visual–speech, auditory–speech). For example, students with visual–motor and/or auditory–motor processing deficits often have great difficulty representing accurately through writing what they know because what they have seen or heard is misrepresented by the motor movements that are involved in writing. Often, the student will be able to represent accurately what he or she saw or heard when asked to say it rather than write it. Therefore, processing deficits can be caused by deficits in one or more of the input processing areas (e.g., visual, auditory, tactile, kinesthetic), by deficits in one or more of the output processing areas (e.g., motor, speech), and by deficits in the integration of multiple input and output perceptual processes (e.g., visual–motor, auditory–speech). In some cases, the speed with which students process information is the issue; that is, they may be able to process information accurately, but it takes a longer time than usual. Students with an auditory processing speed deficit often believe that the teacher is talking too fast. By the time the teacher moves to the next point or idea, the student is still processing what was said first. Students miss important information because they are busy processing information that they have already heard and are not inputting the auditory information that is currently being spoken by the teacher.

Providing multimodal instruction (both teacher input and student response) can help alleviate the effects of a processing deficit. Hands-on, kinesthetic learning will provide students with opportunities to integrate information across modalities, thereby engaging multiple senses. Providing wait time for students is another effective approach when students are to respond to questions. Teachers provide wait time by letting a student know that they are going to ask him or her a question (cuing), asking the question (auditory input), then providing the student time to process the question before expecting an answer or moving to the next part of the question (allowing extended processing time). In addition, when teachers are able to discuss tasks with students and how the student reasoned about completing the task, the teachers can prompt student thinking with purposeful questions. When teachers are explicit with students about using this process to make sense of how they are thinking, students can begin to realize that mathematics is more than just right and wrong answers. Also, students' responses provide the teacher a framework for pinpointing each student's understanding and possible misconceptions. The use of a flexible mathematics interview as a technique for assessing student understanding and misconceptions is discussed in more detail in Chapter 8. Chapters 9 and 10 provide more detail on other instructional strategies that address processing deficits.

Low Level of Academic Achievement   Struggling learners often have low levels of academic achievement, not only in mathematics but also in other subjects such as reading (Mercer & Mercer, 2005). Reading difficulties not only affect students' ability to comprehend written text but also affect their mathematics achievement because reading difficulties result in limited vocabulary development, which in turn affects students' understanding of the language of mathematics (Cawley et al., 2001). For example, students with limited vocabulary development may have difficulty understanding the differences in the following two problems:

Maria and Antoine each have 4 cupcakes. How many do they have all together?

Maria has 4 cupcakes. Antoine has 4 more cupcakes than Maria. How many do they have all together?

In each of these problems, the words *all together* could cue the students to combine objects. However, for students with reading and language difficulties, the words *all together* may be synonymous to adding, so they arrive, incorrectly, at the same answer for each problem. Their difficulties with vocabulary and understanding the semantic features of language impede their problem-solving abilities. Difficulties with language also can make it difficult for students to generate questions that could help the teacher better pinpoint what they do not understand.

As has been discussed, teaching students to solve word problems using cue words is not an effective strategy, even when students do not have limited vocabulary. When taught to look for cue words, students do not read to make sense of the context, but scan the text for numbers and then use the operation "implied" by the cue words. If this strategy always worked, it might be a somewhat effective strategy to complete the task. But as shown in the word problems just mentioned, cue words do not always work. Consequently, teaching students to use cue words to solve word problems can actually continue the vicious circle in which students meet failure in mathematics.

Struggling learners often have difficulty with remembering basic math facts. Some research indicates that students' difficulty with basic math facts is related to the development of phonological processing skills (Hecht, Torgesen, Wagner, & Rashotte, 2001). The traditional method of teaching numbers and number facts in the United States is to have students practice repeating them orally. This is similar to students' ability to encode a string of phonological representations. If a student has delayed phonological awareness skills, then he or she may have concomitant delays in the ability to link oral representations of numbers to their visual shapes.

Gaps inevitably occur in mathematical understanding for these students, only compounding the impact of low levels of academic achievement. As students move beyond second and third grades, these gaps in knowledge/skills have a profound effect because the curriculum begins to build quickly on previous understandings. Without a foundation on which to build, students begin to have greater levels of difficulty, putting them at risk for failure. A word of caution is provided here. Sometimes teachers identify these "holes" in knowledge as a lack of "basic skills." Teachers will often say that students need to know their basic facts before they can do any higher level problems and so the instructional focus becomes having students "learn" these "skills" via drill and memorization (i.e., the traditional method of teaching number facts). In actuality, the holes may be there because students' only exposure to these ideas was through drill and memorization, not through concept development. Mathematics builds on ideas, and when the foundation consists of isolated bits of information, holes will be present. Helping students make connections by focusing on concepts first will close up those holes and shore up the foundation.

To help students build meaningful connections, teachers must teach mathematics with a focus on making sense of the mathematics. Using language that is relevant, understandable, and directly tied to concepts is a must. Using multiple representations for mathematical concepts and combining concrete experiences with authentic contexts that engage students to use their own language to describe what they are learning is also important. Providing students with multiple opportunities to use their developing understanding of mathematical concepts in meaningful ways (what we call *practice*), so that proficiency and mastery of new concepts and skills are attained is essential, as is planning periodic review and practice of concepts and skills that students have mastered previously so that students maintain what they have learned. Chapters 9 and 10 provide additional details for how to address low-level academic achievement.

Math Anxiety   The learning characteristics that have been discussed in this chapter can make math time a very anxiety-ridden experience. In many ways, this anxiety only intensifies the impact of the other seven learning characteristics. For example, a student's use of learned helplessness behaviors is only going to increase when he or she is anxious about attempting something new. Anxiety also can make memory and processing tasks more difficult because fear and stress inhibit students' use of any strategies that they have developed for dealing with memory or processing deficits.

The best cure for math anxiety is success. Providing success starts first with the teacher. By understanding why students are having the difficulties that they are having, teachers are less inclined to place blame on the students for their lack of success in mathematics. These students already believe that they are not capable. The attitude with which teachers approach these students can be a crucial first step in rectifying the mathematical difficulties that they are having. Providing these students with nonthreatening, risk-free opportunities to learn and practice mathematical skills lays a critical foundation. Celebrating both small and great advances also is important. Last, if teachers provide instruction that is effective for these students, then they will help them to learn mathematics, thereby helping them to experience the success that they deserve. Section IV explores responsive teaching strategies that can lead to student success.

HOW THE EIGHT CHARACTERISTICS RELATE TO STUDENTS' DEVELOPING MATHEMATICAL UNDERSTANDING

When teachers understand these eight learning characteristics and how they can affect learning, it is possible to appreciate how they affect students' ability to develop mathematical understandings across the five big ideas of mathematics and using the five processes for mathematics. Table 5.1 shows how the eight learning characteristics affect students' development of mathematical understanding. The marked boxes delineate the big ideas and processes that most likely are affected by a specific characteristic. Because learning is a complex process that involves the interrelationship among many attributes and characteristics and the aforementioned interconnectivity between the mathematical big ideas and processes, it is neither possible nor advisable to state that characteristic A will always affect area B. However, the chart does help to show the pervasiveness of the impact in terms of students' acquiring and developing mathematical understanding. Section IV provides a more in-depth exploration of the impact of each characteristic.

Table 5.1. Impact of eight learning characteristics on students' developing mathematics understanding of the five content big ideas in mathematics and the five process big ideas for using mathematics

Learning Characteristics	Big content ideas					Big process ideas				
	Number and operations	Algebra	Geometry	Measurement	Data analysis and probability	Problem solving	Reasoning and proof	Communication	Representation	Connections
Learned helplessness	X	X	X	X	X	X	X	X		X
Passive learning	X	X	X		X	X	X			X
Memory difficulties	X		X	X						
Attention difficulties			X	X		X		X	X	
Cognitive/Metacognitive thinking deficits	X	X	X	X	X	X	X		X	X
Processing deficits	X	X	X		X	X	X		X	X
Low achievement	X	X	X	X	X	X	X	X	X	X
Math anxiety	X	X	X	X	X	X	X	X	X	X

6

Curriculum Barriers to Learning Mathematics

This chapter describes five curriculum/instructional approaches that are barriers to mathematics learning for struggling learners. These curriculum/instructional approaches are common in pre-K–12 education, and whereas some or all may benefit students who are typical learners, they can have a negative impact on struggling learners. How these approaches can be barriers to students with learning difficulties is described and related to the eight learning characteristics described in Chapter 5.

To understand this chapter more fully, it will be helpful to complete Activity 6.1. Use Figure 6.1 to guide your completion of this activity. Doing so

---

Activity 6.1
Evaluating and Comparing Textbooks

1. Choose a textbook series that you use in your classes or that an instructor provides to you and list several of the key mathematical concepts and procedural understandings that are addressed by the textbook in the first column in a chart similar to Figure 6.1. A blank copy of this figure is included in Appendix A.
2. Now evaluate the same textbook series for another grade and record key mathematical concepts and procedural understandings in that textbook.
3. Compare the first and second columns. Check for similarities and differences. Highlight the similarities across grade levels.
4. What does your highlighted chart indicate? How might this affect students with mathematics learning difficulties?
5. As you continue to read this chapter, reflect on the chart:
   a. What are the instructional ramifications for the information that you collected?
   b. How might this information interact with the characteristics described in Chapter 5?

Grade 2	Grade 3	Similarities and differences
Develop <u>flexible methods of adding whole numbers,</u> one to three digits each.	Develop <u>flexible methods for adding</u> and subtracting <u>whole numbers</u> by taking apart and combining numbers in a variety of ways, with major emphasis on place value.	**Similarities:** Flexible methods, adding whole numbers **Differences:** Subtracting whole numbers; taking apart and combining numbers in a variety of ways, w/emphasis on place value
Determine <u>sum or difference</u> of two whole numbers, each 999 or less, <u>with and without regrouping.</u>	Determine <u>sum or difference</u> of two whole numbers, each 9,999 or less, <u>with and without regrouping.</u>	**Similarities:** Sum or difference, with and without regrouping **Differences:** Numbers to compute are higher

Figure 6.1. Textbook Curriculum Chart showing similarities and differences in concepts described for teaching in second and third grades.

will enhance your understanding of how the information discussed in this chapter might relate to the curriculum that you currently use or will use in the future.

FIVE CURRICULUM BARRIERS

Five curriculum barriers are common to students who struggle with mathematics: 1) spiraling curriculum, 2) teaching to mastery, 3) teaching understanding versus algorithm-driven instruction, 4), reforms that are cyclical in nature, and 5) lack of implementation of effective teaching practices for struggling learners.

Spiraling Curriculum

Within a spiraling curriculum, students are exposed to a number of important mathematical concepts in the first year. As is evident from the chart developed in Activity 6.1, students return to those math concepts in the next year, expanding on the foundation that was established the year before. This cycle continues with each successive year. Although the purpose of this approach is logical and may be appropriate for students who are average to above-average achievers, the spiraling curriculum can be a significant impediment for struggling learners.

The primary problem with this curricular approach for struggling learners is the limited time that is devoted to each concept. Students who have learning difficulties that hinder their ability to learn mathematics may never truly be able to master the concept or skill being taught. For these students, exposure to foundational skills is not enough. Without having multiple opportunities to use their developing understandings of mathematical concepts in meaningful ways (i.e., "practice"), these students will only partially acquire an understanding of the concept or skill. When the concept or skill is revisited in the next year, the student is at a great disadvantage because the foundation that they are expected to have is incomplete. After several years, the student not only has not mastered earlier skills but also has not been able to make the important connections between those earlier concepts and skills and the higher level mathematics concepts and skills that are being taught as the student moves through the elementary, middle, and secondary grades.

This lack of sound foundational knowledge and understanding contribute to students' low levels of achievement. In addition, the affect of a spiraling curriculum can be a major contributor to the development of math anxiety. As students progress through school, they are faced with similar concepts and understandings but do not have a sound foundation to work with these concepts. If in reading, a student's phonological understanding has a negative impact on his or her ability to comprehend written material as he or she moves up through the grades, then why should mathematics not be similar? A student who fails to develop the earlier foundational ideas in the five strands of the mathematics curriculum will certainly have difficulty comprehending material at a higher level. As the student progresses through the curriculum, the holes in his or her understanding become greater. Think of the difficulty of building a tower if the foundation is not set. The same idea holds true for struggling learners and mathematics.

Spiraling curricula can be beneficial when teachers are aware of the curricular expectations, determine potential mismatches between these expectations and their students' learning needs, and make appropriate instructional adjustments. For example, when the linkages and connections between concepts are made explicit, students with learning difficulties are provided a way to build on their previous knowledge, thereby positively influencing their development of mathematical understandings. However, when students are not provided with such explicit connection building, the needed linkages are not made and the intended purpose for the spiraling curriculum is not achieved.

Teaching to Mastery

Struggling learners need many and varied opportunities to respond to specific mathematical ideas to master them (i.e., to have facility with the idea and be able to use it meaningfully; Fuchs & Fuchs 2001). Teaching to mastery requires that both the teacher and the student monitor the student's learning progress. For example, attention and memory deficits can present significant barriers to long-term retention of new information. When teachers provide students with multiple opportunities to respond to learning tasks that involve new information, it enables students to strengthen the neural pathways in memory. By involving students in monitoring their progress as they learn, teachers activate metacognition, thereby enhancing students' ability to think about what they are learning as they continue to make connections between ideas. This process also helps strengthen retention.

Struggling learners often demonstrate uneven performance levels. Because of the learning characteristics that are common for these students, it is possible that a student might do well on a mathematics test one day but not do as well if given the same test another day. Mastery (i.e., relational understanding of mathematics) can be inferred only when the student demonstrates consistent understanding over time. Moreover, instructional changes can be made quickly when continuous progress monitoring indicates that a student is not progressing. Unfortunately, such continuous assessment is rare in mathematics classrooms.

When the significance and potential negative effects of teaching to mastery are not considered, one can understand that the sequential nature of mathematics can be both a blessing and a curse. Although it can provide struggling learners many linkages and connections, it also can lull teachers into thinking that students have mastered concepts because of the repeated exposure that they receive (e.g., spiraling curriculum). However, repeated exposure in and of itself will not be sufficient without multiple opportunities for students to use their developing mathematical knowledge in meaningful ways, without close monitoring of student performance, and without identifying specific areas of weakness and misunderstandings. A struggling learner may have been exposed to a concept several times. However, because of attention difficulties, he or she may understand only part of the concept or because of memory difficulties may not be able to retain or retrieve the full sequence of needed steps in problem solving. Students with metacognitive difficulties may use a strategy for one context but cannot truly demonstrate understanding by applying the strategy to another context.

Struggling learners need multiple practice opportunities in addition to multiple opportunities to demonstrate mastery. They need to demonstrate mastery, not just recognition, of mathematical concepts and to do so within a variety of problem-solving contexts. Students who are passive learners and who struggle with math anxiety will need multiple opportunities to demonstrate not only to their teachers but also to themselves that they can be successful at learning mathematics.

Teaching Understanding Versus Algorithm-Driven Instruction

Although the NCTM strongly encourages teaching for mathematical understanding and reasoning, the reality for struggling learners is that they spend most of their mathematics time learning and practicing particular computational procedures that are demonstrated by the teacher as steps to memorize and are typically the only strategy focused on. Because of their memory difficulties, attention difficulties, and metacognitive deficits, these students have difficulty accurately performing multistep computations "learned" in this manner. It is likely that teachers focus on fixing this area because computation mistakes are so readily observable. In addition, because many teachers experience a lack of preparation in mathematics education, the procedural aspect of mathematics may be what these teachers know about or what they learned about when they were students. Therefore, these teachers tend to place emphasis on procedural accuracy rather than on conceptual understanding for their students.

This emphasis on algorithmic (i.e., procedural) proficiency supersedes emphasis on conceptual understanding, which is unfortunate because conceptual understanding is primary to making mathematics meaningful. A lack of conceptual understanding then results in difficulties with higher order mathematics and in applying and generalizing existing knowledge in meaningful ways. Students may be able to do the steps but, when asked, are unable to explain the mathematics behind the steps. When required to use the conceptual knowledge that underlies the procedure to learn something new, students are unable to do so because they lack the conceptual knowledge.

This lack of conceptual knowledge can lead to a passive approach to mathematics and contributes to the development of math anxiety. It is similar to following a recipe without knowing what you are making. You can read the steps and measure the ingredients, but your interest will wane if you performed this task repeatedly without ever knowing what you were making. In addition, if you were being assessed on the end result of what you made but you were not sure what it was, why it was or was not edible, and how you could change the product to make it better if needed, then you might become very anxious and avoid the task. It is likely that few people would want to eat what you cooked! Similarly, students who are walked through the steps without being given opportunities that enable them to understand the concept underlying the procedure likely will lose their motivation to explore and expand their knowledge of the task at hand because it holds no meaning for them.

For *all* students, but especially for struggling learners in mathematics, instruction should always be grounded in concepts, in making sense of the mathematics. This may mean that the teacher has to become an advocate for this type of learning environment for struggling learners, particularly if a purely algorithmic approach to mathematics is emphasized where they teach.

Reforms that Are Cyclical in Nature

The cyclical nature of mathematics curriculum/instruction reforms creates changing instructional practices that confuse struggling learners. Like reforms for reading instruction, reforms in mathematics instruction can swing from a primarily skills-based emphasis to a primarily meaning-based emphasis that depends on the philosophical and political trends of the day. Most students experience at least one of these shifts as they move through grades K–12. Whereas students who are average to above-average achievers are able to manage these changes in instruction, struggling learners do not adjust well to such change. Struggling learners need support for learning the procedural *and* conceptual aspects of mathematics. Without emphasizing both in ways that respond to the learning needs of these students, students will not be successful.

Lack of Implementation of Effective Teaching Practices for Struggling Learners

A fifth curriculum barrier is a lack of implementation of effective teaching practices. For a variety of reasons, teachers are often more focused on the product than on the process when teaching mathematics. This results in teachers using a purely teacher-centered approach to learning mathematics and being unaware that students think about mathematics differently than do adults. All too frequently, teachers are unaware that there are different ways to think about mathematics and that effective instruction begins with understanding how students think about mathematics in order to avoid imposing one's own way of thinking during instruction. If a student is struggling with coming up with a way to reason through a task, a teacher should be able to share an approach that he or she knows is closer to how the student thinks about mathematics and to make it very clear that this is just *one* way to do it; and then to share another way that is again a way that the student would think about the concept. For example, prior to being taught the standard algorithm, students typically start with the larger numbers when they are asked to add multidigit numbers. When teachers engage in ineffective instruction, they teach students to start with the numbers in the ones place, the smaller numbers. By doing so, teachers are starting out of the students' zone of proximal development (i.e., the difference between what a child can do by him- or herself and what he or she can do with help). Compounding this problem is the use of instructional strategies that do not account for learning characteristics of struggling learners. Many students, particularly struggling learners, have difficulty with the concept of place value. However, when students are allowed to do computations in meaningful ways first, they readily use place value to make sense of the numbers and the operation.

THE VIEW OF THE FUTURE

By this time, it should be apparent that struggling learners have unique needs related to both learning characteristics and how the mathematics curriculum is taught. Fortunately, research has identified mathematics instructional practices that are effective for struggling learners. However, these instructional practices are not always implemented in schools, and many educators are unaware of the needs that these students have, particularly the needs that have been addressed in this chapter and in Chapter 5. When teachers are not aware of the learning characteristics of struggling learners or how students think about mathematics in ways that differ from how adults view mathematics, the result may be frustrated students and frustrated teachers. The remaining chapters in this book describe research-supported instructional practices that address these students' needs, which can help to alleviate the frustration.

7

How Struggling Learners
Can Learn Mathematics

Chapters 5 and 6 discussed several important learning characteristics and curriculum issues that can create mathematics learning barriers for struggling learners. This chapter builds on this knowledge base by explaining how struggling learners *can* learn mathematics despite the learning barriers previously described, thereby providing a solid foundation for implementing instructional practices that meet the learning needs of struggling learners. These instructional practices are described in Section IV.

This chapter is organized into three sections. The first section discusses a framework for thinking about how struggling learners typically learn new mathematics concepts and skills. The second section provides several tips for facilitating understanding of mathematics for struggling learners. The last section describes some general teaching techniques that address the learning needs of these students.

STAGES OF LEARNING: A FRAMEWORK
FOR HOW STRUGGLING LEARNERS LEARN

Teaching struggling learners effectively would be easier with a map, or conceptual framework, for how these students typically learn. Such a framework has been proposed and found to be useful by many educators. Mercer and Mercer (2005) described six stages of learning through which students progress from initial understanding of a new concept (initial acquisition) to adapting this understanding to learning other concepts and applying them to other subject areas (adaption) (Table 7.1). These six stages of learning are not meant to be absolute; that is, struggling learners do not always move through each stage in a lock-step manner. However, teachers, by conceptualizing student learning in this way, provide students with the nuts and bolts of a meaningful framework for planning mathematics instruction and for evaluating their students' learning progress. Rather than think of each stage as a discrete and separate entity, it is helpful to view them as key points across a continuum for learning mathematics. Figure 7.1 shows this continuum of learning and where each stage might occur.

Table 7.1.   Six stages of learning

Stage 1: Initial acquisition. Students develop a beginning level of understanding, moving from understanding nothing about the target concept to understanding approximately 50% of the concept.

Stage 2: Advanced acquisition. Students develop and can demonstrate a complete or near-complete understanding of the target concept (i.e., 50%–95%).

Stage 3: Proficiency. Students become fluent with using the target concept with a high level of accuracy.

Stage 4: Maintenance. Students demonstrate the ability to maintain a high level of proficiency over time, such as being able to demonstrate a high level of understanding when required to use the concept later in the school year or in subsequent years.

Stage 5: Generalization. Students are able to apply proficiently the use of the concept in contexts that are different from the one in which they learned it. For example, students learn to apply their classroom-based knowledge of percentage to a real-life setting where they buy clothes that are on sale at 35% off the ticketed price.

Stage 6: Adaption. Students are able to apply the understanding of a learned concept to understanding other concepts, thereby expanding their understanding of the concept and being able to conceptualize how the two concepts relate. For example, students show adaption when they are able to adapt their understanding of an "unknown" in a simple expression such as $4 \times 3 =$ ___; to understand the concept of a "variable" in the algebraic expression $4a + 2b = 14$; and to understand how a variable can be applied to other subject areas, such as economics, physics, and statistics.

Source: Mercer & Mercer (2005).

Depending on their previous knowledge and experiences and their ability to retrieve from memory such previous knowledge, students may be at any of the points on this continuum when teachers first introduce a mathematics concept or skill. Moreover, students may vary in their ability to move independently from one point on the continuum to another point (less understanding to more advanced understanding). The progress that a particular student makes is highly dependent on how the learning barriers discussed in Chapters 5 and 6 affect the student and the degree to which effective instructional practices for struggling learners are implemented.

Initial Acquisition and Advanced Acquisition

There are several important ideas to remember in relation to the instructional goal or purpose of each stage of learning. At the initial acquisition and advanced acquisition stages, the instructional emphasis is on *accuracy of understanding*. Because students are developing a beginning understanding of the concept, teachers should focus instruction such that it promotes greater under-

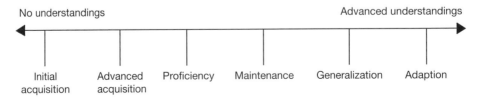

Figure 7.1.   Six stages on a continuum of learning. (*Source:* Mercer & Mercer [2005]).

standing of the target concept or learning objective. It is important to remember that accuracy does not equate to the percentage of problems that a student gets correct on a worksheet (i.e., whether students write the correct answer to a multitude of computational tasks). Accuracy should be conceptualized in a broader sense. *Accuracy in understanding* means the intended target concept is what is important. For example, let's say that a teacher is interested in his or her student's developing an accurate understanding of area related to rectangles. A student may get the correct "answer" 9 out of 10 times on a worksheet that requires the student to compute the area of various rectangular figures given the length and width of each figure. The teacher might think that the student understands how to find the area of rectangles. However, when given a set of different rectangles without their lengths and widths provided and asked to identify the rectangle with the greatest area and the rectangle with the smallest area, and to describe why their choices are good ones, the student is unable to provide a rationale for his choices. The student can accurately use a formula (length $\times$ width = area) to compute an answer (procedural accuracy) but they are not able to truly demonstrate accuracy of the target mathematical concept, which was area of rectangles (conceptual accuracy).

Basically, accuracy at these stages of learning has to do with the student's ability to demonstrate accurate understanding of the key mathematical concept. Take, for example, the concept of *a right angle.* A right angle has particular characteristics that make it a right angle. By definition, a right angle is formed by two intersecting rays and measures 90 degrees. Embedded within these characteristics are the ideas of rays, intersection, what it means to measure an angle, and how that is accomplished. We can also include the connection of where one might find right angles (e.g., corners of sheets of paper, corners of rooms, squares, triangles). A teacher might decide that the learning objective is to understand all of these ideas about a right angle or a subset of these characteristics. Initial and advanced acquisition of the concept of a right angle would be determined on the basis of the degree to which students can demonstrate that they understand all of the ideas about a right angle as stated by the target learning objective. Whatever the nature of the learning objective or target concept, it is important that the teacher be able to break it into key parts or features so that a determination can be made as to the level of accuracy in understanding that his or her students achieve.

Proficiency and Maintenance

At the proficiency and maintenance stages, an emphasis is placed on fluency. Fluency combines accuracy with rate of responding; that is, teachers should be promoting students' ability to use the newly learned concept multiple times in a timely manner and with a high degree of accuracy. For example, students might be exposed to 15 geometric shapes that are placed around the room and be asked to locate all of the right angles. The teacher could determine easily both how long it took the students to complete the activity (rate) and the percentage of correct responses (accuracy). Proficiency and maintenance are important stages of learning because they are the bridge between understanding a concept and use of the concept. In the sport of skateboarding for example, a person can be accurate at making both left and right turns and can describe what is necessary to do so. However, when on a ramp, he or she turns so slowly and deliberately that it takes him or her too long to go down it, meanwhile causing other skateboarders to maneuver around him or her and making the experience less enjoyable for others. Moreover, if a person cannot maintain his or her skateboarding from one year to the next, then it is less likely that he or she will continue because it will become less and less fun.

As students become proficient, they also become more efficient. For example, look at the following problem:

If Sue has 5 cookies and her brother gives her 8 more, how many does she have?

Young children typically will complete this task by modeling all of the numbers with objects and then counting all of the objects. Eventually, students begin to develop more efficient ways of operating on numbers by counting on and then using number sense. At this point they begin to break numbers apart to solve a task. For example, knowing that 8 is 2 away from 10, students will separate the 5 into 2 and 3, then combine the 2 with the 8 to get 10. Then they will add 3 more. As students progress in their understanding, they no longer have to "unpack" what the 5 means, then what the 8 means, and count them all. Eventually, students should be able to operate even more efficiently and not have to use much, if any, cognitive demand to determine 5 + 8. Fluency with mathematical ideas and skills enables students to progress further down the continuum of mathematical understanding because they can use this knowledge without having to unpack it. This frees the students to focus on extending their understanding by applying their knowledge to a variety of contexts and new ideas. For students to see the value in mathematics and to be able to generalize and adapt their mathematical understanding to other mathematics or subject areas, they not only must be proficient in demonstrating understanding of the mathematics concepts and skills but also must be able to maintain a high level of proficiency.

Generalization and Adaption

The generalization and adaption stages emphasize extension of what a student understands about a concept and is able to do with that understanding. During generalization, students extend their understanding of a concept or skill by using it ably in contexts that are different and gaining proficiency with using it. During adaption, students actually cognitively transform what they know about a concept and extend its meaning and application in ways that differ from how they have understood and used it previously. For example, students learn early on what it means to breathe even though they do not know a name for it. Later, they learn about the respiratory system and how oxygen is taken in and carbon dioxide is released when breathing. Still later, students learn about how the body uses oxygen and how oxygen is transported throughout the body by the circulatory system. As they learn about the environment in which they live, students begin to understand the significance of clean air and its potential impact on their health, and of practices such as smoking, which can

Activity 7.1
Finding the Area

Task 1: Find the area and perimeter of each of the rectangles using Figure 7.2.
Task 2: Suppose you have 36 feet of fencing and you want to use it all to build a rectangular pen for your dog. Find all the possible rectangular pens you could build.

have a negative impact on one's ability to breathe and take in enough oxygen. Students also learn about other animals and find out that some animals breathe under water, which leads to the knowledge that oxygen is found not only in the air. We could go on, but the point is that students' initial understanding of breathing has been extended and transformed in a way that has greatly enhanced what they initially understood, and it has helped them to understand other concepts and processes.

Consider how the notion of area can be developed with more understanding throughout the grades. Students begin in earlier grades to develop an understanding of the concept of area as the attribute that covers a two-dimensional region. They then begin to learn what it means to measure area and then how to measure area. Later, students work toward more efficient ways to measure area than simply counting all of the units (e.g., lima beans, square tiles, squares on grid paper), hopefully developing area formulas in meaningful ways and eventually learning procedures such as $A = L \times W$ for finding area of a rectangle. Carefully chosen tasks can provide rich contexts for helping students continue to generalize and extend their understanding of mathematical ideas. In Activity 7.1, compare the following two tasks in terms of how each one helps students extend their understanding of the notion of area of a rectangle.

The first task in Activity 7.1 provides opportunities for students to practice the procedures for calculating perimeter and area. However, the opportunities to generalize and extend understanding of area and its relationship to perimeter are just not there with this first task. As students work on the second task, they are not only calculating perimeter and area but also they are generating different examples that show that given a constant perimeter, as the rectangle becomes closer to being square shaped, the area captured within the perimeter is the maximum area possible for that given perimeter.

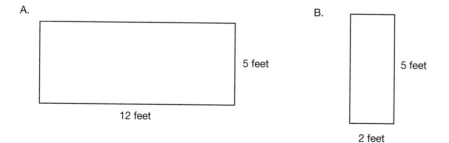

Figure 7.2.   Examples of math problem asking students to find the area of two rectangles.

An important teaching idea for generalization and adaption is that students with learning difficulties do not naturally or automatically generalize and adapt their mathematical understandings. One of the benefits of using tasks such as the perimeter and area problem just described is that the students are already familiar with how to find the area and perimeter of rectangles, so they are more willing to take risks when there is something familiar about the tasks (Malone & Lepper, 1987). Asking good questions that require students to work on skills while at the same time working to extend their current understanding of mathematical ideas is also an efficient way to do math problems because it prompts students to work on skill review while it provides opportunities to move further down the continuum of understanding toward a more relational understanding of mathematical ideas.

It is imperative that teachers plan instruction to support their students to move through these stages successfully. Therefore, purposeful instruction eventually should be focused on generalization and adaption of mathematics already mastered by students. Think about how to modify tasks to ensure that they provide opportunities to generalize and extend understanding, as in the area and perimeter problems in Activity 7.1 and Figure 7.2. Sullivan and Lilburn (2002) provide wonderful ideas for helping teachers modify tasks to allow such opportunities for learning.

TIPS FOR FACILITATING MATHEMATICAL UNDERSTANDING FOR STRUGGLING LEARNERS

Once teachers understand how struggling learners move through these stages of learning, the next step is to learn two simple yet important tips for facilitating learning. These tips are most useful as students move from the initial acquisition stage of learning through the proficiency and maintenance stages.

Building from the work of a number of education theorists, such as Piaget, Bruner, and Montessori, and later researchers who have studied how the application of their theories affect the mathematical learning of students with learning difficulties, educators have at their disposal some powerful research-supported teaching techniques that promote students' mathematical understandings. Two such teaching techniques, or tips, are discussed in this chapter. These teaching ideas are ones that can and should be considered no matter what mathematics content is being learned.

Teaching Tip 1: Scaffold Learning Experiences from Concrete to Abstract

Piaget, Bruner, Montessori, and others helped educators understand that learning is a developmental process, one that moves fluidly from lesser to greater levels of understanding and complexity. As applied to mathematics, the use of a Concrete-Representational-Abstract (CRA) sequence of instruction captures this understanding and should be used when teaching mathematics to struggling learners. This teaching strategy is so significant in terms of facilitating the mathematical learning process that it is discussed here and then described in much greater detail in Chapter 9.

Students can demonstrate understanding of a mathematical concept at various levels. At the concrete level, students can demonstrate understanding through use of concrete materials such as counting objects, plates, base 10 sticks, fraction pieces, and so forth. At the representational (semiconcrete) level, students can demonstrate understanding by drawing or using pictures. At the abstract level, students can demonstrate understanding by using the written symbols that represent mathematical constructs (e.g., numbers, operation signs, variables).

In basic terms, students typically move sequentially from concrete levels of understanding initially, to representational levels, to abstract levels. Although this can be true for many students, teachers cannot always assume that their students have fully developed understandings of a particular mathematics concept at each level, even if they are able to solve problems accurately at the abstract level. For example, a student may be able to say or write the product of two numbers (e.g., $3 \times 5 = 15$) but be unable to demonstrate the same multiplication process using concrete materials (e.g., making three groups of five counting objects and then counting the total number of counting objects among the three groups). Likewise, a student may be able to solve 3×5 by using concrete objects but be unable to solve the problem without them, so students may possess understanding of a particular mathematical idea at one level but not be able to translate that understanding to another level. This is very important for a teacher of struggling learners to remember. Teachers must be aware that their students may have only partial understandings of the mathematics that they are supposed to have learned in previous grades. Sometimes this means that they have attained only a concrete or representational level of understanding and no abstract understanding. Sometimes this means that they have some level of abstract understanding but no concrete understanding (i.e., understanding tied to concepts).

Even though abstract-level understanding generally is thought to represent the highest level of understanding (with representational understanding the next highest and concrete understanding the lowest level), this may be misleading when evaluating mathematical understanding for struggling learners. For example, a student may be able to follow the *procedure* to solve for the variable in the simple expression

$$4x = 12:$$

$$4x = 12$$

$$x = 12/4$$

$$x = 3$$

But when asked to describe what the variable x represents in the expression, they are unable to do so. The student is able to find the answer or solution by using a memorized procedure but does not possess *conceptual knowledge*. It is important that teachers promote conceptual knowledge as well as procedural knowledge when working with struggling learners. Research suggests that students who move through a CRA sequence of instruction are more successful in fully learning mathematics (e.g., Allsopp, 1999; Burns, 1996; Harris, Miller, & Mercer, 1995; Maccini & Gagnon, 2000; Mercer & Mercer, 2005;

Miller et al., 1998; Miller & Mercer, 1993; Miller, Mercer, & Dillon, 1992; Peterson, Mercer, & O'Shea, 1988). Emphasizing concrete experiences with new mathematical concepts and skills is an important aspect of helping students develop conceptual knowledge of the target concept. Refer to Chapter 9 to learn more about how to provide effective CRA instruction for struggling learners.

Teaching Tip 2: Incorporate Both Receptive and Expressive Response Formats When Asking Students to Demonstrate Mathematical Understandings

Educators often make the mistake of assuming that the answer they get from students accurately represents what they understand about a particular mathematics concept or skill. This mistake is even more likely in the age of high-stakes testing, in which evaluation of student learning is based on a single measure that is administered at a single point in time. The reality of learning is that it is not an all-or-nothing phenomenon. Students can learn more about a particular concept as they develop a more relational understanding of the mathematics (see the area and perimeter task from the previous section). Also, students learn at different rates and at different levels of insight and understanding. This is especially true of struggling learners because of the various barriers that can affect learning. Teachers should incorporate both receptive response tasks and expressive response tasks as students move through the six stages of learning.

Receptive tasks are recognition-type activities in which students are given a mathematics-related task and are then provided several choices, one of which is the solution or answer. Receptive tasks require students to have some level of understanding but do not require them to generate the solution on their own. Students are provided cuing through the choices that are made available to them.

Expressive response tasks are those in which students are given a mathematics-related task and are required to solve this on their own without choices. In comparison with receptive response tasks, expressive response tasks require students to demonstrate greater levels of understanding of the target concept.

Teachers should be conscious of the manner in which they ask students to demonstrate their mathematical understandings and to be mindful of what students' responses might or might not tell about where they are on the stages of the learning continuum. Consider the following equation involving order of operations that is an expressive-type response task:

$$4 + 5 \times 3 = \underline{\quad}$$

This task requires the student to solve the problem without support or cuing. When confronted with open-ended kinds of response expectations early in the acquisition stage of learning, struggling learners often are placed in an uncomfortable position because of the learning barriers that they face. For these individuals, a high level of anxiety can set in easily at the prospect of not being able to find the solution.

Referring to the learning characteristics of learned helplessness, metacognitive deficits, and memory difficulties, discussed in Chapter 5, consider what the impact of these learning characteristics can be for students who are given the problem $4 + 5 \times 3 =$ ___. First, students may not respond at all, usually because of their fear of failure resulting from previous negative learning experiences (learned helplessness). Second, students may respond but may do so in an unthoughtful or nonreflective way, such as by simply adding all of the numbers together because that is the first operation symbol in the equation or not noticing that their solution does not account for the multiplication step (metacognitive deficits). Third, students may have difficulty recalling the multiplication fact 5×3 and become frustrated to the point of quitting or just blurting out whatever answer comes to mind (memory difficulties). When students with learning difficulties are confronted with situations that are uncomfortable, their reaction typically is to do whatever they can to remove themselves, to stop that uncomfortable feeling as quickly as they can.

However, teachers can support students to take more risks by providing them with cues in the form of choices when they are not yet proficient with the newly acquired concept or skill. By giving the student the same equation with carefully selected choices (receptive response format), teachers may find that students are less likely to shut down as a result of high levels of anxiety or frustration and more likely to activate their previous knowledge. Either way, teachers are more likely to get a meaningful response that provides some information about students' levels of understanding. Let's look at the following problem:

$$4 + 5 \times 3 = \underline{\quad}?$$

a. 12

b. 1,003

c. 27

d. 19

e. −4

In this situation, students may be able to demonstrate at least some level of understanding of order of operations because the choices provide cuing. In this case, students may quickly omit 1,003 because 1,003 is much too great in value given the numbers in the equation. They also might realize that −4 is unlikely to be the solution because there is no minus sign in the equation. Students are then left with three choices: one that follows order of operations and two that do not. This type of response activity supports students to use what they do understand about order of operations and number and number sense to solve the equation. In this case, the teacher is provided a level of information about what the students understand whether they choose 12, 27, or 19. A quick follow-up question or two by the teacher about why the students thought their choice was correct can help determine their understanding even

---

Expressive:

1. $4 + 5 \times 3 - 4 \times 8 =$ ___?
2. Given the following equation and its solution, describe why the solution is correct:

   $4 + 5 \times 3 - 4 \times 8 = -13$?

Receptive:

3. Which is the correct solution for $4 + 5 \times 3 - 4 \times 8 =$ ___?

    184

    13

    −13

    2

4. Which number completes the pattern 2, 4, 7, 11, 16, ___?

    18

    4

    22

    32

Figure 7.3. Examples of mathematical tasks that require expressive or receptive responses (abstract level of understanding).

further. Moreover, students can be reinforced positively for their decision making. In other words, the teacher can remind them that even if they did not select the correct solution, they did make several good choices. If students select 12 or 27 as their solution, then the teacher can reinforce them for correctly omitting 1,003 and –4 from potential choices. Such experiences both inform the teacher about what students really understand and provide students with a more inviting learning experience that helps them circumvent the negative impact of the learning characteristics they may possess.

When thinking about what the choices to a particular receptive response task should be, a teacher should choose those that provide subtle cuing for students and that are most likely to result in students' recognizing the best choice. In the previous example, two choices (1,003 and –4) are very unlikely to be correct if students possess at least some level of understanding of number and number sense. The choices 12, 19, and 27 are more likely given the value of the numbers in the equation and the operation symbols. The choice 12 assumes the potential of students to add the three numbers in order to reach the solution, a common error pattern that is observed with struggling learners. The choice 27 results from simply doing the operations from left to right, another common error when students are learning about order of operations. The choice 19 is the correct solution because it is the result of multiplying 5 × 3 first and then adding 4. The degree to which the choices should be more or less obvious examples or nonexamples depends on students' level of understanding and the types of learning characteristics that most affect their learning of mathematics in a negative way.

Figures 7.3 and 7.4 show several examples of mathematical tasks that require expressive or receptive responses. Think about how each choice can

Expressive:
1. Draw a picture to show ½ + ⅔.
2. Draw a picture to compare ⅗ and ⅚.

Receptive:
1. Which of the following pictures show ½ + ⅔?

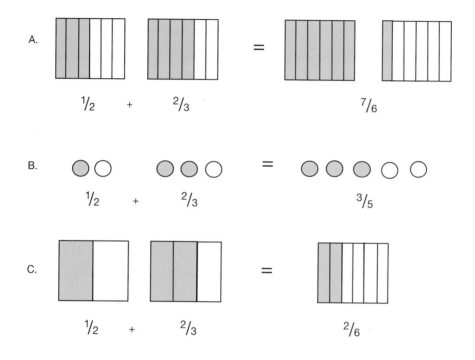

A.

$$\tfrac{1}{2} \quad + \quad \tfrac{2}{3} \qquad\qquad \tfrac{7}{6}$$

B.

$$\tfrac{1}{2} \quad + \quad \tfrac{2}{3} \qquad\qquad \tfrac{3}{5}$$

C.

$$\tfrac{1}{2} \quad + \quad \tfrac{2}{3} \qquad\qquad \tfrac{2}{6}$$

2. Which of the following pictures show ⅗ < ⅚

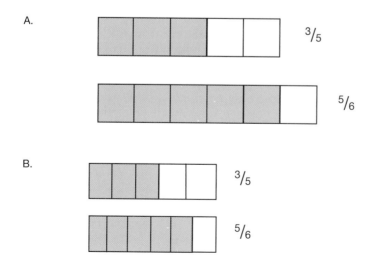

A.

$\tfrac{3}{5}$

$\tfrac{5}{6}$

B.

$\tfrac{3}{5}$

$\tfrac{5}{6}$

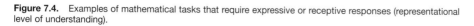

Figure 7.4.   Examples of mathematical tasks that require expressive or receptive responses (representational level of understanding).

inform a teacher about a student's understanding of the target mathematical idea. Although receptive type tasks are helpful in the beginning to provide the needed support to encourage students to take risks and to build connections, sometimes the given concrete objects, pictures, or symbols in a receptive task mask significant misconceptions. For example, students may be able to successfully respond to fraction comparison and/or addition questions when given a receptive task because the given objects or drawings set some of the parameters for the student (e.g., the notion of the whole in fractions). However, when asked to draw a picture to compare or add fractions, it can become more apparent if the student has not developed the idea that the wholes must be congruent. Consider what the representations in Figure 7.4 1B and 2A would tell a teacher if these were student-generated drawings.

The more familiar that teachers become with the major learning characteristics and curriculum barriers described in Chapters 5 and 6 and the potential impact that they can have on the mathematics curriculum taught, the better able teachers will be to create receptive response tasks that support risk taking and success for their students, two necessary ingredients to becoming proficient with mathematics. Although the end goal is for struggling learners to *do* mathematics independently, teachers cannot forget that many students need support to manage the learning characteristics that make learning mathematics difficult for them. By incorporating the use of both receptive and expressive response tasks, teachers can achieve this goal and do so in a supportive way that empowers students to take risks and learn from doing so, eventually developing the skills, knowledge, and belief that they can do mathematics independently.

To provide a better understanding of why the practices described in these chapters are effective, Table 7.2 summarizes several general effective teaching strategies that apply to any content area for struggling learners. Importantly, Table 7.2 also summarizes how each of these teaching strategies can help struggling learners to overcome the learning characteristics that make learning difficult for them. Finally, Table 7.2 shows at which stage(s) of learning (i.e., initial acquisition, advanced acquisition, proficiency, mastery, generalization, or adaption) the strategy most strongly affects student learning. All of these strategies are integrated into the research-supported instructional practices described in the remaining chapters. The purpose of Table 7.2 is to provide a foundation for a better understanding of why the research-supported instructional practices that are described in the remaining chapters are effective for struggling learners.

Understanding how struggling learners learn is important but is not useful if teachers do not understand how to implement those instructional methods that respond to the learning needs of students and facilitate their learning across the learning stage continuum. Chapters 8 through 11 describe specific mathematics instructional practices that do this very thing.

Table 7.2. General effective teaching strategies for struggling learners and how they help

Teaching strategy	Description	Example	How it helps students with learning difficulties
Link new concepts to students' previous knowledge	Teacher clearly connects a new concept to information that students already know and/or to experiences that students have had.	Introduce the purpose of a problem-solving learning strategy by wearing a tool belt and connecting learning strategies to tools used to fix something.	Activates students' memory so that they can better use what they already know to help them learn new concepts. Stage of learning: Initial acquisition Primary learning characteristics addressed: memory deficits, passive learning
Model using multiple modalities	Teacher uses multiple modalities (visual, auditory, tactile, kinesthetic) to make new concept clear and accessible to students.	Think aloud: Teacher says her thinking aloud as she solves for the variable in $2x + 5 = 45$.	Provides students with a clear and accessible (i.e., learnable) model of a target concept/skill. Stage of learning: Initial to advanced acquisition Primary learning characteristics addressed: Processing deficits, memory deficits, metacognitive deficits, attention problems
Teach strategies	Teacher models strategies that help students to learn, to do a skill, or to problem solve and provides opportunities for students to practice applying strategies.	The mnemonic phrase, "**P**lease **e**xcuse **m**y **d**ear **A**unt **S**ally" for helping students remember the rule for order of operations (**p**arentheses and **e**xponents before **m**ultiplication, and **d**ivision before **a**ddition and **s**ubtraction)	Activates metacognitive awareness and promotes independence for attacking problem solving situations. Stage of learning: Proficiency, generalization, adaption Primary learning characteristics addressed: Memory deficits, metacognitive deficits, attention problems
Practice multisensory cuing	Teacher uses visual, auditory, tactile, and kinesthetic modalities to cue students to important features of a concept or skill.	Visual cuing: Teacher uses visual cuing to help students process that they need to use the addition operation in an equation by enlarging the "+" sign: $2 + 5 = \underline{\quad}$ Examples and nonexamples: Teacher cues students to what a triangle is by comparing it with several figures that are not triangles, thereby emphasizing the features that make a triangle a triangle (e.g., comparing a triangle with a square or a pentagon and emphasizing the number of sides that the triangle has compared with the other figures).	Helps students discriminate and cognitively process the features of a concept or skill that are critical to understanding/performance of concept or skill Stage of learning: Initial acquisition to advanced acquisition Primary learning characteristics addressed: Processing deficits, attention problems, memory deficits

(continued)

Table 7.2. (continued)

Teaching strategy	Description	Example	How it helps students with learning difficulties
Provide corrective feedback and positive reinforcement	Teacher provides students with feedback about their responses that helps clarify what they understand correctly and how to improve on what they do not understand and teacher verbally reinforces the specific behavior that students engaged in that was successful.	Teacher uses a calm voice to describe clearly what students did well and provides them guidance for how to correct what they did not do well (e.g., "It makes a lot of sense how you added the two numbers 15 and 4 in the equation $15 + 4 \times 3$, because there is an addition sign [positive reinforcement]. Now, when I see that there are two different signs, I remember the phrase that helps me remember which operation to do first: Please excuse my dear Aunt Sally. When I remember the phrase, I know that multiplication (**my**) comes before addition (**Aunt**) [corrective feedback].")	In a nonthreatening and supportive way helps students to understand clearly what they are doing that demonstrates understanding of a target concept/skill as well as what they can do to improve their level of understanding. Stage of learning: Initial acquisition, advanced acquisition, proficiency, mastery Primary learning characteristics addressed: Learned helplessness, metacognitive deficits
Provide students many opportunities to respond	The teacher provides multiple practice opportunities for students to help them become proficient with a target concept or skill.	Rapid-fire verbal rehearsal: Teacher helps students remember the steps to the word problem-solving strategy FASTDRAW by randomly asking individual students to say what a letter stands for after the strategy has been introduced and modeled initially. The teacher reviews each step multiple times and ensures that all students have opportunities to respond. Response cards: Students have at their seats index cards, cardboard squares, and so forth, with numbers, symbols, or terms written on them. Teacher presents relevant question or problem, provides time for students to determine the best response, and then cues students simultaneously to raise the response card that they think best addresses the question or problem.	Provides students tangible ways to practice using newly acquired understandings of a concept/skill multiple times and in different ways so that they can 1) become proficient at using it in meaningful ways and 2) feel what it is like to be successful. Stage of learning: Advanced acquisition, proficiency, mastery Primary learning characteristics addressed: Learned helplessness, memory deficits, passive learning
Make concepts meaningful/relevant	Teacher incorporates students' interests and/or clearly shows students how the new concept can be used by them in their current lives.	Graphing data: Teacher brings in or asks students to bring in boxes of their favorite video games. Teacher and/or students create a bar chart with a box representing each video placed at the top of each column. Students raise their hands to identify their favorite video game. The data are tallied, and the bar graph is completed.	Helps students to connect meaning to newly acquired concepts/skills and provides them a way to understand the relevance of the concept/skill to their current lives, thereby increasing motivation for learning Stage of learning: All stages Primary learning characteristics addressed: Learned helplessness, memory deficits, passive learning, attention problems

IV

Assessment and Teaching Strategies for Making Mathematics Meaningful

8

Making Instructional Decisions

Determining What and How to Teach

The third anchor of the universal features model of meaningful mathematics instruction for struggling learners involves making informed decisions about instruction based on continuous assessment data (see Figure 8.1). This chapter emphasizes the importance of teacher decision making in the selection and implementation of effective mathematics instruction for struggling learners based on this assessment data. In this chapter, a practical decision-making process that incorporates three methods for gathering information is described. Use of this decision-making process can result in appropriate and responsive mathematics instruction that addresses the mathematics learning needs of struggling learners.

The first method or component of the process is use of a Mathematics Student Interest Inventory (MSII). This inventory provides teachers with valuable information about student interests and experiences and a structure for creating authentic contexts for any target mathematics concept or skill. The second method, the Mathematics Instructional Decision-Making Inventory for Diverse Learners (MIDMIDL), helps teachers to determine the degree of structure that is best suited for their students' learning needs and for the particular mathematics concept or skill being taught. The third method, Mathematics Dynamic Assessment (MDA), integrates the use of three informal assessment techniques, Concrete-Representational-Abstract (CRA) assessment, error pattern analysis, and flexible interviews. The MDA provides teachers with information that shows what students understand about the target mathematics content, what misconceptions they have, and at which level of understanding they are in relation to the target mathematics concept.

These three assessment methods are discussed according to two phases of teacher decision making. The first phase involves making decisions about how to incorporate student interests and experiences in mathematics instruction to make mathematics meaningful and relevant. The second phase involves making decisions about what and how to teach on the basis of students' learning needs.

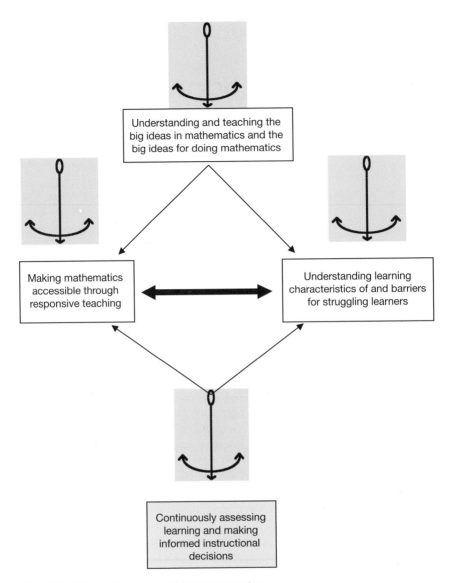

Figure 8.1.   Universal features model: Assessment anchor.

PHASE 1: CREATING MEANINGFUL LEARNING CONTEXTS USING THE MATHEMATICS STUDENT INTEREST INVENTORY

Research clearly supports the effectiveness of anchoring instruction by integrating students' interests and experiences (e.g., Gersten, 1998; Schumm et al., 1995; Wehmeyer, Palmer, & Agran, 1998). Doing so creates meaningful learning contexts for students, and meaning affects learning in several positive ways, including enhancing memory retrieval, increasing attention, and helping students

Student name: *Delaney Wright*

Age/grade level: *9th grade*

Period/class: *4th*

Things I like to do on my own	My special hobbies	Things I like to learn about	Things I like to do with my friends	Fun things my family does
Play video games Listen to hip-hop music	Sing in the church choir Drawing	Things about my African heritage How to make web pages on the internet using a computer Graphics software on a computer to design sports logos for teams	Go to the movies Hang out just talking about stuff Listen to music and dancing	We have a family reunion every year where my relatives from all over the country come to celebrate Going to the river to swim and fish

Figure 8.2. Example of a completed Individual Mathematics Student Interest Inventory Form.

with diverse backgrounds and experiences find relevance in learning. The MSII has two steps and is used most effectively at the beginning of the school year and also perhaps during the year if several new students join the class. The first step involves the teacher asking students to describe the kinds of things that they do in various situations (e.g., at home, with friends, in church/synagogue/ temple, in their neighborhood/apartment complex). Each student in the class writes this information or dictates it to a teacher or peer using an Individual Mathematics Student Interest Inventory Form shown in Figure 8.2.

The next step involves the teacher reviewing all student responses and selecting interests and experiences that best represent all of the students in the class. Selected interests and experiences then are listed on the Class Mathematics Student Interest Inventory Form (see Figure 8.3 for an example) under each of the areas identified in Column 1. The second column in Figure 8.3 provides a place for teachers to identify the specific mathematics concepts or objectives that they teach and that relate to the interests listed under each interest area. The final step is for teachers to think about the type of authentic contexts that can be created given selected mathematics concepts (second column) and related student interests/experiences (first column). The third column in Figure 8.3 provides space for teachers to do this.

Using this tool, teachers can develop a powerful database to create meaningful mathematics learning experiences that are embedded in contexts that are interesting and relevant to their students. The Individual and Class Student Mathematics Interest Inventory Forms provide teachers with an efficient and practical format for capturing this important information and planning how to use it for the specific mathematics concepts that they teach (these Inventories are in Appendix A).

Period/class: 4th period		
School Year: 2006–2007		
Interests	Relevant mathematics concepts/skills I teach that match interest	Ideas for creating authentic contexts
Individual interests/activities *(Columns 1–3 on Individual Mathematics Student Interest Inventory)*		
1. Video games	Data analysis/statistics: Graphing	Develop a bar graph on dry-erase board depicting favorite video games/types of video games of students in the class. Bring in video game boxes/containers to use as "headers" for each type of game.
Peer-related interests/activities *(Column 4 on Student Interest Inventory)*		
1. The local college football team	Fractions: Comparing fractions	Create story problems involving the team playing its big rival where they determine who gained the most yards in a play or quarter based on the fractional parts of the field (e.g., the home team gained yardage equivalent to 7/10's the length of the 100 yard football field while the visiting team gained yardage equivalent to 3/5's the length of the field).

Figure 8.3. Items from a Class Mathematics Student Interest Inventory Form. Shows examples of how mathematics class interest form might be used to identify authentic contexts in two areas, "individual interests/ activities" (e.g., video games), and "peer-related interests/activities" (e.g., local college football team).

PHASE 2: DECIDING WHAT AND HOW TO TEACH: THE MIDMIDL AND THE MDA

Struggling learners benefit from teachers who choose instructional methods on the basis of their learning needs. Such responsive teaching can be a daunting task given the many learning barriers that potentially can affect these students. Phase 2 of this instructional decision-making process provides teachers an efficient, data-driven process for making effective mathematics instructional decisions for struggling learners. There are two steps to complete in phase 2. Step 1 is to use the MIDMIDL to determine which level of structure and explicitness most likely is needed by students. This determination is based on a set of student characteristics that are linked to learning success and a set of content characteristics that are related to the nature of the particular mathematics concept that students will be learning. Step 2 in phase 2 is to use the MDA to determine what students understand about a target mathematics concept and the level of understanding that they have (concrete, representational, abstract, receptive/expressive).

Step 1: Mathematics Instructional Decision-Making Inventory for Diverse Learners

The purpose of the MIDMIDL is to determine which level of structure and explicitness most likely is needed by students given the particular mathematics concept that they will be expected to learn. Structure is the amount of support that a teacher provides students as they are learning a new concept. Higher levels of structure are characterized by teaching methods such as breaking a learning objective into smaller, more learnable parts; sustained teacher scaffolding (i.e., the teacher provides greater levels of direction initially and fades his or her direction less rapidly than he or she might otherwise); a lot of visual, auditory, tactile, and kinesthetic cuing; ample amounts of corrective feedback and positive reinforcement; multiple opportunities for students to use their developing understanding of mathematical concepts in meaningful ways with teacher support (guided practice) before expecting students to do so independently; and visual displays of student learning so that students can see their learning progress. Lower levels of structure are characterized as minimal teacher scaffolding (i.e., the teacher provides less direction initially and quickly fades his or her direction), little or no cuing, minimal amounts of corrective feedback and positive reinforcement, limited or no guided practice before independent practice, and expectation that students can evaluate their learning progress independently. *Explicitness* refers to the extent to which a concept is made clear and accessible to students. High levels of effective instructional explicitness are characterized by teachers who provide modeling of concepts by using methods such as multisensory teaching, saying aloud their thinking as they demonstrate problem solving (think-alouds), showing nonexamples as well as examples of a concept to help students discriminate between what the concept is and what it is not, and emphasizing concrete experiences. Teachers who provide explicit models should not be confused with teachers who "talk at students," who simply tell students how to do something, or who rely on drill and memorization. The idea here is to use the instructional strategies that target struggling students' learning characteristics. While students have to mentally make the connection to concepts for themselves, these are strategies that teachers can use to help increase the likelihood that students will make these connections and develop metacognitive awareness to become more independent learners.

The more difficulty that students have in learning, the more likely it is that they will benefit from instruction that is more structured and more explicit in nature compared with instruction that is less structured and less explicit in nature (Mercer, Lane, et al., 1996). However, struggling learners can benefit from effective instruction that represents various levels of structure and explicitness across an explicit to implicit instructional continuum. How much any one student or group of students needs in terms of structure and explicitness depends on learning needs and the nature of the particular mathematics concept to be learned.

The MIDMIDL is composed of three steps. First, the appropriate Student Characteristics Inventory Form is completed. The score for this section of the inventory provides a teacher with guidance about the level of structure or explicitness that most likely is needed by the students. This score is based on a defined set of characteristics. These student characteristics are linked to learning variables that the literature demonstrates can affect school success and failure (e.g., number of students with identified learning difficulties, percentage of students with history of difficulty in mathematics, percentage of students who meet Title I requirements). There are two Student Characteristics Inventory Forms from which to choose. The Whole-Class Student Characteristics Inventory Form (Figure 8.4) is used to assess the learning variables for an entire class and the Individual and Small-Group Form is used to evaluate these variables for an individual or a particular group of students. Only the Whole-Class Form is included here but blank forms of both are provided in Appendix A). These two forms provide flexibility and allow individual teachers or teachers who are working in co-teaching situations to differentiate instruction as appropriate.

A classroom teacher can answer each of the eight items on the Student Characteristics Inventory Form through consulting typical classroom records, through gathering relevant student information that is readily available from student files, and through experiences with the students. Most, if not all, of the required information is typically known by most teachers. Once the information is gathered, the form can be completed in only a few minutes. At the bottom of the form is a space for the total score. After obtaining the total score, the teacher refers to the Student Characteristics Rating Guide shown in Appendix A to determine the appropriate level of structure and explicitness (teacher support most likely needed by the students). Because these student characteristics are fairly stable across a typical school year, this determination will need to be made only once or at the most twice during a school year (beginning and mid-year).

The next step is to determine the level of teacher support that is indicated by the particular mathematics concept being learned by students. Because the nature of mathematics concepts that a teacher may cover during a school year will vary, it is important that a teacher complete this form each time a new concept is covered. As a teacher gets more accustomed to thinking about these content characteristics, it is likely that he or she will be able to determine the level of teacher support that is indicated without actually completing the form each time a new concept is introduced. Basically, the characteristics that a teacher will want to evaluate about a mathematics concept are its level of complexity, the level of accuracy required, the amount of instructional time available, and the extent to which the concept is foundational to students' understanding of mathematics concepts to be learned later. As a general rule, concepts that are more complex, that require a high degree of accuracy, that are covered when less instructional time is available, and that are foundational to later mathematics understanding correlate with the need for higher levels of teacher support. In contrast, concepts that are less complex, that do not require a high degree of accuracy, that are covered when more instructional time is available, and that are less foundational in nature correlate with the need for lower levels of teacher support.

Mathematical concepts, processes, and skills that involve multiple features or steps and/or that rely on knowledge of many other mathematics concepts are complex in nature. Problem-solving strategies for story problems are examples of mathematical processes that are high in complexity. They require multiple steps/skills (e.g., reading fluently, comprehending, discriminating important information from less important information, drawing relevant and helpful

Student learning characteristics	Rating scale			Score
1. Number of students receiving special education services	**Zero** 0	**One to three** (5)	**Four or more** 10	5
2. Number of students receiving Title I services and/or who are "at-risk" for school failure	**Zero** 0	**One to three** 5	**Four or more** (10)	10
3. Number of students receiving free or reduced lunches	**Zero** 0	**One to three** 5	**Four or more** (10)	10
4. Number of students whose previous math grades are less than satisfactory (e.g. below a "C" or "S" level)	**Zero to two** 0	**Three to five** 5	**Five or more** (10)	10
5. General achievement level of your class considering, all students	**High** The majority of students maintain a "B+" to "A" average. 0	**Average** The majority of students maintain a "C" or "B" average. (5)	**Low** The majority of students maintain grades below average. 10	5
6. Number of students with a "history" of behavior/discipline problems	**Zero** 0	**One to three** (5)	**Four or more** 10	5
7. Level of absenteeism for students in your class	**Low** There are very few absences in my class. 0	**Medium** There are more absences in my class than I would like. (5)	**High** The number of absences in my class is a significant problem. 10	5
8. General degree of intrinsic/internal motivation of students in your class toward math	**High** A majority of students express that they like math and that they value math as something relevant to their lives. 0	**Medium** An equal mix of students who do and do not like math and who do and do not value math as something relevant to their lives. 5	**Low** A majority of students do not like math and do not value math as something relevant to their lives. (10)	10
Total score				60
Appropriate level of teacher support				High

Figure 8.4. Example of completed Whole-Class Student Characteristics Inventory Form (The Mathematics Instruction Decision-Making Inventory for Diverse Learners [MIDMIDL]). Scores of 60–80 indicate a high level of teacher support is needed. Scores of 0–29 indicate a lower level of support is needed.

diagrams, listing all possibilities), and students must be able to relate previously learned mathematics to the particular context in the story problem to determine which process or operation is needed. Mathematics tasks that are highly procedural in nature and for which the purpose is to find a particular solution represent concepts that require a high degree of accuracy. At the elementary level, long division is an example of a skill that requires a high degree of accuracy. The amount of time available is an important variable, particularly as it relates to struggling learners. For example, students with cognitive processing and memory deficits require more time to learn because information does not move from input (e.g., hearing what is said or seeing what is demonstrated) to output (e.g., responding to what is heard or seen) in as rapid a manner as students without learning difficulties. Instruction that emphasizes helping students process information in efficient ways is crucial when instructional time is limited. Mathematics concepts that students will need to understand fully and be able to use effectively so that they can learn other mathematics are foundational in nature. For example, place value is such a concept because it permeates mathematics throughout the elementary and secondary grades. Figure 8.5 shows the Mathematics Curriculum/Content Characteristics Inventory Form; the corresponding rating guide for determining which level of teacher support is indicated by the target mathematics content appears in Appendix A.

Once a teacher has determined the level of teacher support suggested by the Student Characteristics and Mathematics Curriculum/Content forms, the Instructional Planning Guide, shown in Appendix A, provides the teacher guidance in terms of the level of teacher support that is most likely to lead to success for students during the initial/advanced acquisition and proficiency stages of learning.

When examining the planning guide in Appendix A, you might notice that sometimes the same level of teacher support is indicated for both teacher instruction and student practice, whereas in other situations, different levels of teacher support are indicated. This variability should not be surprising, because both the learning needs of the students and the nature of the particular mathematics that students are expected to learn need to be considered when making instructional decisions. Moreover, as discussed in Chapter 7, the goals of instruction are different as students move from one stage of learning to the next. Therefore, when multiple learning factors such as student learning characteristics, curriculum/content characteristics, and the instructional goal of a particular stage of learning are taken into account, it is to be expected that different levels of teacher support will be required in different combinations on the basis of these learning factors.

Once the level of teacher support that students might need has been determined, the types of instruction to provide to students who need a higher or lower level of teacher support need to be ascertained. Chapters 9 through 11 provide descriptions of instructional strategies that will help, but Table 8.1 provides some general characteristics of instruction that represent higher and lower levels of teacher support (i.e., structure and explicitness) during the initial/advanced acquisition (teacher instruction) and proficiency (student practice) stages of learning. A copy of the complete MIDMIDL is in Appendix A.

Curriculum/content characteristics	Rating scale		Score
1. Degree of content complexity: simple versus complex	**Simple** The content is well-defined, is primarily conceptual in nature, and does not require multiple steps/complex procedures (e.g., comparing attributes of shapes). (0)	**Complex** The content is not well-defined, is factual in nature, and/or requires multiple steps/complex procedures (e.g., algorithms, word problems). 10	*0*
2. Degree of accuracy required	**Low** Procedural accuracy is not relevant; emphasis is not on getting the right answer; multiple responses may be appropriate (e.g., estimation, classification). (0)	**High** Procedural accuracy is expected (e.g., solving equations using a specific algorithm, solving word problems that have one solution). 5	*0*
3. Amount of instructional time available	**Unrestricted** Time allows for students to extend their understanding of a concept; students have ample time to learn and practice essential skills but also have time for extending their acquired knowledge through games, brain teasers, and other extension activities. 0	**Limited** Time constraints dictate that students acquire concept in an efficient and timely manner. (5)	*5*
4. Foundational nature of content	**Not foundational** Content is not foundational to understanding future math concepts; primarily relies on students' using concepts already acquired (e.g., commutative property of addition and multiplication). (0)	**Foundational** Content is foundational to understanding future math concepts (e.g., concept of order/seriation, conservation, place value); primarily relies on new concepts or concepts that are complex in nature (e.g., long division, regrouping with $+$, $-$, $\times$, $\div$ computation). 10	*0*
Total score			*5*
Appropriate level of teacher support			*Low*

Figure 8.5. Example of a completed Mathematics Curriculum/Content Characteristics Inventory Form. Scores of 15–30 indicate a high level of teacher support is needed. Scores of 0–14 indicate a low level of teacher support is needed.

Table 8.1.   Instructional features for higher and lower levels of teacher support

Stage of learning	Higher level of teacher support	Lower level of teacher support
Initial/advanced stage of learning (teacher instruction)	Concepts are broken down into learnable parts CRA sequence of instruction are used with all concepts Concepts to be learned are identified and clearly linked to students' previous knowledge/experiences Teacher modeling provided Multisensory cuing (visual, auditory, tactile, kinesthetic) is used Teacher "thinks aloud" what he or she is thinking as he or she demonstrates a concept or skill Examples and nonexamples of concepts are provided Teachers carefully prompt student thinking with questions Teachers gradually fade direction (scaffolding) as students increasingly demonstrate understanding	Concept may be presented in a more wholistic manner Students may need fewer concrete-level experiences and may be able to move directly from concrete to abstract understanding with minimal representational experiences Minimum level of teacher modeling and cuing: Students are provided with activities in which they "discover" the concept either individually or with peers Moving from teacher direction to student direction occurs much quicker
Proficiency stage (student practice)	Practice occurs at same level of understanding as teacher instruction occurred (concrete, representational, or abstract) Multiple practice opportunities are provided Cuing of the concept is provided in the form of an example or model (i.e., a visual example of how to solve a particular mathematics equation is provided including cuing that highlights important steps or features of the equation, e.g., color-coding numerators and denominators in fraction equations) Directions are clear for all practice activities Teacher models how to perform skill within the context of the particular practice activity All peer tutoring or cooperative group activities are planned/structured carefully to ensure that all students have equal opportunities to practice the skill (e.g., specific roles are assigned and modeled, and students have chance to perform each role) Teacher continually monitors practice and provides corrective feedback as needed Ample amounts of positive reinforcement are provided for both accuracy and effort. Various types of positive reinforcement should be considered (tangible, social/verbal, natural) Methods for evaluating individual student performance are included Practice opportunities are provided until students reach a high level of proficiency (90%–100% accuracy)	Practice occurs at same level of understanding as teacher instruction, but students are challenged to make more immediate connections between concrete levels of understanding and more abstract ones Fewer practice opportunities required to reach high level of proficiency Less explicit cuing is needed Directions are clear for all practice activities Less teacher modeling of concept within context of practice activity needed Peer tutoring and cooperative group learning are appropriate and require less structure (certain features should remain, e.g., roles) Teacher monitors practice and provides corrective feedback as needed Mainly social/verbal positive reinforcement is provided Methods for evaluating individual or group performance are included Practice opportunities are provided until students reach a high level of proficiency (90%–100% accuracy) Extension activities that challenge students to enhance their understanding of concept and to adapt it to other concepts are included

Step 2: Mathematics Dynamic Assessment

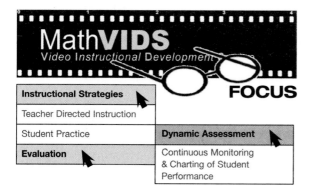

The MathVIDS Focus feature alerts you to additional information that is available at the MathVIDS web site, including video/digital pictures that model the instructional practices and expand on the ideas that are presented in this chapter. The MathVIDS Focus feature shows you where in the web site's navigation menu to find information related to the topic being discussed in that section of the book. In this chapter, the MathVIDS Focus feature will alert you to where further information and resources on the MDA is located.

The second step in Phase 2 is to assess what students understand about each target concept that is taught, what misconceptions they have about the concept, and at which level of understanding (CRA; receptive/expressive) they are. To do this effectively, teachers must have a reliable process that provides in-depth information, that can be completed practically in a classroom context, and that is flexible enough to be used with whatever mathematics they teach. The MDA provides teachers with such a process. In addition to evaluating students' interests (See Step 1), the MDA integrates three research-supported effective assessment approaches in mathematics: 1) CRA assessment, 2) error pattern analysis, and 3) flexible mathematics interviews. This section summarizes each of these three assessment strategies and then describes how a teacher can integrate these assessments in a classroom context. Last is a discussion of the types of data that can come from the MDA and how these data can inform teachers about what and how to teach struggling learners.

Concrete-Representational-Abstract Assessment CRA assessment provides students the opportunity to demonstrate their knowledge of a mathematical concept or skill at any of the three levels of mathematical understanding (concrete, representational, and abstract). Often, teachers assess students at an abstract level of understanding (e.g., using only numbers and math symbols; problem solving in their heads), and if a student does not demonstrate proficiency at the abstract level, then the teacher might assume that the student does not understand the concept. If the teacher also assessed students at the concrete and representational levels of understanding, then he or she might find that they do indeed have some understanding of the concept. Conversely, the teacher might find students who are able to "do" the mathematical procedure at the abstract level but are not able to demonstrate understanding when requested to use objects or drawings. By building on students' levels of understanding, the teacher can provide specific instruction that will enable students to move forward and acquire needed procedural and conceptual knowledge. Therefore, in order to plan meaningful instruction, a CRA assessment incorporates assessment of mathematics at all three levels of understanding.

How to Do It   The following steps provide a framework for implementing a CRA assessment effectively:

1.   Determine the specific concepts or skills to be assessed.

2.   Write down on a piece of paper the major components of the concepts or
     skills to be assessed. (Ask yourself, "What would I do and think to describe
     the concept or perform the skill? How do students think about this con-
     cept as opposed to adults?") This will provide a reference when evaluating
     a student's performance, particularly if the concepts are ones with which
     a teacher has had little experience teaching. If difficulty is experienced
     with this step, then sources such as the district or state curriculum frame-
     work, an enhanced scope and sequence chart, a listing of essential knowl-
     edge and skills for mathematical concepts, and resources that describe how
     students think about the mathematical ideas should be consulted.

3.   On the basis of previous assessment information and other knowledge
     about the student's abilities (previous teaching experience with the stu-
     dent; the student's developmental level), decide at which level of under-
     standing the student should be performing: concrete, representational, or
     abstract. Also be prepared with appropriate items or tasks that allow the
     student to demonstrate understanding at the other two levels. For exam-
     ple, if the assessment is begun at the abstract level, then have prepared
     items or tasks that reflect concrete (e.g., objects, math manipulatives) and
     representational (e.g., pictures, opportunities to draw) understanding.

4.   Prepare assessment items that accurately reflect the mathematics con-
     cept or skill to be assessed. For example, if multiplication of fractions is
     being assessed, then including items that require division of fractions is
     not appropriate.

5.   Provide a sufficient number of items or tasks to determine a pattern of per-
     formance. Too few items (e.g., one or two items) may provide inaccurate in-
     formation because both successful and unsuccessful student performances
     may be random (e.g., careless mistakes). With this said, time and potential
     student fatigue preclude the inclusion of a large number of items. A good
     rule is to include at least three to five items or tasks for each concept to be
     assessed. Figure 8.6 shows a CRA Assessment Planning Form to help teach-
     ers to structure their CRA assessments and align them with district/state
     mathematics standards, mathematics big ideas, and an authentic assess-
     ment context (from Mathematics Student Interest Inventory). A blank copy
     of the CRA Assessment Planning Form is in Appendix A.

6.   Explain to the students the purpose of the assessment and the process that
     will be used. It is important to create as comfortable and nonthreatening
     an atmosphere as possible. Students who are not used to explaining their
     thinking will tend to think their answer is incorrect when a teacher asks
     them about it because in the past that was usually the only time a teacher
     had asked them to explain. Keep the focus on making sense of the students'
     thinking. For example, tell the students, "I'm interested in understanding
     how you solve math problems. I might ask you to solve them using objects,
     such as these Unifix cubes, or I might ask you to draw pictures that show

CRA Assessment Planning Form

Authentic context (from Interest Inventory)	How much money people make in particular jobs/careers		
Relevant standard(s)	Virginia Standard of Learning 7.1		
Identified big ideas	Decimals and fractions are both ways to represent parts of a whole.		
Key problem (based on identified authentic context)	Comparing the rate of pay for different jobs of interest to students.		
Target objective	Students will rewrite decimals as fractions using numbers less than 1.0.		
		Concrete	Representational	Abstract

CRA Assessment Table	Receptive			
	Task 1	Look at the fractions pieces shown in the box. Now look at the decimals written on your paper. On your paper, write whether fraction A, B, or C shows Decimal 1 (repeat for Decimal 2 and 3).	Put a check on each picture that shows a fractional equivalent for 0.6	For each decimal, choose the equivalent fraction: .25: 2/5 25/100 5/10 .04: 4/10 40/100 4/100
	Task 2			
	Task 3			
	Expressive			
	Task 1	Make 3 fractions that are equivalent to the decimal .5.	Draw a picture in each box that shows a fractional equivalent for the decimal.	Write the fractional representation for: .25 .06 .10 .50 .49
	Task 2			
	Task 3			

Figure 8.6. Concrete-Representational-Abstract (CRA) Assessment Planning Form example.

me what you know. I also may ask you to try to solve problems in your head or with paper and pencil. Today we're going to see how you think about solving _____. Do you have any questions?"

7.   On the basis of the students' performance, decide whether a change in level of understanding is needed. For example, if students are having difficulty solving items at the abstract level, then have students solve them by drawing pictures or by using concrete objects. Conversely, if it is obvious that students understand the concept or skill at the concrete or representational level, then move to the abstract level (using only numbers and math symbols). With this said, although it is beneficial and indeed often essential to assess students' understanding at all three levels even if students demonstrate abstract-level understanding, you may find that students have procedural knowledge but lack conceptual knowledge. Sometimes students learn how to apply a procedure but do not really understand the concept behind the procedure. The use of concrete materials and representational drawings can bring this to light, providing important information for instruction. There are no hard-and-fast rules for what percentage of items a student must answer accurately to demonstrate mastery. Teaching experience and the specific observations that are made while the student performs are the best guides. However, a helpful rule of thumb is that the student should demonstrate proficiency on at least two of three items, three of four items, or four of five items, depending on the number of items included for each concept. It should be remembered, though, that there is less certainty about what students understand, the fewer the number of total items to which they respond. More confidence can be applied when a student responds correctly to four or five items compared to two of three items. As the student works through the tasks, try to make sense of how the student is approaching the tasks. Be careful of imposing an adult's perspective of thinking about the problem. Ask yourself if the student's approach is mathematically valid. Consider the different student approaches to the fraction multiplication task in Chapter 5 (⅔ of 15 Valentine cards). Both approaches were mathematically valid and built from the meaning of ⅔.

8.   Determine at which level of understanding instruction should begin. Instruction should begin at the level of understanding at which students are somewhat proficient but have not mastered the concept. At the frustration level, students demonstrate accuracy below 75%. At the instructional level, students typically demonstrate 75% to 95% accuracy. Mastery is achieved when the student is accurate more than 95% of the time. Instruction should not be initiated at a level of understanding at which students perform below an accuracy rate of 70% to 75% because of the likelihood of failure and frustration.

9.   When the level of understanding at which the student understands the concept or skill has been determined, instruction is begun at that level of understanding (with the intent of moving to the next level in the sequence of CRA). If the student does not demonstrate an instructional level of understanding of the concept at any of the three levels of understanding, then determine whether he or she has the prerequisite concepts and skills to understand the pertinent concept/skill. If not, then teach those prerequisite concepts and skills.

Why This Approach Is Helpful to Struggling Learners CRA assessment is helpful to struggling learners and to teachers who teach them because the information that is obtained through this assessment pinpoints the level of mathematical understanding at which the student can complete the mathematical task. Students who have learning difficulties too often are assessed only at the abstract level of mathematical understanding. This can lead to misinformation about the student's true mathematical understanding. When students do not perform successfully at the abstract level, it often is assumed that they do not understand the particular mathematical concept being assessed. Although a student may not be able to complete the mathematical task at the abstract level, he or she may indeed understand the underlying concept and/or procedures for the situation at the concrete or representational level of understanding. If the teacher underestimates the student's knowledge base in this situation, it leads to student frustration and affirmation of the student's negative academic self-concept. Instead of spending additional instructional time reteaching the mathematical concept, the student actually may need specific teacher instruction and meaningful practice for performing the abstract computation, explicitly relating the procedure to the student's concrete or representational understanding.

Moreover, "apparent" student demonstration of understanding at the abstract level also may misinform the teacher. As a result of the cognitive processing difficulties of some students who have learning difficulties, they may never have really understood the mathematical concept that underlies the particular mathematics operation/algorithm. In this case, the teacher may assume that the student truly has mastered the mathematical concept or skill and move ahead with instruction. This creates the situation in which the student's lack of conceptual knowledge will prove an insurmountable obstacle for future mathematics success. If the teacher suspects that the student may have procedural proficiency but lacks true understanding of the mathematical concept, then assessing the student at the concrete level of understanding is warranted. Consider, for example, a student who is able to memorize and write multiplication facts correctly. It might be logical to assume that he understands the concept of multiplication. However, when that student is asked to demonstrate multiplication using Unifix cubes or counting blocks (e.g., for 3×2, the student could use repeated addition by making three groups of two Unifix cubes each and counting the total: 2 cubes + 2 cubes + 2 cubes = 6 cubes), the student may not be able to do it. He may never have learned what multiplication really means. Without this conceptual understanding, the student will encounter much difficulty as he moves through the mathematics curriculum. Because the concept of multiplication is an important component to many future mathematical skills (e.g., multiplication of fractions), the student will be at a great disadvantage and at risk for future failure in mathematics.

Error Pattern Analysis Error pattern analysis is an assessment approach that allows for determining whether students are making consistent mistakes when performing computations. In a general sense, the teacher is trying to determine if the student is using a mathematically valid approach. If the student is not, then the teacher has to determine what is mathematically invalid or flawed with the student's approach. This type of analysis can provide insight into a student's mathematical thinking and provide the teacher with the information needed to address students' misunderstandings.

Why This Approach Is Important for Struggling Learners   Error pattern analysis provides an effective and efficient method for pinpointing specific difficulties that students are having with computation. By determining that a student is consistently using an inaccurate procedure for solving computation problems, a teacher can then provide specific instruction and monitoring to assist the student in using an effective procedure for solving specific types of computation situations. However, error pattern analysis is much more than a diagnostic tool for determining students' procedural accuracy; this type of analysis can provide insight into a student's misconceptions if the teacher asks him- or herself why the student's approach would make sense to the student. Specific types of error patterns can be a cue that a student not only uses an ineffective procedure to do computation but also does not understand an important mathematical concept. Students who have difficulty learning mathematics typically lack important conceptual knowledge. This is the result of various student learning characteristics as well as instructional factors, including a student's slow rate of processing information relative to instructional pace, lack of sufficient opportunities to respond in meaningful ways (practice), lack of specific feedback regarding misunderstanding, anxiety about mathematics, and visual as well as auditory processing difficulties.

How to Do It   The following steps describe the process for completing error pattern analysis (Howell, Fox, & Morehead, 1993):

1. Collect a sufficient number of student computation samples for each type of problem (at least three to five samples for each type of problem).

2. Review the responses and look for patterns among common problem types.

3. Look for examples of exceptions to an apparent pattern. Accurate exceptions may indicate that the student has partial understanding of the procedure or of a basic concept.

4. List in simple words the patterns that you discover, then write beside each pattern why you think that it is causing the student difficulties (e.g., if a student fails to regroup double-digit addition problems, then it *may* indicate that he or she does not understand the concept of place value. It *may* also signal that the student is attempting to follow a procedure that does not make sense to him or her.).

5. Interview the student by asking him or her to explain how he or she solved the problem. Hearing what a student was thinking can help you confirm suspected error patterns and how they are affecting your student's success (techniques for interviewing students are described in the next section, Flexible Interview).

What to Look for   Common types of error patterns for the basic operations include number fact errors, "slips," and "bugs" (Ginsburg, 1987). Number fact errors occur because a student has not mastered the basic facts. Slips refer to mistakes made as a result of lapse in memory or impulsivity. These errors usually do not indicate misunderstanding; they usually occur because of particular learning characteristics that a student possesses (e.g., memory deficits, impulsivity, visual/motor integration difficulties). Bugs are most serious because they indicate that a student is systematically using an inaccurate or inefficient procedure or strategy. Typically, this type of error pattern indicates an instrumental misunderstanding of an important mathematical concept such as number sense.

Common Error Patterns   Following are some error patterns that are commonly made by students with learning difficulties (Mercer & Mercer, 2005).

- The sums of the ones and tens each are recorded without regrouping. This error pattern reflects a lack of regard for or misunderstanding of place value.

$$
\begin{array}{r} 83 \\ +\ \ 67 \\ \hline 1410 \end{array}
\qquad
\begin{array}{r} 66 \\ +\ 29 \\ \hline 815 \end{array}
$$

- All digits are added together. This error pattern reflects inaccurate procedural knowledge of an algorithm and a lack of regard for place value.

$$
\begin{array}{r} 67 \\ +\ \ 31 \\ \hline 17 \end{array}
\qquad
\begin{array}{r} 58 \\ +\ 12 \\ \hline 16 \end{array}
$$

- Digits are added from left to right. When the sum of a column is greater than 10, the unit, or ones, placeholder is carried to the column on the right. This error pattern reflects inaccurate procedural knowledge of an algorithm and a lack of regard for place value.

$$
\begin{array}{r} 24 \\ 476 \\ +\ 851 \\ \hline 1111 \end{array}
\qquad
\begin{array}{r} 38 \\ 763 \\ +\ 693 \\ \hline 1114 \end{array}
$$

- The smaller number is always subtracted from the larger number without regard for placement of the number (whether it is the upper number [the minuend] or the lower number [the subtrahend] is irrelevant). This error pattern reflects inaccurate procedural knowledge of an algorithm. In addition, the student may be using this procedure to avoid regrouping. This may indicate either misunderstanding of the importance of place value or a visual/motor deficit that makes the regrouping process difficult.

$$
\begin{array}{r} 627 \\ -\ 486 \\ \hline 261 \end{array}
\qquad
\begin{array}{r} 861 \\ -\ 489 \\ \hline 428 \end{array}
$$

- Regrouping is used when it is not needed, meaning that the student may not understand place value, may not have good number sense, and/or

may not understand the computational procedure they are being asked
to use.

$$
\begin{array}{cc}
61 & 71 \\
175 & 185 \\
-54 & -22 \\
\hline
1111 & 1513 \\
\end{array}
$$

- When regrouping is needed more than once, the correct value is not subtracted from the column borrowed from in the second regrouping (e.g.,
  when the upper numbers in the tens and hundreds column are borrowed
  from, the values of those upper numbers are not changed). Such errors
  show lack of understanding of place value and/or the computational procedure they are being asked to use.

$$
\begin{array}{ccc}
511 & 411 & 411 \\
632 & 523 & 563 \\
-147 & -366 & -382 \\
\hline
495 & 167 & 181 \\
\end{array}
$$

- The regrouped number is added to the multiplicand in the tens column before the multiplication operation is performed. Again, this error pattern
  shows lack of number sense, place value, and/or the computational procedure they are being asked to use.

$$
\begin{array}{cc}
2 & 4 \\
17 & 46 \\
\times4 & \times8 \\
\hline
128 & 648 \\
\end{array}
$$

- The zero in the quotient is omitted, showing the student's disregard for
  place value and lack of the ability to judge the reasonableness of his or her
  answer (e.g., number sense).

$$
\begin{array}{r}
21 \\
6\overline{)1206} \\
1200 \\
\hline
6 \\
6 \\
\hline
\end{array}
$$

These error patterns are common errors students make when they are only
taught standard procedures for computation. The standard algorithms are very
efficient ways to do computations. They use fewer pencil strokes than extended algorithms because they are digit-oriented. The problem with this efficiency is that they can mask or leave implicit faulty place value concepts.
Think about how the standard algorithm for adding multidigit numbers is typically taught. Let's look at the example of adding 57 and 94. The usual procedure would go like this: Add 4 and 7 to get 11, then write down the 1 and carry
the 1 (actually 10). Add 1 and 5 and 9 to get 15. Write down the 5 (actually 50)
and carry the 1 (actually 100). Research in mathematics education (e.g., Carpenter et al., 1999; Kami, 1985; Kami, 1989) indicates that when students are
allowed and encouraged to perform computations using approaches that make

sense to them, they typically use number sense based on place value to look for ways to pull numbers apart and start adding the larger numbers first. Students can use a variety of ways to perform the computations in meaningful ways and can share these different strategies with the class. As students attempt to apply other strategies they have seen others use, error pattern analysis can be used to help students become proficient with these new strategies.

Flexible Interview   In a flexible interview, a teacher asks a student, in a nonthreatening way, how he or she solved a particular mathematical problem or set of problems and provides the student, given his or her expressive language needs, an appropriate way to respond. The purpose of the flexible interview is to gain insight into a student's mathematical thinking.

How to Do It   Although the flexible interview should be a comfortable experience, this does not mean that it should be without structure and purpose (Bryant, 1996). Several approaches can be selected. The teacher can give a student a problem and ask him or her to think aloud as he or she solves it. As the student thinks aloud, the teacher notes errors and potential misconceptions, always attempting to make sense of how the student is thinking about it (i.e., is the student's way of thinking mathematically valid?). On the basis of these data, the teacher then reteaches the concept. It is important for the teacher to refrain from interrupting the student during the explanation (Kennedy & Tipps, 1994). Interruptions can distract the student's thought process, thereby confounding the information gathered. In addition, the teacher must refrain from cuing students with subtle verbal and nonverbal behaviors. Some struggling learners are adept at responding on the basis of these cues, potentially leading to an incomplete or misleading picture of the student's problem-solving abilities. Although this interview approach can be helpful, verbal expression deficits of many struggling learners can make thinking aloud difficult (Bryant, 1996).

A second interview approach, engaged dialogue, provides students structure for expressing their thoughts (Zigmond, Vallecorsa, & Silverman, 1981). This semistructured dialogue between the teacher and the student involves teacher questions that prompt student thinking. Because the purpose of the flexible interview is to understand student thinking, it is important to avoid questions that tempt students to refuse to respond (Liedtke, 1988). For example, questions that take the form of, "Can you . . . ?" or, "Could you . . . ?" offer students the opportunity to say, "No." Because struggling learners typically are passive learners and/or have learned helplessness, the likelihood of their refusing to answer or to say, "I don't know," is great. Types of questions that can avoid such responses include, "Show me how you would . . . ," and, "Try to . . . ." Sometimes, starting with one or two problems with which students have had success can build momentum because students are more likely to respond positively and with greater confidence. An alternative approach for establishing a dialogue with students is to ask them to represent a concept or to define it in more concrete terms (Liedtke, 1988). Students can be provided with concrete objects to show their thoughts. They also can be encouraged to illustrate their thinking by drawing pictures.

A third interview approach occurs when the student takes the role of teacher and demonstrates (teaches) how to solve the problem to the teacher.

As the student teaches, the teacher notes errors and misconceptions. It is important that the teacher not stop the student in the middle of teaching for correction purposes. To stop and reteach at this point prevents the teacher from completely understanding the student's faulty mathematical thinking. Only after completely observing the student teaching does the teacher get a complete picture of the student's faulty mathematical thinking.

Why This Approach Is Helpful to Struggling Learners   Flexible interviews help the teacher gain insight into a student's thinking if the teacher remains open to the *student's* reasoning and allows for multiple approaches (that are mathematically valid) to solving the task. Because the various learning characteristics of struggling learners can have a negative impact on learning, their mathematical thinking may be flawed. Conversely, sometimes these students develop alternative approaches to solving mathematical tasks that are mathematically sound but that are different from what typically is taught. In either case, a teacher can learn a lot about a student's math problem-solving abilities by implementing any of the techniques described. When a teacher discovers faulty mathematical thinking, the teacher then can plan and implement appropriate instruction. The teacher also may gain insight into successful problem-solving strategies that the student uses. For example, a student may find it easier and more meaningful to use an alternative procedure for solving multidigit multiplication tasks, such as multiplying using place value. Consider the following example:

$$
\begin{array}{r}
22 \\
\times\ \underline{15} \\
10\ \text{(5 ones} \times \text{2 ones)} \\
100\ \text{(5 ones} \times \text{2 tens)} \\
20\ \text{(1 ten} \times \text{2 ones)} \\
\underline{200}\ \text{(one ten} \times \text{2 tens)} \\
330
\end{array}
$$

If a teacher was not familiar with this alternative procedure, then he or she may believe that a student did not really understand how to multiply. However, when the student explains that he or she uses this procedure because he or she has difficulty remembering to use zero as a placeholder (when using the traditional procedure) or in lining up the numbers accurately, the teacher learns important instructional information. When other concepts or skills are taught, the teacher can help the student to implement similar strategies that do not require extensive memory skills or the ability to write numbers in a linear spatial form. The more information about a student's understanding that a teacher has, the more likely he or she will be able to implement instruction that accommodates that student's learning strengths and weaknesses.

Implementing the Mathematics Dynamic Assessment

A teacher can implement an MDA by integrating the student interest inventory, CRA assessment, error pattern analysis, and flexible mathematics interviews by following 10 steps. These 10 steps are summarized next, and some include examples to illustrate the steps:

1. The teacher identifies the mathematics concept/skill for assessment. *Example:* Comparing fractions with like and unlike denominators

2. The teacher selects a relevant authentic context (from Mathematics Student Interest Inventory [see Figure 8.3]). *Example:* The hometown college football team playing a game against their big rival

3. The teacher introduces an authentic context to which assessment items will relate. The teacher needs to ensure that all students understand the relevant information in the context (e.g., how many yards are on a football field, how many quarters are played in a game). The selected authentic context can then be used the next day when instruction begins, thereby providing a link for students from the previous day's assessment. *Example:* Story problem written on dry-erase board: During the second half of the Florida–Florida State football game on Saturday, the Gators began to move the ball both on the ground and in the air. In the fourth quarter, the Gators gained ⅝ of the football field and the Seminoles gained ¾ of the football field. The television announcer said that Florida really out-gained the Seminoles during the quarter.

4. The teacher develops three to five receptive-level and three to five expressive-level assessment tasks that incorporate a relevant authentic context at each of the concrete, representational, and abstract levels of understanding. The assessment items should relate directly to the authentic context created in step number 3 (e.g., football game story problem). A method for students recording their responses is determined (e.g., response sheet on which students write [abstract level] or draw [representational level] their answers; digital camera for students to take pictures of concrete representations). Figures 8.7 through 8.12 show examples of tasks and possible student responses on CRA Response Sheets. Student responses are underlined.

5. The teacher constructs three assessment centers: a concrete center, a representational center, and an abstract center. Each center contains the appropriate number of response sheets and necessary materials. A relevant independent learning activity is made available for students when they are not working at one of the three assessment centers (e.g., instructional game, self-correcting material).

6. The teacher introduces the purpose of the MDA activity and provides directions (e.g., students will work on tasks individually, students will move through the centers at their own pace but there should only be four students at each center, and so on).

7. The teacher reviews the key problem with the whole class and tells students that the problems at each center relate directly to this key problem. The teacher briefly models how to complete tasks at each center (e.g., in the concrete center, use the manipulatives to think through the problem. Take a digital picture of the final arrangement of your materials).

Name: _____

**Concrete Center
Response Sheet**

1. Below each item, use your fraction bars to show the first fraction and then show a fraction that makes each statement true. You can use any of the fractional parts listed in the parentheses for each item. *Take a picture of your answer sheet when you've shown all your answers.*

   1a.   (Use halves, thirds, sixths, eighths, tenths, or twelfths)

   ¾   is less than   ⅞

   Student response:

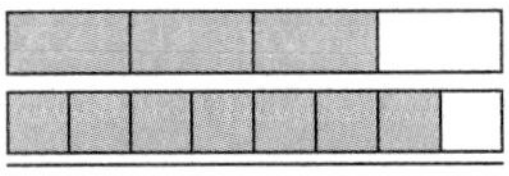

Figure 8.7.   CRA Assessment Response Sheet example: Concrete expressive level.

2. For each set of fraction bars given, write "greater than" (>), "less than" (<), or "equal to" (=) between the two fraction bars.

   2a.

                                          (=)

                              Student response

Figure 8.8.   CRA Assessment Response Sheet example: Concrete receptive level.

Name: _____

**Representational Center
Response Sheet**

1. Below each item, draw a fraction that shows the first fraction and then draw a fraction that makes each statement true. You can use any of the fractional parts listed in the parentheses for each item.

   1a.   (Use halves, thirds, sixths, eighths, tenths, or twelfths)

   ¼   is greater than   ⅛

   Student response:

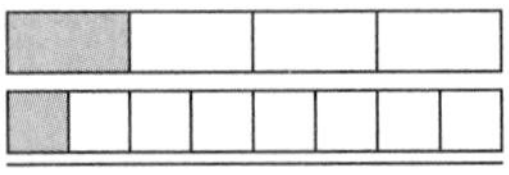

Figure 8.9.   CRA Assessment Response Sheet example: Representational expressive level.

8.   Students progress through the centers in three different groups.

   •   Grouping should be random (i.e., do not group students on the basis of skill level) so that struggling learners do not feel stigmatized.

2. For each set of fraction bar drawings given, write "greater than" (>), "less than" (<), or "equal to" (=) between the two fraction bars.

2a.

Figure 8.10. CRA Assessment Response Sheet example: Representational receptive level.

Name: _____

Abstract Center
Response Sheet

1. For each written fraction, write a fraction in the space provided that makes each statement true. You can use any of the fractional parts listed in the parentheses for each item.

   1a. (Use halves, thirds, sixths, eighths, tenths, or twelfths)

   $\frac{1}{4}$ < $\frac{3}{6}$

Figure 8.11. CRA Assessment Response Sheet example: Abstract expressive level.

---

2. For each set of written fractions given, circle the comparison that is true.

   2a.

   $\frac{2}{3} = \frac{2}{4}$ $\frac{4}{5} < \frac{2}{3}$ $\left(\frac{2}{4} > \frac{3}{8}\right)$

Figure 8.12. CRA Assessment Response Sheet example: Abstract receptive level.

- Stagger the starting time of each group.

- Students start at the abstract center, then move to the representational center and then to the concrete center. Students progress at their own pace, as space allows at the next center. This progression for assessment is suggested so that a more accurate picture of students' abstract-level understanding can be obtained. When students respond to concrete and representational tasks before the abstract center, these experiences could cue the student when responding at the abstract level, thereby biasing the results. For example, by seeing and manipulating fraction pieces to compare the fractions $\frac{1}{8}$ and $\frac{1}{3}$, they may remember the visual comparison when confronted with $\frac{1}{8}$ or $\frac{1}{3}$ at the abstract center, given the short time interval between the concrete and abstract centers. Without the visual image, students may not be able to compare accurately these fractions at the abstract level. The very conceptual nature of concrete- and representational-level experiences has a positive impact on abstract-level understanding. This is the reason that a CRA sequence of instruction is recommended as an effective mathematics instructional practice in Chapter 9. It is important to remember that the purpose of dynamic assessment is to find out what students really know. It is not meant to be a time for teaching. This is not to say that students cannot learn from the assessment, just that teaching is not the primary purpose for doing the assessment.

- Students record their responses as determined by the teacher (e.g., response sheets, digital camera) and place their response sheets in a designated place after each center.

- Students work at an independent activity when not working at the assessment centers.

- The teacher monitors student activity; probes students as needed; and notes significant misconceptions, ideas, errors, and so forth. The teacher can make notes about specific students on a checksheet or notesheet, a personal digital assistant (PDA), or other method. This information can be used later to inform flexible interviews and whole-class instruction.

9. The teacher conducts brief flexible interviews with particular students as they are responding, as determined by his or her observations.

10. The teacher examines students' work, noting common error patterns and whether students are at the mastery, instructional, or frustration level for each level of understanding (concrete, representational, and abstract). The teacher also notes whether student responses reflect receptive or expressive understanding. If needed, the teacher conducts additional flexible interviews with students at the next instructional period.

In the comparing fractions example, the teacher used an analysis of patterns strategy to observe several interesting patterns in the students' work. Many students chose to use fractions that had like denominators even though the directions asked them to use fractions that had unlike denominators. This was true for responses at the concrete, representational, and abstract levels of understanding. In several follow-up flexible interviews, the teacher found that students had difficulty using fractions with unlike denominators when prompted.

For representational-level expressive response items, students did not draw fractions so that fractional parts were equivalent (e.g., when drawing $\frac{2}{3}$, the size/area of the third pieces were not equivalent). Moreover, the size/area of the wholes that students represented were not equivalent (the total size/area of the whole showing $\frac{2}{3}$ was not equivalent to the size/area of the whole for the comparison fraction $\frac{4}{5}$). When the teacher followed up using a flexible interview, she found that students did not consider the actual area of the fractional parts or their relationship to the whole when describing why their drawings were greater than, less than, or equal to another drawing. This was an important concept that the teacher believed that she would need to emphasize during instruction.

Another interesting pattern that the teacher noted was that at the abstract level, students mostly wrote fractions that were common multiples of the comparison fractions (e.g., to show an equivalent fraction to $\frac{2}{3}$, students would write $\frac{4}{6}$). When students attempted to write a fraction that was not a common multiple (e.g., writing $\frac{4}{5}$ to show a fraction greater than $\frac{2}{3}$), they typically were incorrect. During a flexible interview, the teacher found that students used their procedural understanding of how to convert common multiple fractions

Name	Abstract		Representational		Concrete	
	Expressive	Receptive	Expressive	Receptive	Expressive	Receptive
SA	F	I	I	M	I	M
ZD	F	I	I	M	I	M
JD	F	I	I	M	I	M
AD	M	M	I	M	M	M
RF	I	M	M	M	M	M
FJ	M	M	I	M	M	M
RJ	M	M	I	M	M	M
SK	F	I	I	M	I	M
NM	I	M	M	M	M	M
JM	I	M	M	M	M	M
XM	I	M	M	M	M	M
TR	F	I	I	I	I	M
JT	M	M	I	M	M	M
TW	M	M	I	M	M	M

Figure 8.13. Class results from MDA: Level of understanding and instructional level. (*Key:* M = mastery, I = instructional, and F = functional.)

(e.g., $\frac{2}{3}$ to $\frac{4}{6}$ by doubling the numerator and the denominator). In addition, she found that students used only fractions that they had memorized as being equivalent or not equivalent (e.g., $\frac{2}{4}$ is the same as $\frac{1}{2}$; $\frac{1}{4}$ is less than $\frac{3}{4}$). When asked to explain why the fractions were or were not equivalent, students could not provide a rationale other than that is what they had memorized.

Figure 8.13 shows the class results for the level of understanding (concrete, representational, or abstract) that these students have for the concept of comparing fractions, including the corresponding instructional phases (mastery, instructional, or frustration). For example, the first student (initials SA) is at the mastery phase (+95% accuracy) for concrete and representational receptive understanding; at the instructional phase (70%/75%–95%) for concrete and representational expressive understanding and abstract receptive understanding; and at the functional level (below 70%) for abstract expressive understanding. This information allows the teacher to know that SA will benefit from instruction that begins at the representational level. In addition, the teacher knows that the student's concrete understandings can be used to facilitate understanding at the representational level and eventually understanding at the abstract level.

On the basis of the observations made by a teacher through error pattern analyses and relevant flexible interviews, insight into students' mathematical thinking can be gained. These insights, combined with information gained from a CRA assessment, can help a teacher plan instruction. Figure 8.14 shows the insights that Mrs. Carlson noted about her students on the basis of observations that she made while completing an error pattern analysis of her students' responses, including observations that were made by completing several flexible interviews during the assessment (when she observed

VIDEO FOCUS
Dynamic Assessment

You can see a teacher modeling this dynamic assessment process in the MathVIDS web site by navigating to the Dynamic Assessment web page. The video links on the Dynamic Assessment web page include a teacher and her students doing dynamic assessment. In addition, the teacher describes why she finds implementing dynamic assessment in her mathematics classroom helpful and what kind of information she learns about her students' mathematical understandings through doing dynamic assessments.

students responding in interesting and perhaps unexpected ways) as well as follow-up flexible interviews that she completed with a few individual students after she completed her error pattern analyses of students' responses.

Determining What and How to Teach

When teachers know the interests and experiences of their students (e.g., by using a Mathematics Student Interest Inventory), the level of teacher support that best meets students' needs for particular mathematics content (MIDMIDL), and what students understand about a target mathematics concept (MDA), they are equipped to determine effectively what their students need to learn and how best to approach instruction. The teacher determines *what* to teach on the basis of the results of the MDA; that is, from the results of the MDA, the teacher has a clear understanding about what his or her students do and do not understand about the target mathematics concept. In particular, he or she knows the level of understanding that his or her students have (concrete, representational, or abstract); whether they are at a mastery, instructional, or frustration level of understanding; and whether they demonstrate their understanding receptively or expressively. This information provides the teacher with a concrete way to determine at which level of understanding instruction should begin (i.e., the instructional level at which students are functioning) and which level of understanding he or she can use to support more advanced understanding of the target concept.

Judging from the data generated by the MDA and shown in Figure 8.14, students in a classroom typically fall into three groups, with each group demonstrating understanding at different levels. Students in one group demonstrate understanding of comparing fractions at the mastery level of instruction at the *concrete* level of understanding, but at the instructional level of instruction at the *representational* level of understanding. Students in another group demonstrate understanding at the mastery level of instruction at the *representational* level of understanding and at the instructional phase of instruction at the *abstract* level of understanding. Students in the third group demonstrate instructional understanding at the *representational* and *concrete* levels of understanding.

The teacher determines *how* to teach on the basis of the information gathered from the three assessment approaches. An authentic context within

—Difficulty representing fractions that are greater than, less than, equal to using unlike denominators (abstract and representational)

—Difficulty determining greater than, less than, equal to using symbols between fractions with unlike denominators (abstract and representational)

—Have some ability to do this with fractions that have natural relationships—$\frac{2}{4}$ and $\frac{1}{2}$; $\frac{4}{6}$ and $\frac{2}{3}$ (abstract)

—Difficulty relating written fractions to drawings; "meaning" of what a fraction actually represents may be lacking

—Concept of "equivalent area" of whole to part when drawing not evident

Figure 8.14.   Mrs. Carlson's conclusions about student mathematical thinking from error pattern analysis and flexible mathematics interviews.

which she will embed instruction is determined through the Mathematics Student Interest Inventory. The level of structure and explicitness (i.e., level of teacher support) that will be used as she teaches is determined through the results of the MIDMIDL. The extent to which she will teach using the determined level of support at the concrete, representational, or abstract level depends on the results of the MDA. One last piece of information that can help the teacher decide how to teach is through the development of an instructional hypothesis.

Instructional Hypothesis

On the basis of observations that a teacher makes as his or her students respond at the MDA centers and on the basis of misconceptions that were revealed through error pattern analyses and flexible mathematics interviews (see Figure 8.14), the teacher determines the reason or reasons for the current level of each students' understanding. Instruction then can be directed toward addressing those misconceptions and gaps in understanding. By combining insights gained from both an error pattern analysis and flexible mathematics interviews, the teacher can develop an instructional hypothesis easily.

On the basis of her students' responses (CRA assessment), common error patterns (error pattern analysis), and their verbalization of their mathematical thinking (flexible mathematics interview), Mrs. Carlson was able to confirm her assumption about why students responded as they did, thereby providing her with a rationale for their current level of understanding of fractions and of comparing fractions with like and unlike denominators. Figure 8.15 shows Mrs. Carlson's instructional hypothesis about her students' current level of understanding about fractions and comparing fractions with like and unlike denominators.

Mrs. Carlson's instructional hypothesis includes four important pieces of information: 1) the context ("given two fractions"), 2) what students are able to do, 3) what students are unable to do, and 4) a rationale for the students' understandings. Given this information, an instructional hypothesis can help Mrs. Carlson purposefully plan how to teach in ways that address her students' mathematical learning needs relative to the particular concept of focus. The instructional plan that Mrs. Carlson developed on the basis of her instructional hypothesis is described in detail in Chapter 11. One instructional hypothesis can be made for an entire class, or several instructional hypotheses might be made for different groups of students depending on assessment results and the degree to which students are in need of differentiated instruction.

Given two fractions . . .

Students are able to determine >, <, or = when fractions have like denominators at concrete, representational, and abstract levels.

Students are unable to determine >, <, and = when fractions have unlike denominators at concrete, representational, and abstract levels.

. . . because they lack understanding of the area that fractions represent (proportionality)

Figure 8.15.   Mrs. Carlson's instructional hypothesis.

The Frequency with Which a Mathematics Dynamic Assessment Should Be Administered

The MDA can be implemented within a typical 40- to 50-minute class period. The frequency with which a teacher implements an MDA will vary based on his or her own instructional needs, relevant curriculum pacing guides, and student needs. Two tips can help teachers think about implementing MDA in their classrooms. As a general tip or rule, it is suggested that teachers select the major mathematical concepts (i.e., big ideas) covered during a school year and plan on completing an MDA prior to introducing each identified concept. The teacher can then use what he or she learns through the MDA to guide instruction for each big idea and its related instructional objectives. For example, *fractions* was a major number and number sense concept that Mrs. Carlson's students would be learning during the first half of the school year. She selected the concept of comparing fractions as the primary focus of the MDA because she thought such a focus would give her insight into both her students' understanding of fractions and their understanding of how fractions can be manipulated. With the information she learned about her students from this MDA, she had valuable information to use as she introduced her students to related instructional objectives (e.g., operations with fractions; mixed numbers). Mrs. Carlson might implement an MDA every 1 or 2 months depending on her particular school's grade-level curriculum structure. Other teachers might implement an MDA more or less frequently depending on their own curriculum and the learning needs of their students. For some teachers, thinking of completing an MDA at the beginning of each major mathematics "unit" might be helpful. Another tip is that teachers should save copies of all materials used for each MDA that they implement. By creating folders that contain materials for each MDA, a library can be created that the teacher can use for future years. Grade-level teams can share MDA materials so that each teacher actually develops one or two, saving planning time.

Through integrating the assessment approaches described in this chapter, a teacher is provided with valuable information for deciding what to teach and how to teach target mathematical concepts effectively. Six primary pieces of information are obtained from this assessment and decision-making process: 1) student interests/experiences, 2) the level of structure and explicitness (teacher support) required by students, 3) the level of understanding (concrete, representational, or abstract) that students have regarding a target concept, 4) whether students have receptive or expressive response abilities, 5) where to begin instruction (on the basis of the level of understanding that students demonstrate with instructional-level accuracy), and 6) what misconceptions students might have regarding the target concept. This information allows the teacher to develop an instructional hypothesis to guide his or her instruction and provides relevant and meaningful contexts in which to teach. An example of how Mrs. Carlson used the data collected from her implementation of an MDA to plan instruction is provided in Chapter 11.

9

Teaching for Initial Understanding

Using Effective Instructional Practices

hapter 8 described how to use various assessment techniques to determine both *what* to teach and *how* to teach. By using these assessment techniques, teachers can tailor their instruction to respond to students' individual needs. However, effective instruction does not end with assessment. To gain real success for struggling learners, teachers must use instructional practices that are planned and deliberate. The first stage of instruction must be geared toward helping students *acquire understanding* of target mathematical concepts and skills (i.e., initial and advanced acquisition stages of learning). This chapter describes four instructional practices that provide students with powerful opportunities to acquire this understanding:

1. Teaching within authentic contexts

2. Building meaningful student connections

3. Modeling and scaffolding instruction using a Concrete-Representational-Abstract (CRA) sequence

4. Teaching problem-solving strategies.

You will see the MathVIDS Focus feature periodically throughout this chapter to alert you to additional information that is available at the MathVIDS web site, including video/digital pictures that model the instructional practices and expand on the ideas that are presented. In this chapter, the MathVIDS Focus feature will alert you to where each of the teacher instruction strategies for developing initial understanding is located.

As explained in Chapter 7, struggling learners need support during the initial and advanced acquisition stages of learning. The teacher's role is to assist students to link new knowledge to previous knowledge and experiences, to understand the relevance of the target concept, and to gain as accurate an understanding of the concept as possible so that they can apply their conceptual knowledge when confronted with related problem-solving situations. During this stage of instruction, when students are gaining initial understanding of a mathematical concept or skill, it is important to integrate those general effective teaching strategies that were identified in Chapter 7 (Table 7.2) within the four instructional practices described in this chapter. Each of these four instructional practices integrates one or more of these general effective teaching strategies. To assist in planning for and implementing these four practices, each description includes the purpose of the specific practice and a description of how the instructional practice affects struggling learners, the critical instructional features and components that are embedded in each instructional practice, and implementation ideas. Before reading this chapter, review summaries of the four instructional practices in Table 9.1 and note some ideas that you have for each instructional practice. A version is included in Appendix A that supplies an extra column in which to make notes. After reading this chapter, return to your notes and revise them on the basis of additional information that you learned.

INSTRUCTIONAL PRACTICE 1: TEACHING WITHIN AUTHENTIC CONTEXTS

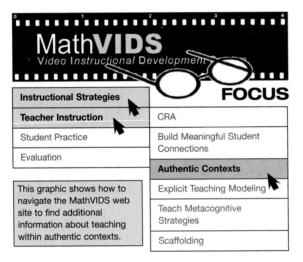

Once the teacher has assessed students' interests (see Figures 8.1 and 8.2) and has decided what to teach, he or she can plan how to introduce the new mathematical concept in an authentic and meaningful context. Instruction that is anchored in rich and meaningful contexts enhances learning outcomes for struggling learners (Bottge, 1999; Bottge, Heinrichs, Chan, & Serlin, 2001; Bottge et al., 2002). When mathematical concepts are introduced in contexts that are meaningful to students, it is more likely that students will 1) see value in learning the mathematical concept, 2) have greater capacity to remember what they have learned, and 3) be more likely to have cognitive access to the meaning of the concept.

Purpose and Description

One way to learn about students' interests and experiences is to have them write their ideas in a journal or in a letter to the teacher at the beginning of the school year. Observing what students do in the classroom; what they talk about in- and outside class; and what they do during recess, breaks, and lunch

Table 9.1. Instructional practices descriptions

Practices	Explanation	Purpose for students	Features	Research support
Teach within authentic contexts	Introduction to all new mathematics concepts are embedded within contexts that are authentic and meaningful to the students.	Provides students a meaningful context to • Understand the significance of mathematics that they learn • Promote interest/ engagement and enhance memory	Authentic contexts selected from use of Mathematics Student Interest Inventory. Target concept or skill is introduced within selected context in tangible way (e.g., story problem, using props, video). Teacher describes explicitly how target concept relates to selected context.	Baroody (1987); Bottge (1999); Bottge et al. (2001, 2002); Kennedy & Tipps (1998); Mercer, Jordan, et al. (1996); NCTM (2000); Van de Walle (1994)
Build meaningful student connections	Teacher links students' previous knowledge and experiences to new mathematics concepts and skills.	Provides students support for using what they already know to help them to learn a new mathematical concept.	Teacher links previous knowledge to new concept; identifies learning objective; provides learning rationale for the new concept's importance to students' lives.	Baroody (1987); Kennedy & Tipps (1994); Mercer, Jordan, et al. (1996); Mercer, Lane, et al. (1996); Mercer & Mercer (2005); Van de Walle (1994)
Provide explicit Concrete-Representational-Abstract (CRA) instruction with modeling/scaffolding instruction	**CRA instruction:** Mathematics concepts are introduced and practiced at the level of understanding that is most appropriate for students (concrete, representational, or abstract). At the concrete level, students engage in use of manipulatives to do mathematics and to demonstrate their understandings. At the representational level, students draw solutions. At the abstract level, students do mathematics using numbers and symbols only.	When students are provided instruction that matches their current level of understanding, they are provided a process for truly developing conceptual understanding. Students' concrete experiences provide a meaningful foundation for developing more abstract yet still meaningful understandings of a concept.	Depending on the results of the MDA, the teacher incorporates the appropriate concrete materials, representational strategy, or abstract strategy.	Allsopp (1999); Baroody (1987); Butler et al. (2003); Harris et al. (1995); Kennedy & Tipps (1998); Mercer, Jordan, et al. (1996); Mercer & Mercer (2005); Miller & Mercer, 1995; Peterson et al. (1988); Van de Walle (1994); Witzel et al. (2003)

(continued)

Table 9.1. *(continued)*

Practices	Explanation	Purpose for students	Features	Research support
Explicit modeling/scaffolding:	When students are initially acquiring an understanding of a concept or skill, the teacher takes responsibility for ensuring that the concept or skill is modeled clearly, meaningfully, and accurately using a variety of techniques (e.g., multisensory teaching, cuing essential features of a concept, providing examples and nonexamples, thinking aloud, prompting student thinking). As students demonstrate greater and greater understanding, the teacher fades direction and encourages the students to take on more and more responsibility for demonstrating/doing the mathematics concept.	Depending on where the students are in terms of their understanding of a concept, the teacher is able to meet them where they are, providing them the level of support that is needed for them to demonstrate complete understanding (advanced acquisition) and a beginning level of proficiency. Specific feedback is provided as needed, which prompts students' thinking and promotes understanding.	The teacher supports students' initial and advanced acquisition of the concept at three levels: high teacher support, medium teacher support, and low teacher support. As students demonstrate greater understanding, the teacher moves from high to medium to low levels of support.	Baroody (1987); Borkowski (1992); Brophy & Good (1986); Carnine et al. (1998); Cobb et al. (1992); Kennedy & Tipps (1994); Mercer, Jordan, et al. (1996); Mercer & Mercer (2005); Miller et al. (1998); Montague (1992); Paris & Winograd (1990); Polloway & Patton (1993); Swanson (1999)
Teach problem-solving strategies	Develop students' metacognitive (thinking) processes by teaching students learnable/memorable strategies that they can apply to particular types of problem-solving situations.	Develops students' metacognitive abilities and allows them to become independent problem solvers.	Teacher explicitly models an appropriate strategy and provides opportunities for students to apply the strategy to relevant problem-solving situations.	Allsopp (1997); Borkowski (1992); Jitendra, Hoff, & Beck (1999); Lenz, Ellis, & Scanlon (1996); Miller & Mercer (1993); Miller, Strawser, & Mercer (1996); Montague (1992); Owen & Fuchs (2002); Paris & Winograd (1990); Strichart, Mangrum, & Iannuzzi (1998); Swanson (1999)

also can provide ideas. In addition, meaningful contexts can be found in other content areas that are part of the students' curriculum (e.g., technology, fine arts). Once ideas for authentic contexts have been collected, they can be matched with appropriate mathematical concepts that will be taught during the year. The Mathematics Student Interest Inventory described in Chapter 8 provides a helpful structure for doing such planning.

When teaching struggling learners, it often is tempting to ignore the NCTM process standards outlined in Chapter 3 and move students rapidly to "doing" mathematics (i.e., procedures). However, as noted previously, this approach typically results in understanding that is disconnected and incomplete (i.e., instrumental understanding). Students may learn a specific sequential procedure but fail to be able to relate and apply it to real-life problem-solving situations. It also is true that struggling learners often need more structure as they are learning, particularly during initial instruction. Although these two statements may seem like a paradox, they actually are complementary. Teachers cannot directly format any student's conceptual schema (i.e., the framework for connecting and understanding a concept). Indeed, when they attempt to do this, the result is that the student has typically gained only surface knowledge and understanding and is unable to use conceptual knowledge in ways that extend meaning. However, teachers *can* provide planned, purposeful, systematic instruction to improve the likelihood that students see the connections and use their knowledge and experiences (their contextual understanding) to meaningfully explore and ultimately to make sense of the mathematical concepts and skills that are being taught. If teachers can structure their instruction to enable struggling learners to look for and realize the connections between what they are learning and their reality, then instruction is more effective and students' understanding is enriched.

Critical Features/Components

Although the manner in which authentic contexts are created can vary greatly, four important components should be incorporated when teaching struggling learners:

1. The context must be age appropriate/relevant. Students' cognitive/mental age should be considered as well as their chronological age.

2. The context must be culturally responsive. The context created should resonate with students' language, family, and community experiences.

3. The context must be of interest to students.

4. The concept to be learned must be depicted clearly through the context, not hidden. The context features should not distract students from seeing the purpose or being able to focus on those aspects of the context that highlight the target mathematical concept.

Instructional Implementation

When using this instructional strategy, the teacher must make the following decisions.

What Is the Appropriate Context that Matches the Targeted Mathematical Concept or Skill?   When making the decision of what the appropriate context that matches the target concept or skill is, it is important to consider factors such as appropriateness, responsiveness, and relevance. It also is important to consider accessibility and permanence. For example, if the teacher considers using the problem context of a farmer needing enough seed to plant his rows of corn to discover patterns in multiplication problems, then he or she needs to consider not only the familiarity of this concept for his or her students but also the accessibility of their observing the problem. During the initial acquisition stage of learning, this would not be a good context to use during the winter because students could not observe and make real connections. If students do not live in an agricultural community where farming is a common occurrence, the teacher might use the number of rows in a car parking lot as a relevant context, if that is something that would be a common sight to them. The point here is that the context has to be something with which students are familiar.

How Will Students' Previous Knowledge of the Authentic Context Be Activated?   One of the most effective ways to activate students' previous knowledge of the authentic context is to embed the mathematical context into familiar, interactive content. For example, students can be introduced to the concept of extending patterns while stringing popcorn and cranberries or making a paper quilt when studying Colonial American customs. Similarly, students can extend a given core of dance movements or musical notes, based on appropriate dance moves and music popular to students. These activities then become the basis for introducing the new mathematical concept. Making use of video imagery that engages students and creates a relevant context also is an effective approach (Bottge, 1999; Bottge et al., 2001).

How Will the Target Mathematical Concept/Skill Be Related Explicitly to the Meaningful Context?   Students with learning difficulties will benefit from having the target mathematical concept related explicitly to the authentic context. Due to the learning characteristics described in Chapter 5, the target mathematical concept can get "lost" within the authentic context and the associated activities. For example, students with attention difficulties may be distracted by various stimuli in the presented context, thereby missing the connection to the target mathematical context. However, explicitly relating the authentic context to the mathematical concept does not mean that students are not given the opportunity to problem solve. Indeed, providing the authentic context actually helps students to problem solve because students can use the context to help provide structure to the situation. To develop the deep mathematical conceptual understandings that are necessary for success, struggling learners need opportunities to problem solve, reason, represent, and communicate, and using authentic contexts can help with this development of understanding.

To support students' abilities to connect and relate concepts, teachers must be very explicit in their introduction of the authentic contexts. For example, when introducing the concept of collecting, organizing, and graphing data to fourth graders, all of the following would be possible authentic contexts: number and types of video games owned by students, most visited or favorite fast food restaurant, favorite movie or book character, and most frequently packed sandwich for lunch. As the teacher introduces one of these contexts, it will be important to display representations used in the authentic context (e.g., boxes from video games, picture menus from restaurants, types of sandwiches) and to reference these visual displays in a discussion as the problem situation is developed (e.g., "The local video store wants to know which video games to stock"; "The librarian wants to know which books to order"). It is equally important to ensure that the students understand the context and have opportunities to work with the mathematical concept in this context during both acquisition and practice. Once an authentic context is chosen, the lesson plan should continually provide opportunities for students to further develop and apply their understanding of the mathematical concepts in meaningful ways within that context (i.e., practice). Table 9.2 shows a variety of approaches and examples for creating authentic contexts within which mathematical concepts can be taught.

INSTRUCTIONAL PRACTICE 2: BUILDING MEANINGFUL STUDENT CONNECTIONS

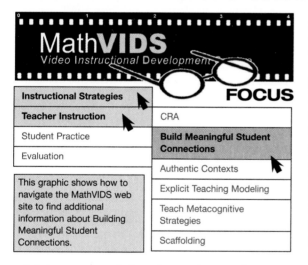

Many struggling learners have difficulty with memory, attention, and metacognition. These difficulties can interfere with struggling learners' ability to relate and connect concepts to each other. It is important to plan and then teach explicitly *how* what is being taught links to students' previous knowledge and experiences. Using this instructional practice in combination with teaching in authentic contexts can provide a very powerful instructional foundation for teaching any mathematical concept to students who have learning difficulties.

Purpose and Description

The purpose of building meaningful student connections is to assist students to make meaningful connections between what they already know and what they are to learn in the present instructional lesson or instructional activity. By activating students' previous knowledge, they are more able to make full use of their cognitive processing abilities because they are thinking about the kinds of ideas that will help them the most. Think of navigating an unfamiliar city. If you find that the streets are laid out like a city in which you have already traveled, then you already have a partial map to help with your navigation. If

Table 9.2. Ways to create authentic contexts

Approach	Examples
Video/digital photography	Select scenes from appropriate movie videos and PBS documentaries that depict a context for the particular mathematics concept that you are teaching.
	Use anchored instruction video (e.g., Bottge et al., 2001) to contextualize a desired mathematical situation.
	Shoot video/take digital pictures of students engaging in various everyday activities at school, and categorize shots on the basis of activities that represent mathematics concepts, principles, or processes.
	Have students shoot their own video or take digital pictures that depict a target mathematical concept or process.
WebQuests	Use problem-based Internet searches that provide a guided structure for solving simulated real-life problems. Students explore various links that relate to the problem and solve the problem on the basis of the information that they collect.
	WebQuest sites: The WebQuest Page (http://webquest.sdsu.edu/); the WebQuest Portal (http://webquest.org/); Techtrekers webquest page (http://www.techtrekers.com/webquests/)
Simple props/ classroom materials, and classroom/school activities	Use everyday materials to simulate action that occurs in given story problems; for example: *One warm day, John and Emily Bear walked down to the forest to go swimming in one of the many swimming holes close to their den. As they came to a place where two swimming holes are side by side, they saw eight bears swimming. Each swimming hole is big enough to hold only five bears. If the same number of bears were swimming in each swimming hole, then was there enough room for John and Emily Bear in the two swimming holes?* (Two plastic containers with water and eight counting bears can be used to simulate this story problem that represents the expression $2x = 8$.)
Skits/plays/drama	Develop short skits that involve acting out a real-life situation that represents a particular mathematics concept or problem-solving situation; for example: *Several students act out an algebra situation in which students determine how much one CD costs. Students buy various CDs from favorite singers or groups and pay a total sum. . . Jerome buys two rap CDs, Genie buys one rock CD, and Mike buys three country CDs for total of $42. How much did each CD cost?*
Literature	Select from books, magazines, and newspapers readings that reflect a particular mathematical concept or situation (e.g., newspaper: descriptions of sporting events in which points are scored in periods, quarters, or innings; examining the trends of stock prices over the course of a certain number of days).
Art	Use various works of art to explore relationships, patterns, and geometric representations: pictures of famous paintings and sculptures; photographs that depict distinct textures and colors; cartoon characters that have distinct facial, body, or clothing features (e.g., the pattern of Charlie Brown's zig-zag shirt; determine the slope of Mona Lisa's smile; estimate the real height of the man depicted in Michelangelo's sculpture "David" on the basis of the parameters of various body parts in relation to those of the average-height man).

someone points out the similarities of the two cities, then your ability to find your way increases, as does your confidence. Correspondingly, if a student has a strong understanding or knowledge of a mathematical concept or skill, then linking new information to this previous knowledge provides students with a road map to follow (in contrast to starting without direction). One way this can be accomplished is to have students think about a simpler task that connects to the learning objective of the lesson (see lesson plan in Chapter 11 for using alternative strategies to add multidigit numbers). Of note, linking the current lesson to previous knowledge assists students in two additional ways: It provides students with needed periodic reviews of previously learned concepts, and it helps to alleviate the anxiety that these students experience when tackling a new concept or novel situation.

Critical Features/Components

There are many different ways to build meaningful student connections and provide linkages. It is vital that this instructional strategy be done *after* the authentic context to be used has been decided and planned and *before* the initial stage of instruction. This strategy, closely related to what the literature refers to as an *advance organizer* (e.g., Mercer & Mercer, 2005), is designed to occur at the beginning of a lesson and to provide a structure for introducing a new mathematical concept or skill. This strategy incorporates three important components (adapted from suggestions presented in Mercer & Mercer, 2005):

1. *Link the concept to be taught to students' previous knowledge and experiences.* In other words, connect the new ideas to previously learned and experienced information. For struggling learners, even if teachers want them to discover the linkages, they need to provide ways for them to structure their observations and thinking so that the linkages are not lost as a result of distractibility, memory difficulties, or metacognitive deficits.

2. *Identify what students will learn.* Clearly state what students will be doing and learning in the day's lesson. This does not mean telling the students the outcomes of problems or automatically using prescribed or scripted lesson objectives. What it does mean is to provide a focal point for the students' attention. For example, when teaching young students to identify patterns, the teacher would not necessarily tell them the type or the number of patterns that they are expected to identify. However, the teacher would identify that they will be working with patterns and will discover different types of patterns. Part of this introduction should involve students discussing what a pattern is so that the teacher can capitalize on students' ideas to further clarify for all students the *meaning* of the concept of *pattern*. For students who have attention and memory difficulties, the close proximity of restating the learning objective to the actual learning activity helps them to focus on the purpose for what they are getting ready to do. The learning objective should be communicated using multiple sensory inputs. To communicate with auditory and visual inputs, for example, say and write the objective on the dry-erase board, or show a concrete example of the target concept and say that this is what they will learn about.

3. *Provide students a meaning, or a rationale, for learning the skill.* Struggling learners often have passive approaches to mathematics because they are unable to see the connections between what they are doing in class and what they do outside of class or school. Using authentic contexts will help with this, but until teachers are able to articulate to their students *why*

what they will be learning relates to their lives, students who struggle will see it as just another hurdle to overcome, one that has little or no meaning outside the classroom.

By doing these three things, teachers stimulate active learning in their students. Teachers help them to actively connect to information that they already know, providing them with a meaningful foundation for learning the new math concept.

Instructional Implementation

For maximization of the effectiveness of this strategy, several teacher behaviors can make this teaching technique effective for struggling learners.

1. *Capture students' attention by using visual and kinesthetic cues.* Such cuing helps students who have attention difficulties focus on the concepts. Because struggling learners often have difficulty with attending to the relevant features of a concept, using cues helps them to filter out extraneous information and leads them to understand and connect concepts more readily. Cuing also provides support for students who have memory difficulties and who have difficulty with organizing and retrieving information. Cuing provides students with additional structure for storing in memory the important features of a concept, and it enhances meaning. When information is stored in memory with structure and meaning, it is more likely that students will be able to retrieve that information efficiently when needed. For example, when teaching about repeating patterns, a teacher can use a simpler task to discuss what constitutes a repeating pattern. In the discussion, the teacher can use brackets to "capture" the repeating elements in the pattern to help cue students to the notion that they are looking for replicas (see Figure 9.1).

2. *Make use of multisensory cues.* Multisensory cues (e.g., visual displays of video game boxes, sandwich ingredients, place value materials, color-coded operation symbols, directional cues) also can assist students with processing difficulties (Bley & Thornton, 1995). Although students who have visual and auditory processing deficits may actually know the previous mathematical concept being referenced, their processing difficulties may prevent them from hearing or seeing the key linkages. By cuing these students, the teacher increases the possibility that they will process accurately what they see and hear.

3. *Clearly identify the learning objective and what students will be expected to do.* Struggling learners often lose sight of the learning objective during the course of a particular mathematics lesson or activity because of attention difficulties, cognitive processing difficulties, and memory difficulties.

Figure 9.1.   Illustration depicting the practice of using visual cues to help students focus on the significant ideas of a concept. The brackets cue students that the circles and triangles represent repeating patterns.

By making explicit what students will be learning during the lesson, the teacher can help students who have these learning difficulties recognize and cognitively process the learning objective. For students who can read efficiently, an effective technique can be for the teacher to write the learning objective on the chalkboard or other visible place. Referring to this visual cue as the teacher states the learning objective provides students with multiple sensory modalities through which to capture the learning objective and store it in memory. The teacher can support this effect further by periodically referring to this visual cue and restating the learning objective throughout the lesson. Communicating to students the learning objective clearly does not mean telling students *how* to solve a problem; rather, it is a way to identify explicitly for students the concept that is targeted for instruction and assist them to connect it to previous knowledge. For example, during a lesson on alternative strategies for addition, the teacher can briefly review what addition means by having students indicate whether each of the problems displayed on the board is an addition problem. Students can hold up index cards with an addition or a subtraction sign and the corresponding mathematical term to indicate which operation they think should be used. In a secondary classroom, students could display "thumbs up" or "thumbs down" when the teacher shows several examples of algebraic equations in which like terms have been combined in preparation for a corresponding algebra lesson. This method of communication helps students connect to relevant previous knowledge, which can encourage more risk-taking on their part because they know that they already understand something about what they are getting ready to learn. This also provides the teacher with an efficient way to evaluate student understanding. After students have shown their cards or displayed thumbs up or thumbs down, several volunteers can be asked to explain why the situation does or does not require addition or does or does not represent combined like terms. For extra emphasis, the teacher can restate the objective in words used by student volunteers.

4. *Integrate other relevant content and skills into the lesson's introduction.* As a part of introducing a lesson, students also can develop "math talk" notebooks for individual reference. By helping students organize their notebooks by mathematical concept, problem-solving strategy, or other scheme, students will have a meaningful reference to mathematical language using their own words to build connections.

By building meaningful student connections in an age- and interest-appropriate manner for students, teachers can lay the foundation for success. Each advance organizer should include the three essential components for assisting struggling learners to build meaningful connections to the concept that they are about to learn.

1. *Link* what students already know by demonstrating or identifying familiar patterns, operations, problems, concepts, and/or relevant contexts of interest.

2. *Identify* what students will be doing/learning that day.

3. *Provide* students a rationale or meaning for learning the concept.

VIDEO FOCUS

**Building Meaningful
Student Connections**

See a teacher implementing
building meaningful student
connections at the MathVIDS
web site, and learn more about
why this instructional practice
addresses the mathematical
learning needs of students with
learning difficulties.

Providing an advance organizer such as this sets the stage for learning because it activates student thinking in a way that is planned and focused. An easy way to remember these three essential elements for building meaningful student connections is the mnemonic LIP for *link* to student prior knowledge, *identify* the learning objective, and *provide* meaning/rationale for learning the concept or skill. Implementing LIP prepares students for learning the target mathematical concept or skill.

INSTRUCTIONAL PRACTICE 3: EXPLICIT CONCRETE-REPRESENTATIONAL-ABSTRACT INSTRUCTION WITH TEACHER MODELING/SCAFFOLDING

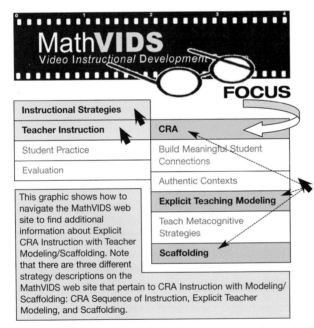

This graphic shows how to navigate the MathVIDS web site to find additional information about Explicit CRA Instruction with Teacher Modeling/Scaffolding. Note that there are three different strategy descriptions on the MathVIDS web site that pertain to CRA Instruction with Modeling/Scaffolding: CRA Sequence of Instruction, Explicit Teacher Modeling, and Scaffolding.

Learning mathematics involves learning how to communicate about mathematical ideas in the world by using different representations such as graphs, pictures, variables, numbers, and other kinds of symbols. For struggling learners, it is important to provide structure for learning how to communicate mathematically. A CRA sequence of instruction is one important framework for thinking about how to help students develop understandings of mathematical ideas. Struggling learners often have "Swiss cheese" mathematical knowledge; that is, their knowledge and skill base has holes throughout. Such a situation creates a shaky foundation on which to develop more complex and sophisticated mathematical understanding. However, when struggling learners are allowed first to develop a concrete (i.e., meaningful) understanding of mathematical concepts, they are much more likely to be able to learn more efficient and sophisticated ways of operating at the abstract level.

The effectiveness of teaching mathematics through a CRA sequence of instruction to students who have disabilities as well as students without disabilities is well-substantiated in the literature (e.g., Allsopp, 1999; Baroody, 1987;

Butler, Miller, Crehan, Babbitt, & Pierce, 2003; Harris, Miller, & Mercer, 1995; Kennedy & Tipps, 1998; Mercer, Jordan, et al., 1996; Mercer & Mercer, 2005; Miller & Mercer, 1993; Peterson et al., 1988; Van de Walle 2006a,b,c; Witzel, Mercer, & Miller, 2003). Like authentic contexts, CRA instruction helps students establish meaning for mathematics. Explicit CRA instruction provides a rich environment to make mathematics both meaningful and accessible to struggling learners. By integrating *explicit teacher modeling and scaffolding* during the CRA sequence, accessibility is enhanced for struggling learners in mathematics.

Purpose/Description

Using an explicit CRA instruction with teacher modeling/scaffolding means providing students with opportunities to understand each mathematical concept by first working with *concrete materials* (e.g., chips, straws, Unifix cubes, base-10 blocks, beans and bean sticks, pattern blocks), then working with representations (drawings), and finally working at the abstract level (numbers and symbols/"mental math"). The concrete level of understanding is the most basic level of mathematical understanding in that it is inherently tied to the mathematical concept via a model of the mathematical idea. It is the most crucial level for developing conceptual knowledge of mathematical concepts, particularly for struggling learners.

Concrete objects (i.e., manipulatives) can be useful when teachers understand the purpose of using them and how students perceive them in understanding mathematical ideas. Unfortunately, some students can just as mindlessly manipulate concrete objects as they can mindlessly manipulate abstract symbols. First of all, mathematical ideas are about relationships. These relationships have to be constructed in one's mind and then imposed on (or seen in) the concrete objects. One of the problematic issues with using manipulatives is that adults who have already constructed and understood particular mathematical relationships "see" these relationships in the manipulatives and assume that students "see" these relationships as well. This is not necessarily the case. For example, teachers often believe that base-10 materials are such wonderful concrete objects because the 10–1 relationship of our number system is so "clearly" exhibited in the materials. One only has to have a student "count" 3 ten sticks and 5 ones as 8 objects to understand that the student does not "see" this 10–1 relationship in the concrete manipulatives. Concrete objects can help students make sense of a mathematical relationship by providing structure to the idea. By having students explore the mathematical relationship using several different kinds of manipulatives, teachers can help students look for the significant and common element that is the mathematical idea the students are working to construct. The teacher's role is to get students to reflect on the significant attributes of the model and on *how* the model reflects the mathematical idea. That's when students are able to "see" the concepts in the concrete materials.

Concrete learning occurs when students have ample opportunities to use concrete objects to reflect on how the mathematical ideas are manifested in the model or concrete objects. Through the use of concrete materials, students have a tangible way to see, touch, and feel the mathematical concept. In addition, concrete materials provide students a way in which to interact with the mathematical concept using multiple senses (visual, auditory, tactile, and kinesthetic), ensuring that students with specific cognitive processing deficits have alternative means for gaining understanding of mathematics. For example, if a student has an auditory processing deficit, then the student can still see, touch, and move the concrete representation of the mathematical concept, thereby making it more likely that his or her auditory processing deficit will not block his or her ability to understand. The use of simple, discrete concrete materials (i.e., objects that have a definite beginning and end such as counting objects, paper plates) has been found to be effective for teaching struggling learners (e.g., Allsopp, 1997; Harris et al., 1995; Miller et al., 1992; Witzel et al., 2003).

When students become proficient at the concrete level, the mathematical concept or skill next is modeled at the *representational* (i.e., semiconcrete) level. At this level, students learn to draw pictures that represent the concrete objects that were used previously (e.g., tallies, dots, circles, stamps that imprint pictures for counting). Again, students are provided with many opportunities to practice and demonstrate mastery by drawing solutions. Several processes occur at the representational level of instruction that are especially helpful to struggling learners and that support these students' transition from concrete to abstract mathematical understanding. One of these important processes is that the representations can provide a supported way to extend their concrete understanding. An issue with concrete manipulatives is that they can offer so much structure that their use actually masks significant attributes of a mathematical idea. When students begin to draw representations, some of the structure is removed and if students have not picked up on particular significant ideas with manipulatives (e.g., the wholes must be the same when comparing fractions), this can become quite apparent when students draw their own representations. By teaching students to draw pictures that represent previously used concrete materials (e.g., tallies or dots to represent Unifix cubes or counting chips), they can connect, in a one-to-one manner, their drawings of newly learned concepts to the concrete materials with which they are already familiar.

Teachers should show explicitly how the drawings relate to the concrete materials that were used previously, first by reviewing the concrete-level process and then by demonstrating how the process can be replicated by drawing pictures. The drawing level provides students with an intermediate transition point between the concrete and abstract levels of understanding. Therefore, students are not expected to move automatically to an abstract level of understanding from the concrete level, something that often results in frustration and failure for struggling learners. Learning to draw solutions to problems also is an excellent general problem-solving strategy, one that struggling learners often do not use. Drawing solutions in this context is an excellent experience for later instruction on how to apply this strategy to general problem-solving situations. At the representational level, students also are provided a process for replicating the movements that are used when manipulating concrete objects. Many struggling learners benefit from learning that includes a kinesthetic (i.e., movement) component. Reproducing these movements while drawing provides students with additional replications of the process that they eventually will use at the abstract level through procedural algorithms.

When students are proficient at drawing solutions, they may transition to the *abstract* level. The goal at this level is for the teacher to ensure that students explicitly connect their conceptual knowledge gained at the concrete and representational levels to mathematical symbols (e.g., numbers, variables) and related mental processes. Like the transition from the concrete to the representational level, it is helpful initially to associate what students did at the representational level with the mental processes that they will use at the abstract level. At the abstract level of understanding, the goal is to have students internalize their concrete and representational understanding by doing mathematics using mathematical symbols without concrete materials or drawings. It should be emphasized that abstract-level understanding goes beyond the ability to carry out mathematics procedures or algorithms (e.g., solving equations). Students should be able to *describe* what the abstract symbols (e.g., numbers, operation signs, variables) represent and the significance that their representation has to relevant contexts. This means that teachers must capitalize on opportunities in the CRA sequence to highlight these connections. When the teacher believes that the student has a grasp on the concept, abstract symbols and vocabulary can be meaningfully introduced and explicitly tied to the students' representations and concrete materials.

Pairing abstract symbols with the concrete objects and drawings that represent their meaning during the concrete and representational levels of instruction helps struggling learners attach meaning to the abstract representations that are used in mathematics. Encouraging students to use their own language to describe each level of understanding is an effective way to enhance abstract mathematical understanding. Chapter 10 describes how to integrate the use of language experiences in mathematics instruction to enhance meaning for struggling learners.

Struggling learners often have difficulty demonstrating abstract-level understanding. Two common reasons are that 1) they do not really understand the concept or meaning behind the abstract representation (symbols, equations, variables, procedure) and 2) they have difficulty retrieving from memory previously learned mathematical concepts and skills that are needed to understand a new concept or perform a new skill. To avoid these difficulties, it is important to use a CRA sequence of instruction with explicit teacher modeling and scaffolding and provide students many opportunities to practice and demonstrate mastery at the abstract level and to demonstrate their understanding between the various levels before moving to a new mathematical concept or skill. Having students master moving back and forth between levels gives them the skills and confidence needed so that if they cannot remember something, they have a way to derive it.

It is important to remember that the level of explicitness that a teacher provides during the CRA sequence is critical to success for struggling learners. A helpful way to think about this is that the teacher provides students with an accessible "learning bridge" to mathematical understanding (see Figure 9.2) through explicit teacher modeling/scaffolding.

A potential misconception about explicit teacher modeling/scaffolding is that it simply means that the teacher stands in front of the classroom and talks at students, resulting in a unidimensional communication style. Another misconception is that explicit teacher instruction/modeling requires use of a pro-

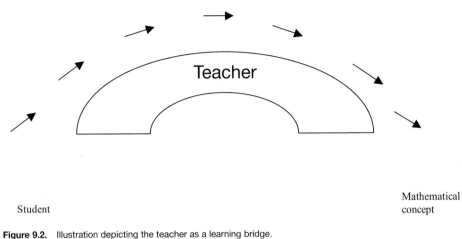

Figure 9.2.   Illustration depicting the teacher as a learning bridge.

grammatic script from which the teacher reads, directing students to parrot back answers to simple questions. When implemented effectively, explicit teacher mathematics instruction/modeling results in engaged learning for struggling learners because the various teaching techniques that are used allow students access to mathematical understanding. For students who often find learning difficult, such an experience is a wonderful feeling, one that encourages them to *want* to learn mathematics. Additional techniques for implementing explicit teacher modeling/scaffolding within a CRA sequence of instruction follows.

Critical Features/Components

There are four important considerations teachers should make when teaching through the CRA sequence.

Consideration 1. Use Appropriate and Various Concrete Objects to Teach the Particular Mathematical Concept or Skill

To use math manipulatives effectively, it is important to understand several basic characteristics of different types of math manipulatives and how these specific characteristics affect struggling learners. There are two distinct types of concrete objects: discrete and continuous.

1. Discrete objects are materials that can be counted (e.g., cookies, children, counting blocks, chips).

2. Continuous objects are not used for counting but are used for measurement (e.g., ruler, measuring cup, weight scale, trundle wheel).

Struggling learners need abundant experiences in using discrete objects before they will benefit from the use of continuous objects. This is because discrete objects have defining characteristics that students can discriminate easily through sight and touch. As students master an understanding of specific readiness concepts for specific measurement concepts and skills through the use of discrete objects (e.g., counting skills), continuous objects can be used.

Figure 9.3. Nonlinked proportional concrete materials including a) ten straws bundled together to make 10 and three single straws equals 13, and b) ten Unifix cubes attached together make 10.

Manipulatives that are used to teach the base-10 number system can be classified into two types: proportional and nonproportional.

1. Proportional materials show relationships by size (e.g., 10 counting blocks grouped together is 10 times the size of one counting block; a bean stick with 10 beans glued to a popsicle stick is 10 times bigger than one bean).There are two distinct types of proportional materials:

    a) Nonlinked proportional materials are single units that are independent of each other but can be bundled together (e.g., straws can be bundled together in groups of 10 with rubber bands; individual Unifix cubes can be attached in rows of 10 Unifix cubes each [see Figure 9.3]).

    b) Linked proportional materials come in single units as well as already-bundled tens units, hundreds units, and thousands units (e.g., base-10 cubes/blocks; beans and bean sticks; see Figure 9.4).

2. Nonproportional materials use units whose size is not indicative of value, whereas other characteristics are indicative of value (e.g., money, for which one dime is worth 10 times the value of one penny; poker chips, for which color indicates value of chip; an abacus, for which location of the row indicates value). A specified number of units that represent one value are

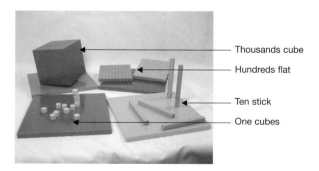

Thousands cube

Hundreds flat

Ten stick

One cubes

Figure 9.4. Linked proportional concrete materials including a) commercially made base-10 materials and b) teacher-made 10 stick (10 beans glued to tongue depressor).

Figure 9.5. Nonproportional concrete materials. Ten yellow cubes equal one blue cube (color denotes value of a cube).

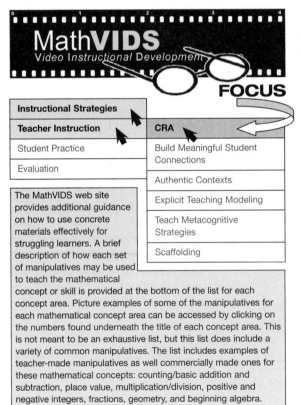

Instructional Strategies	
Teacher Instruction	CRA
Student Practice	Build Meaningful Student Connections
Evaluation	
	Authentic Contexts
The MathVIDS web site provides additional guidance on how to use concrete materials effectively for struggling learners. A brief description of how each set of manipulatives may be used	Explicit Teaching Modeling
	Teach Metacognitive Strategies
	Scaffolding

The MathVIDS web site provides additional guidance on how to use concrete materials effectively for struggling learners. A brief description of how each set of manipulatives may be used to teach the mathematical concept or skill is provided at the bottom of the list for each concept area. Picture examples of some of the manipulatives for each mathematical concept area can be accessed by clicking on the numbers found underneath the title of each concept area. This is not meant to be an exhaustive list, but this list does include a variety of common manipulatives. The list includes examples of teacher-made manipulatives as well commercially made ones for these mathematical concepts: counting/basic addition and subtraction, place value, multiplication/division, positive and negative integers, fractions, geometry, and beginning algebra.

exchanged for one unit of greater value (e.g., 10 pennies for 1 dime, 10 white poker chips for 1 blue poker chip, 10 beads in the first row of an abacus for 1 bead in the second row, 10 yellow cubes for 1 blue cube [see Figure 9.5]).

Struggling learners are more likely to learn the base-10 system and the important concept of place value when they use proportional manipulatives because differences between ones units, tens units, and hundreds units are easy to see and feel. Because of the very nature of nonproportional manipulatives, struggling learners have more difficulty seeing and feeling the differences in unit values and imposing the 10–1 relationship onto the manipulatives.

Consideration 2. Use Appropriate Drawings or Picture Representations of Concrete Objects   It is important to link concrete manipulatives with their representations explicitly. This entails showing students how to represent a set of counting bears with tallies, how to use circles and tally marks for plates and beans, and so forth. Students with learning difficul-

Equation 4x + 2x = 12

1.   Represent the variable "x" with circles. By combining like terms, there are six "x's."

6x = 12

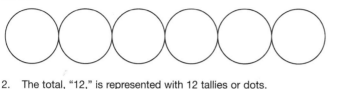

2.   The total, "12," is represented with 12 tallies or dots.

3.   The total, "12," is divided equally among the circles.

x = $\frac{12}{6}$

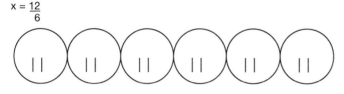

4.   The solution is the number of tallies represented in one circle—the variable "x."

x = 2

Figure 9.6.   Example of drawing the solution to an algebraic equation.

ties need to see these explicit linkages. The pictures that students draw represent the concrete objects that students manipulated when problem solving at the concrete level. It is appropriate for students to begin drawing solutions to problems as soon as they demonstrate mastery of a particular mathematical concept or skill at the concrete level. When students learn to draw solutions, they are provided with an intermediate step between the concrete and abstract levels, and they learn a valuable strategy for solving problems independently. Students should be provided with multiple independent problem-solving practice opportunities at this level. They gain confidence as they experience success, and the multiple practice opportunities assist students in beginning to internalize the problem-solving process that is necessary at the abstract level. In addition, students' concrete understandings of the concept or skill are reinforced because of the similarity of their drawings to the manipulatives that they used previously at the concrete level. Figure 9.6 shows an example of how drawings can be used to solve an algebraic equation.

Consideration 3. Use Appropriate Strategies for Assisting Students to Make the Transition from Concrete to Abstract Level of Understanding   Struggling learners may experience difficulties in

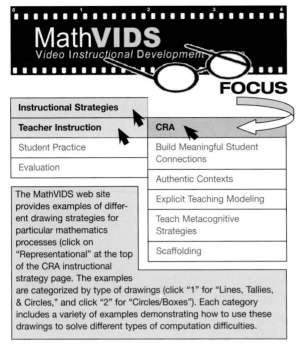

moving to the abstract level. It is important to provide students with multiple experiences at the two previous levels of understanding before moving to the abstract level. In addition, it is important to provide structured linkages between each level of understanding. Struggling learners need to understand that the problem 5×3 is the same as the representation of five boxes with three tallies each as well as a group of five plates with three macaroni pieces on each plate. To enhance students' abstract understandings and reinforce their concrete-level understandings, teachers should provide planned, periodic opportunities for students to "move down" by having them represent and show, with manipulatives, solutions to abstract problems.

Consideraton 4. Determine Students' Understanding at Each Level Before Moving to the Next Level

The key to using CRA instruction effectively for students with learning difficulties is to appreciate their need to move through the CRA sequence in a manner that allows them to master understanding at *each* level. If the expectation is for students to possess conceptual as well as procedural knowledge (the procedures or algorithms that are used to solve particular mathematics tasks), then it is imperative that students develop their mathematical understandings along this developmental sequence. It is equally as important that students demonstrate a mastery level of understanding at each level *before* moving to the next level. To facilitate this understanding, teachers need to encourage students to use their own language to describe their understandings at each level and demonstrate their understanding in a variety of authentic problem-solving contexts. Table 9.3 shows guidelines for determining when students are ready to move from one level of understand-

Table 9.3. Guidelines for determining mastery at the concrete, representational, and abstract levels of understanding

Level of understanding	Mastery guideline
Concrete	Accurately represents mathematics concept or performs mathematics skill correctly 3 of 3 times for 3 consecutive days
Representational	Accurately represents mathematics concept or performs mathematics skill 5 of 5 times for 3 consecutive days
Abstract	Accurately represents mathematics concept or performs mathematics skill 10 of 10 times for 3 consecutive days

ing to another. In conjunction with these four considerations, three additional features of CRA instruction with explicit teacher modeling/scaffolding make this instructional practice effective for struggling learners. These features, summarized below, are described in greater detail in the next section on instructional implementation.

1. Help students build meaningful connections between their existing knowledge and experiences and the mathematics concept to be learned (a description of this practice is provided earlier in this chapter).

2. Describe and model the mathematical concept or skill with the students. This does not mean that students are not able to build their own understandings and connections. What it does mean is that teachers provide the level of support and structure needed for students to build their understandings (Mercer, Lane, et al., 1996).

3. Scaffold your instruction by fading your direction and encouraging graduated levels of student independence (i.e., student assumes more responsibility for doing the skill at graduated levels while teacher simultaneously provides less direction).

Instructional Implementation

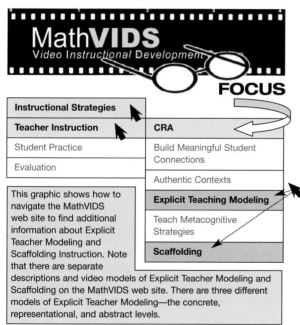

This graphic shows how to navigate the MathVIDS web site to find additional information about Explicit Teacher Modeling and Scaffolding Instruction. Note that there are separate descriptions and video models of Explicit Teacher Modeling and Scaffolding on the MathVIDS web site. There are three different models of Explicit Teacher Modeling—the concrete, representational, and abstract levels.

Explicit teacher modeling/scaffolding is a well-supported instructional strategy for students with high-incidence disabilities in mathematics as well as other content areas (Baroody, 1987; Borkowski, 1992; Brophy & Good, 1986; Carnine et al., 1998; Cobb, Yackel, & Wood, 1992; Kennedy & Tipps, 1994; Mercer, Jordan, et al., 1996; Mercer & Mercer, 2005; Miller et al., 1998; Montague, 1992; Paris & Winograd, 1990; Polloway & Patton, 1993; Swanson, 1999). When explicit teacher modeling/scaffolding is implemented within the CRA sequence, struggling learners are provided a powerful instructional approach.

Several specific modeling and scaffolding techniques are effective when helping students move through the CRA sequence of instruction.

1. *Link to previous knowledge.* It is always important for teachers to link explicitly what students already know to the new mathematics concept that they are going to learn. Using the suggestions described for the instruc-

tional practice Building Meaningful Student Connections will help teachers to do this effectively.

2. *Incorporate multisensory methods.* Teachers incorporate multisensory
    methods by planning how to integrate the use of both multiple sensory in-
    puts (how students receive information) and outputs (how students show
    their understanding). For example, teachers can provide or highlight in stu-
    dents' activities auditory and visual descriptions of mathematical concepts
    and skills (inputs) so that students have opportunities to engage kinesthet-
    ically, tactually, and verbally (inputs and outputs). Providing students with
    visual examples of mathematics (e.g., concrete objects, drawings, display of
    problem-solving steps) and using language to describe the particular con-
    cept's features are excellent ways to start.

3. *Cue key features of a target mathematics concept.* An effective use of mul-
    tisensory methods is cuing students to key features of mathematical con-
    cepts (Bley & Thornton, 1995). This includes using visual cuing, such as
    color-coding to highlight meanings of numbers in mathematical state-
    ments: blue for denominator in a fraction and red for numerator; direc-
    tional arrows that depict where to start and then where to proceed when
    working problems; circling mathematics symbol and connecting it to
    other representations of the same idea to emphasize important features of
    a particular mathematics concept. When using these cues, it is very impor-
    tant to point to and describe explicitly the relationship between the visual
    cue and its meaning. Consistency in cuing through the CRA sequence of
    instruction also can be advantageous. For example, if a teacher begins
    teaching fractions with fraction circles in which the whole (denominator)
    is blue and the fractional part (numerator) is another color, then when he
    or she proceeds to the representational level of understanding, the same
    color coding would be used. Then the same color-coding scheme would be
    maintained when numbers and symbols alone were used to represent var-
    ious fractions.

    Another way to cue students is to support their developing mathemat-
    ical thinking (metacognition) using a structured form with guiding ques-
    tions or prompts to direct student reflection (see Figure 9.7a and b). Cue
    sheets such as these can help students develop independent learning skills.
    Figure 9.7a shows a sheet that cues students on how to write the addition
    statement on the paper and where they can illustrate, with pictures or
    words, the strategy that they used to solve the problem. For students with
    fine motor and/or language difficulties, drawing pictures is an effective al-
    ternative for them to express their understandings. The cue sheet in Figure
    9.7b shows a method for supporting students as they begin to learn to use
    a strategy during independent practice. By checking off each step as they
    complete it, students have a tangible way to monitor their implementation
    of the strategy. As a teacher scaffolds (i.e., fades direction or involvement),
    the number of cues/prompts can be faded over time as students become
    more proficient in their use of the strategy.

4. *Provide examples and nonexamples of a target concept.* Modeling both
    examples and nonexamples of particular mathematics concepts or skills

1. Problem: _____

2. Describe with pictures or words your way for solving the problem.

3. When I solved the problem, I got _____.

4. I used _____ to solve the problem.

a)

Goal: *To solve a math problem.*

Checklist
You are to:

☐   Write the problem at the top of the page.

☐   • Use a strategy to solve the problem.

☐   • Use pictures or words to explain your strategy.

☐   Write your answer in the blank.

☐   Write the items or ideas you used to solve the problem.

b)

Figure 9.7.   Cuing forms that help students work independently: a) structured form with prompts, b) cuing sheet for activity.

at the concrete, representational, and abstract levels also is very helpful to struggling learners. After students demonstrate that they have acquired an initial understanding of the concept or skill, the teacher models a nonexample that differs from the example. This enables the teacher to help students focus on essential features of the target mathematics concept or skill through comparison and contrast. For example, when teaching triangles, use another geometric figure (e.g., square) as a nonexample and guide students through pinpointing the features that distinguish the two concepts (e.g., number of sides, number of vertices or "corners"). The most important aspect of this technique is to help make explicit for the students how the nonexample lacks key features of the example by using multisensory cues. In the previous example, you might have students circle and number the vertices of one shape in red and the other shape in blue and then provide additional cuing by having students come up to the board to point to and count each set of points with the rest of the class. When teaching how to combine like terms in algebraic equations, such cuing can help students distinguish what exemplifies "like terms" from unlike terms. For example, variables with exponents (e.g., x^2) can be circled with the exponent color-coded red, whereas variables with a coefficient (e.g., 4x) can be circled with the coefficient color-coded blue. Similar to the preceding example, students can be guided to point to and describe why certain terms are like terms or unlike terms. Students benefit from this technique because it teaches them discrimination skills. The use of nonexamples helps to highlight key features of the target concept. Struggling learners often do not make such distinctions naturally because their learning characteristics can make discrimination of subtle similarities and differences among mathematics concepts difficult.

5. *Scaffold/fade teacher direction from high to medium to low levels.* Scaffolding complements explicit teacher modeling because it provides a supportive process for students to assume greater levels of responsibility for demonstrating their newly acquired mathematical understandings. This instructional technique is instrumental in helping students move from initial to advanced acquisition of the target mathematics concept, setting the stage for developing learning independence. When scaffolding instruction, the teacher gradually fades his or her direction from high to medium to low levels as students demonstrate increased levels of understanding. A high level of teacher direction is characterized by the teacher's modeling/doing most of the mathematical concept or skill and students' modeling/doing one or two features or procedures with which they are most likely to have success. A medium level of teacher direction is characterized by the teacher's modeling/doing approximately one half of the mathematical concept or skill and students' modeling/doing approximately one half. A low level of teacher direction is characterized by the teacher prompting students to model/do most or all features or procedures of the mathematical concept or skill. It is important for teachers to determine which features or procedures of a target mathematical concept or skill their students are likely to have success with first, which features or procedures are slightly more difficult for students, and which features or procedures are most difficult. By making these determinations, teachers then can select what their students will model/do across these three levels of scaffolding with the intent of ensuring that students experience success at each level. Such decision making is very important; the experience of mathematical success is crucial for struggling learners because of previous learning failures, resulting in learned helplessness and a passive approach to learning mathematics.

6. *Provide immediate and specific corrective feedback.* Throughout modeling/scaffolding process, it is important that teachers provide students with specific corrective feedback and specific positive reinforcement. Corrective feedback that is specific and delivered in a supportive way provides students with a structure for building on their mathematical understandings. An effective way to do this is to acknowledge students' efforts and the features or procedures that they modeled appropriately and then to re-model the features or procedures for which students need additional support.

7. *Provide generous amounts of specific positive reinforcement.* The use of specific positive reinforcement is as important as specific corrective feedback when scaffolding instruction. Doing so confirms to students those aspects of the concept that they do understand. As a result of metacognitive deficits,

struggling learners often do not connect their thoughts and actions to a particular learning objective. In other words, they often do not know when they are or are not understanding. When positive reinforcement is specific, teachers can strengthen the cognitive connections that students have made. Positive reinforcement also can help students to develop metacognitive awareness about why and how what they are doing is helpful.

Following is an example of specific positive reinforcement related to plotting coordinates on a plane:

> "I noticed that when you began to plot the series of x and y coordinates, you first pointed to the first number in a set, then ran your finger along the x axis to find the x coordinate. I find that it helps me, too, when plotting x and y coordinates because it helps me to find the y intercept more easily."

Teachers provide struggling learners with an excellent process to acquire initial mathematical understanding by using explicit modeling/scaffolding techniques. When teachers explicitly link new mathematical concepts to students' previous knowledge, provide students with multiple pathways to input and output new mathematical concepts, use multisensory cues that highlight a concept's key features, and help students distinguish examples of a mathematical concept from nonexamples, struggling learners are less likely to be negatively affected by the various mathematics learning barriers that they experience. When teachers explicitly help students to connect new mathematical concepts to something they already know about, meaning is enhanced. Given the various mathematical learning barriers that these students experience, it is important that they be provided with instruction throughout the CRA sequence that engages them in ways that circumvent their mathematical learning barriers.

VIDEO FOCUS
Explicit Teacher Modeling

View teachers implementing explicit teacher modeling at the MathVIDS web site, and learn more about why this instructional practice addresses the mathematical learning needs of struggling learners. Teachers model this instructional practice at each level of understanding: concrete, representational, and abstract.

Scaffolding instruction helps students to increase their accuracy in understanding a target mathematical concept after they initially have begun to understand it through explicit teacher modeling. Scaffolding is a natural extension of modeling throughout the CRA sequence and helps advance student understanding from *some* understanding of the target concept to full understanding. When students demonstrate full, or complete, understanding, they are ready to apply that understanding by engaging in various student practice activities to build proficiency.

Explicit CRA instruction with teacher modeling/scaffolding is an interactive process between teacher and student in which students are actively engaged in the acquisition of mathematical *understanding* at the concrete, representational, and abstract levels. Through the techniques described in this

VIDEO FOCUS
Scaffolding

See a teacher scaffolding instruction on patterns with kindergarten students at the MathVIDS web site: *Scaffolding Instruction* web page.

section, teachers create interactive learning on the part of struggling learners by making mathematical concepts cognitively accessible; by prompting students' thinking and connection-making through prompts, cues, and questioning; by encouraging students to activate their developing knowledge (i.e., expecting students to use concrete materials, drawings, and thinking skills to demonstrate understanding as the teacher releases his or her direction); and by supporting risk taking and student involvement through specific positive corrective feedback and reinforcement.

INSTRUCTIONAL PRACTICE 4:
TEACH PROBLEM-SOLVING STRATEGIES

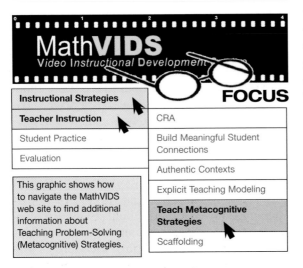

When one interacts with the world or uses language to understand it, one engages in problem solving. When one uses the language of math to gain understanding, one is engaged in problem solving. However, struggling learners frequently have difficulty understanding the message, the communicative intent in mathematical communication (problem solving). Often, this is because they are not able to understand fully the meaning of mathematics as a result of the various learning barriers discussed in Chapters 5 and 6. Even more important is that these students have difficulty repairing their receptive communication difficulties. Generally, if a person does not understand what someone has said, then he or she monitors the context of the conversation, decides what was meant, and determines why he or she did not understand. The individual then takes steps to correct the situation (e.g., a word that had not been heard before was used, and the person realizes it and asks the person speaking what the word means). If one is unsure of what a mathematical problem is asking, or what the communicative intent is, then he or she rereads it, breaking it down into more understandable parts. This ability to monitor one's own understanding and go back and repair it is an important metacognitive skill.

Purpose/Description

Metacognition involves students' ability to monitor their learning cognitively by 1) evaluating whether they are learning, 2) using strategies when needed, 3) knowing whether a strategy is successful, and 4) making changes when needed. These are essential skills for any problem-solving situation. Because mathematics involves problem solving, students who are not metacognitively adept have great difficulty being successful. In fact, most struggling learners do not realize that students who are successful in mathematics use metacognitive strategies when working on mathematical tasks. Struggling learners often need to be taught explicitly how to be metacognitive learners. Teachers can do this by providing structure for learning new strategies and by helping students become aware of and monitor the effectiveness of the strategies that they choose to use. Teachers who model strategies and who have classmates share problem-solving strategies, who reinforce students' use of these strategies, and who teach students to organize themselves so that they can implement strategies will help students who have metacognitive deficits become metacognitive learners (e.g., Allsopp, Minskoff, & Bolt, 2005; Minskoff & Allsopp, 2003; Swanson, 1999; Vaughn et al., 2000).

Critical Features/Components

To assist students to become more metacognitively aware, teachers must purposefully teach strategies for problem solving, and they must teach how and when to use strategies effectively so that students can determine whether their approach is successful. In some cases, this means explicitly teaching strategies for particular concepts and skills. In other cases, this means emphasizing metacognitive thinking as students learn new concepts, apply them, and relate them to previous knowledge and experiences. Creating the expectation that this is a natural part of learning should be a primary goal. By reinforcing risk taking, teachers can encourage struggling learners, who often are reticent to take risks because of past failures, to take a more proactive role in mathematical problem solving.

Metacognitive strategy instruction should incorporate the following teacher-directed components:

1. Model strategies and provide multiple opportunities to practice using strategies in relevant contexts.

2. Ensure that there is an appropriate match between strategy steps and their representation of the concept or skill.

3. Emphasize both the actions and thinking that are needed to solve a problem.

4. Reinforce risk taking when students are problem solving.

5. Teach students to self-monitor and self-evaluate their performance.

Strategy instruction should begin early in the learning cycle and continue as students progress in their understanding. For example, strategy instruction can be helpful in the early grades when teaching simple patterns. Figure 9.8 shows a procedural strategy for extending simple patterns. This strategy guides students to discover the pattern and then to use predictions and organizational skills to complete the task. After modeling of the strategy, the teacher provides guided and independent practice. Teachers can practice multisensory cuing by incorporating visuals for each step of the strategy. As students become more adept at extending patterns, they repeat the strategy rhyme, use a cue card, and finally internalize the steps.

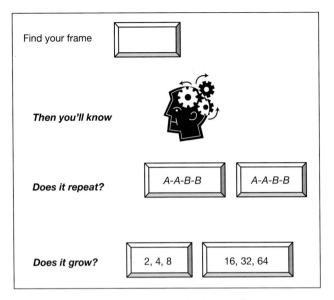

Figure 9.8.   Early grades strategy instruction for extending patterns.

A variety of techniques can be used to enhance strategy instruction. For instance, teachers can cue students to the steps that are being used as they work together on activities. The use of strategy cue sheets that remind students of major problem-solving steps helps them to develop independent use of the strategy. Figure 9.9 shows a cue sheet for the EQUAL strategy, a learning strategy for determining greater than, less than, and equal to.

The components of a strategy must accurately represent the required learning task for it to be helpful to students. For example, if the task requires students to solve a particular mathematical problem, then the steps or procedures that are included in the strategy must provide students an efficient and accurate way to solve that problem. Strategies must be physically as well as cognitively accessible. Some students will be able to remember strategies and their steps. Many strategies, such as mnemonics, use cuing that is memorable. However, some students will have difficulty remembering strategies because of memory retrieval deficits. For these students, encouraging them to develop mathematics strategy notebooks and allowing them access to the notebooks is a critical accommodation. The use of visual cues (color coding, graphics), say-alouds (cuing that prompts students to think out loud), and kinesthetic movement (strategy steps that include student movement) provide students multiple pathways to interact with the strategy and the related mathematical concept. By including both the actions (procedures) and the thinking processes that are needed for mathematical problem solving, effective mathematics strategies help students become more adept at doing mathematics independently. Figure 9.10 shows the integration of a CRA sequence of instruction for the concept of *square root* with the metacognitive strategy "ROOT IT" as one process for learning both the procedures and thinking processes that are necessary for determining the square root of a number.

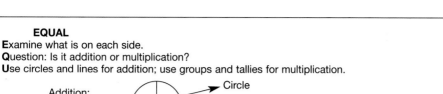

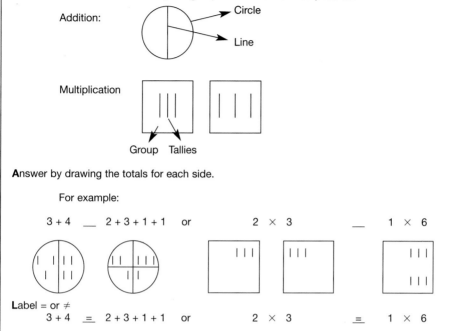

Figure 9.9. EQUAL strategy cue sheet. EQUAL stands for Examine what is on each side; Question: Is it addition or multiplication?; Use circles and lines for addition, use groups and tallies for multiplication; Answer by drawing the totals for each side; and Label (<, >, =, /).

Strategies can be presented in many forms, including acronyms or mnemonics (i.e., words for which each letter represents a step), pictures, acrostics (i.e., phrases in which the first letter in each word of the phrase represents a step), and graphics or concept/semantic maps. Figure 9.11 shows an example of an acronym/mnemonic strategy for adding positive and negative numbers. Strategies can also be used for multiple instructional purposes. Some strategies support students in retrieving information from memory (e.g., acronyms/mnemonics). Other strategies help students structure how they may approach solving a task or performing a skill (e.g., the ADD and ROOT-IT strategies). Still others help students to cognitively connect conceptual knowledge to procedural knowledge. The explicit trading method for long division (Van de Walle, 2006b) is an excellent example of how to explicitly help students connect the concept of fair sharing (i.e., one meaning of division) to the long division algorithm (see Figure 9.12). In the explicit trading method the total (i.e., dividend) is modeled using base-10 pieces. The base-10 materials are then fairly shared (i.e., divided equally) among the number of groups indicated by the divisor, starting with the largest base ten pieces. The pieces are distributed across the groups until there are not enough blocks of the same value to evenly distribute. The leftover pieces

Math skill/concept: Square root

Break down into teachable/learnable steps:

1. Determine the sign and what it represents.
2. Read the equation.
3. Determine the quantity of the number inside the square root sign.
4. Put the quantity into groups. Start with groups of two.
5. Ask, "Does it add up?"
6. Determine whether it is the answer, or continue grouping.
7. Select the square root by identifying the total number of groups.
8. Check the answer by counting if the total number equals the number inside the square root sign.

ABSTRACT level of understanding:

$\sqrt{9} = 3$

REPRESENTATIONAL level of understanding:

$\sqrt{9} = 3$

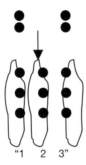

"1   2   3"

CONCRETE level of understanding:

*Same process as with drawing representational, but used with discrete counting objects (e.g., chips, pennies, tees, etc.)

Metacognitive strategy:

<u>R</u>ead the number inside the square root sign.

<u>O</u>rganize the number in groups, starting with groups of two.

<u>O</u>bserve the groups and ask, "Does it add up?"

<u>T</u>ie down the answer, or continue grouping.

<u>I</u>dentify the square root by circling/counting the total number of groups.

<u>T</u>est the answer by counting.

Figure 9.10. Applying CRA instruction and strategy instruction to middle school math skills/concepts. This example shows the ROOT-IT strategy, which include the procedures and thinking aspects of finding square roots.

are then traded for smaller pieces so that the fair sharing across the groups can continue. This process continues until the ones are fairly shared. Any leftover ones represent the remainder. As pieces are fairly shared and traded, the number of pieces is represented in columns that mirror the long division format with place-value columns so that students can match the base ten pieces to the cor-

Strategy: *ADD*—Helps students to add positive and negative numbers.

Ask yourself, "Is this an addition problem?"
  • *Look for an addition sign.*
Decide which signs are given for each number.
  • *Check for positive and negative signs and circle negative integer.*
Determine the problem, what to do, and the sign of the sum.
  • *Use Adding Positive and Negative Integers Cue Sheet*

How to implement the ADD strategy:

9 + − 6   =   _____   1. **A** – student looks for addition sign

9 + ⊖6   =   _____   2. **D** – student determines the sign for each integer and circles the negative integer.

9 + − 6   =   __3__   3. **D** – student decides three things: 1) whether the problem adds a positive and a negative integer or two negative integers, 2) whether to subtract the absolute values of the integers (if they are positive and negative) or add their absolute values (if both are negative integers), and 3) which sign the sum takes (negative if integers are negative or the sign of the integer that has the greatest absolute value). *See cue sheet below.

Adding Positive and Negative Integers Cue Sheet

Problem	What to do	Sign of sum
Positive + positive	Add	+
Negative + negative	Add	−
Positive + negative or negative + positive	Larger number − smaller number	Sign of larger number

Figure 9.11.   Acronym/mnemonic mathematics metacognitive strategy with decision-making cue sheet. (From Minskoff, E., & Allsopp, D. [2003] *Academic success strategies for adolescents with learning disabilities and ADHD* (p. 257). Baltimore: Paul H. Brookes Publishing Co.; reprinted by permission.)

responding numbers and their values. The pictures and text in Figure 9.12 shows each step of the division process. Figure 9.13 shows a cuing sheet to support students as they build facility with the long division algorithm in a meaningful way.

Instructional Implementation

Although the attributes of a mathematics strategy are important, even the best strategy will be of little use to students if they do not learn how to use it. Mathematics strategies should be taught using the explicit modeling/scaffolding methods described earlier in this chapter and by providing multiple practice opportunities using the student practice strategies described in Chapter 10. Simply providing students a copy of the strategy, going over it once or twice, and

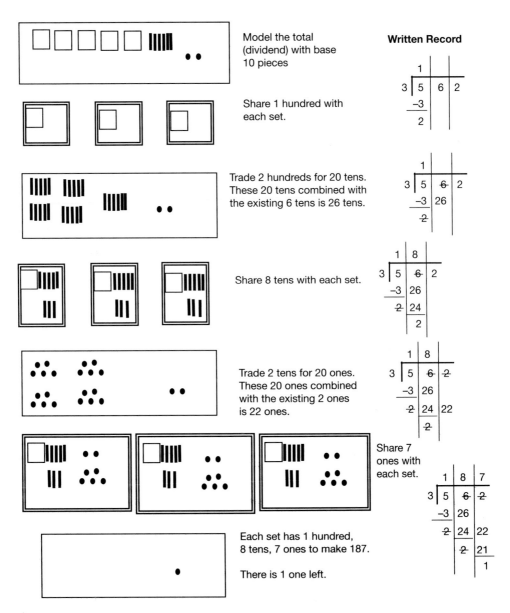

Figure 9.12. Explicit trading method. (*Key:* □ = 100, | = 10, • = 1.)

then expecting them to understand the strategy and how to use it effectively will result in failure for struggling learners. Mathematics strategies should be taught to students using the same effective instructional processes that are used to teach any mathematical concept or skill. Following are important steps for teaching mathematics metacognitive strategies:

- Choose an appropriate metacognitive strategy for the mathematical skill. (For a list of metacognitive strategies by mathematical concept area, go to the Metacognitive Strategies section of the MathVIDS web site.)

Math skill/concept: Long division procedure connected to concepts

Break down into teachable/learnable steps:

To start:
1. Represent the total (dividend) with base ten pieces.
2. Identify how many groups to share pieces among.
3. Share all the pieces until you can no longer fairly share.

Fair-Sharing:
1. Share and record the number of pieces put in each group.
2. Record the number of pieces shared in all. (Multiply to find this number.)
3. Record the number of pieces remaining. (Subtract to find this number.)
4. Trade (if necessary) for smaller pieces, and combine with any that are there already. Record the new total number in the next column.

Written Record

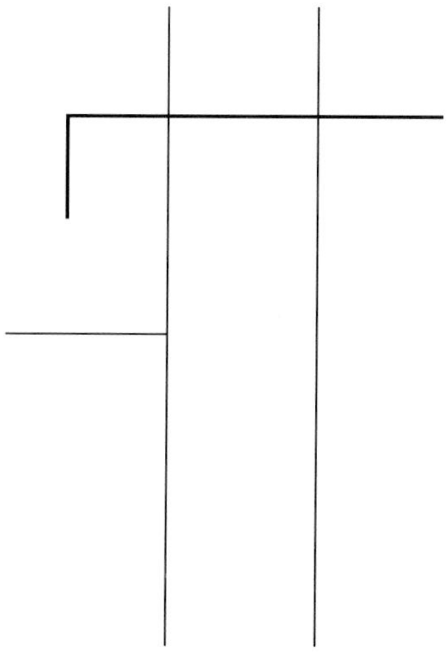

Figure 9.13. Explicit trading method cue sheet.

- Build meaningful student connections among the strategy, the related mathematical concept or skill, and the previous knowledge and experiences of students.

- Describe and model the strategy at least three times.

- Check student understanding. Ensure that they understand both the strategy and how to use it.

- Provide ample opportunities for students to practice using the strategy.

- Provide timely corrective feedback, and remodel use of strategy as needed.

- Provide students with strategy cue sheets (or post the strategy in the classroom) as students begin independently using the strategy.

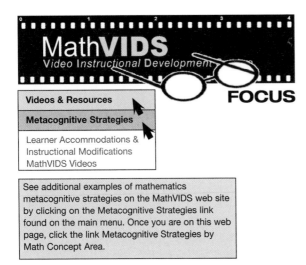

Videos & Resources
Metacognitive Strategies
Learner Accommodations &
Instructional Modifications
MathVIDS Videos

See additional examples of mathematics
metacognitive strategies on the MathVIDS web site
by clicking on the Metacognitive Strategies link
found on the main menu. Once you are on this web
page, click the link Metacognitive Strategies by
Math Concept Area.

- Fade the use of cues as students demonstrate that they have memorized the strategy and how (as well as when) to use it. (Some students will benefit from a "strategy notebook" in which they keep both the strategies that they have learned and the corresponding math skill for which they can use each strategy.)

- Reinforce students for using the strategy appropriately.

VIDEO FOCUS

Teach Metacognitive Strategies

See a teacher implementing these
critical instructional features as she
teaches the ORDER strategy for
order of operations on the MathVIDS
web site.

RESPONSIVE/ACCESSIBLE INSTRUCTION

Students need to learn how to become effective communicators of mathematics. They need to be able to apply their mathematical knowledge and skills to problem solve. The process strands that are listed by the NCTM include the ability to problem solve and to communicate mathematical understandings (NCTM, 2000). To avoid building "Swiss cheese "understanding, to shore up the holes, to enable struggling learners to move beyond a rote and drill approach to mathematics, teachers have to provide structured, systematic, highly effective instruction that is based on communicating mathematical understanding. Such instruction must provide the supports that are needed by struggling learners. Grounding mathematics instruction in relevant, authentic contexts; providing clear linkages and connections; teaching by integrating explicit teacher modeling/scaffolding with a CRA sequence of instruction and; teaching problem-solving strategies will lay the foundation for initial understanding of mathematical concepts and skills.

Now go back to Table 9.1 that you completed at the beginning of the chapter. Review the ideas that you noted for each instructional practice before you began reading. On the basis of what you have learned in this chapter, add to or revise those ideas that you would like to carry with you as you work toward implementing these practices in your school or classroom.

10

Building Proficiency

Using Effective Student Practice Strategies

hapter 9 explored four effective teaching practices to use as students are acquiring mathematical understandings (initial acquisition and advanced acquisition stages of learning). During these stages, the instructional emphasis is on accuracy of understanding. However, as students demonstrate their understanding of the target concept or learning objective, the instructional emphasis must shift to helping students become proficient or fluent.

APPLYING MATHEMATICAL KNOWLEDGE

Fluency involves both accuracy and rate. For students to use their mathematical understanding in relevant, authentic ways, they must be able to demonstrate their knowledge with accuracy and at a rate that supports, not hinders, their efficient application of mathematics. Students can be accurate at doing mathematics, but if they cannot apply their mathematical knowledge in an efficient way, at a usable rate of speed, then they will struggle.

Suppose, for example, that a student can accurately perform the mathematical calculations that are needed to find the product of a multiplication fact (e.g., use the repeated addition process), but if it takes 20 minutes for him or her to complete 10 problems, then he or she will have difficulty applying his or her understanding of multiplication to mathematical processes that require automaticity with facts, such as solving quadratic algebraic equations. Granted, students may use compensatory techniques such as using a calculator or a fact chart, but doing so still requires additional time, making the performance of the task less than automatic. Reliance on such compensatory techniques can prove to be frustrating when higher level mathematics requires repeated use of prerequisite skills in an automatic manner. Moreover, practice opportunities that promote students' proficiency will enhance their ability to maintain their understandings over time. Maintenance of mathematical concepts and skills is essential if students are to be successful in pre-K through 12 mathematics.

Why Practice Matters

Does all of this really matter? Think of learning a new sport such as golf. In the beginning you are conscious of your grip, your stance, and the rules of the game. As you become more adept and the basics become more automatic, you start thinking of nuances, of strategic play. You develop the ability to monitor and adjust your stroke, to look ahead, and to read the course. The same holds true for learning mathematics. As students understand mathematical concepts well and are able to "play the ball," they then can move on to becoming mathematical thinkers who are more strategic and self-aware.

As Publilius Syrus said in 100 BC, "Practice is the best of all instructors." Practice is what builds the bridge between acquisition and application. During practice, students move through the proficiency and maintenance stages referenced in Chapter 7. Struggling learners often require more opportunities to practice a newly learned skill compared with students without learning difficulties. The more opportunities that students have to respond to a problem-solving context and the more occasions that they have to practice what they are learning, the more likely it is that they will master the concept (Brophy & Good, 1986). Moreover, student behavior improves when students are provided with multiple opportunities to respond meaningfully to academic tasks (Sutherland & Wehby, 2001).

Student practice, as meant here, does not simply mean drill and practice. Too often, struggling learners are asked to complete mathematics worksheets day after day. Usually, this involves solving basic mathematics computations with paper and pencil (e.g., addition, subtraction, multiplication, division, fractions). Such an approach creates a lack of interest in students and in many cases promotes frustration because such practice requires students to rely on learning processes that are difficult for them (e.g., memorization, visual-spatial processing, fine motor skills).

Instead, practice should be varied, it should incorporate multiple processes for learning, and it should be motivational. When a variety of practice activities are provided, students have a way to transfer their developing mathematical understandings to multiple contexts. In addition, variety can enhance interest in mathematics rather than discourage it. It is important that practice, like teacher instruction, occurs in authentic contexts. For example, in contrast to measuring a square on a piece of paper to practice measuring perimeter and area, students can measure tiles on the floor, bulletin boards, windows, desk tops, and so forth. Combining such activities with a purpose can enhance the authenticity and meaning of these activities (e.g., determining the area of the entire room for rearranging classroom furniture for a special classroom event; estimating how many pictures can fit on a new bulletin board display given certain dimensions; determining how much paint [area] is needed to paint murals on windows; graphing the number of gold, silver, and bronze medals won by certain countries during the Summer or Winter Olympics).

Guidelines for Effective Student Practice

In Chapters 7 and 8, various levels of understanding were discussed as they relate to how struggling learners learn, how to determine what students know, and how to decide what to teach. In Chapter 9, Concrete-Representational-Abstract (CRA) instruction was described. Levels of understanding also must be considered when providing students practice with mathematics. Students who have initial understanding at the concrete level should be provided practice opportunities using concrete objects. Students who have moved to the representational level of understanding should be provided practice opportunities in which they draw solutions. Students who are at the abstract level of understanding should practice using numbers and symbols, incorporating use of drawing or concrete objects only when needed.

The type of student response also should be considered. At the receptive level, students demonstrate their understanding by choosing an example of a mathematics concept or skill from among several choices. For instance, students may be presented with several sets of fraction circles that represent a particular mixed number. A student then would select the set of fraction circles that represents the mixed number. At the expressive level, students actually perform the mathematics skill or demonstrate the mathematics concept. For this type of response, students would be given the mixed number and would use fraction circles to represent the mixed number.

Struggling learners benefit from response opportunities that occur in a graduated sequence. Seeing possible examples of a mathematics concept that they initially have learned and choosing the one that represents the concept is a less demanding task than actually representing the concept. Providing additional practice at the receptive level gives students both the understanding and the confidence to demonstrate their understanding of mathematics at the expressive level. If a student demonstrates initial understanding of a mathematics skill but cannot express his or her understanding during student practice, then consider providing him or her receptive-level practice first. Figure 10.1 shows an example of both a receptive and an expressive student practice activity.

Although providing a variety of student practice activities is important, all practice activities should include particular characteristics for them to be effective in helping students become proficient at doing mathematics. Following are eight important characteristics or components of effective student practice for struggling learners:

1. Practice activities involve mathematics concepts and skills with which students have already demonstrated initial understanding.

2. Practice activities provide students with multiple opportunities to respond using the target mathematics concept or skill.

3. Practice activities match students' levels of understanding (CRA; receptive or expressive).

4. Practice activities are designed to complement students' unique learning characteristics so that students can best demonstrate their understanding. Students' responses (e.g., writing, speaking, drawing) are not significantly affected by their disability (e.g., if a student has significant visual-motor integration difficulty, then have him or her use a means of responding that does not require fine motor movements such as writing numbers).

5. The teacher provides directions and models how to perform the task required by the practice activity before students begin.

6. The teacher continually monitors students as they practice, providing corrective feedback and positive reinforcement for accuracy and effort.

7. Practice activities include a process for measuring individual student performance.

8. Subsequent instructional planning is based on the degree to which students demonstrate mastery of the concept or skill being practiced (adapted from Allsopp, in press).

Seven student practice instructional strategies are described in the remainder of this chapter. All of these student practice instructional strategies can be used to help students build mastery of mathematics. The student practice strategies described are not the only practice strategies that can be used effectively with struggling learners. However, they represent a variety of activities and are included to provide a forum for expanding one's notion of what mathematics practice can entail. It is important to note that each student practice strategy contains research-based instructional features that result in positive learning outcomes. Each description includes the purpose of the practice strat-

---

Lesson purpose: to provide students with multiple practice opportunities to make groups of ten.

Receptive/Recognition Level

Materials:

Three containers (e.g., box tops) with groups of concrete objects. Containers should be differentiated with a color or symbol, letter or number. Some groups in the containers should show groups of ten; some groups should only show groups of ones.

Activity:

Students will work at tables in groups of three. Each child is assigned a container. Each child should look at his container and decide whether it shows groups of tens or not. When the teacher rings the bell, the children at each table are to take turns telling the others at their table if their container shows groups of ten, and if so, how many groups of ten. After each child at the table has shared his or her decision with his or her tablemates, the teacher will ask one child at each table to share his or her decisions with the entire class before signaling the children to pass the containers around the table. Continue until every child has practiced with each container at the table.

Expressive Level

Materials:

Several containers or envelopes. Each container will have counting objects (e.g., beans). Ten frames (can be made from index cards and then laminated)

Activity:

Students will work in teams of four. Each team will count the items in each of their containers by grouping by tens. Because this activity requires space for the ten frames, it might be best to do this as a table or floor activity. The teacher will ring a bell to signal an end to the activity and at that time, will ask individual students from each team to come to the front to show their solutions. Teams can get points for each correct answer.

Figure 10.1.   Student practice activity at the receptive and expressive levels (concrete objects).

egy, tips about how to implement the strategy effectively, and an example of the strategy. When making decisions regarding which type of practice activity to use, it is important to base the decision on how well the purpose and the procedures of the student practice strategy meet both the needs of the students and the mathematics concept or skill that is being learned.

STRATEGY 1: STRUCTURED LANGUAGE EXPERIENCES

Purpose

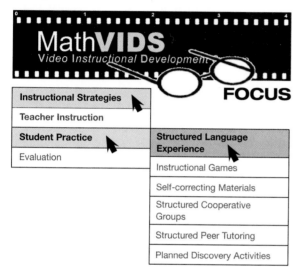

This practice strategy encourages students to use their own language to describe their mathematical understandings, a strategy supported by mathematics educators to enhance understanding (Baroody, 1987; Kennedy & Tipps, 1994). The purpose of this practice strategy is to help students deepen their understanding through talking, writing, performing, or drawing. Suggestions from the mathematics education literature have been adapted to describe how "structured language experiences" can be applied effectively to mathematics for struggling learners. These ideas also have been derived from the literature on enhancing meaningful writing/language development when teaching struggling learners (e.g., Englert et al., 1995; Englert & Mariage, 1991; Gersten, Baker, & Edwards, 1999; Graham & Harris, 1989; Graham, Harris, & Larson, 2001; Mason, Harris, & Graham, 2002) and others who are interested in how language can be applied to mathematics to meet the needs of struggling learners (Baxter, Woodward & Olson, 2005; Tomey, 1998).

Teaching Tips

Structured language experiences are well-planned, systematically applied activities in which students have multiple opportunities to use their own language to describe their mathematical understandings. Structured language experiences are intentional in nature, meaning that an appropriate activity is developed and relevant materials are provided so that students can describe what they know in a supported environment. It is important for the teacher to demonstrate explicitly a clear link between the activity and the target mathematics concept or skill to be practiced. It also is important that students receive feedback from the teacher about their descriptions.

When selecting a math concept or skill for students to practice using a structured language experience, it is important to ensure that students first

VIDEO FOCUS
Structured Language Experiences

See a teacher implementing this instructional strategy by viewing the video that is available on the Structured Language Experiences strategy web page on the MathVIDS web site.

have demonstrated at least initial acquisition understanding of the concept. Providing concrete objects during the activity will link explicitly the practice activity with previous instruction and can reduce the negative effects of students' memory difficulties. It also is important to plan alternative response opportunities for individual students whose learning characteristics create barriers for using one type of response mode (e.g., students who have speech difficulties may prefer to write their explanations; students who have significant writing difficulties may prefer to describe their understanding verbally). Finally, the structured language practice activity should be closed by modeling an accurate description of the math concept or skill, providing appropriate cuing (e.g., think-alouds; visual, auditory, kinesthetic, tactile modalities).

Example

Figure 10.2 shows an example of a structured language experience activity that is appropriate for practice occurring at the concrete or representational level of understanding.

STRATEGY 2: STRUCTURED COOPERATIVE LEARNING GROUPS/PEER TUTORING

Purpose

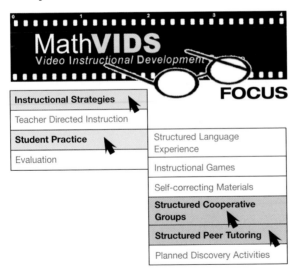

This practice strategy provides students the opportunity to enhance their initial understanding of particular mathematical concepts and skills through practicing with their peers. Cooperative learning/peer tutoring is peer-mediated learning that encourages students to learn from each other (Johnson & Johnson, 1986; Slavin, 1990). For struggling learners, cooperative learning is most effective when the cooperative activity is highly structured. Having students work together simply for the sake of working together will not result in effective learning. Cooperative learning activities should be planned thoughtfully and should incorporate several effective techniques for struggling learners to practice.

Structured Language Experience

Objective: Divide with remainders using concrete objects in measurement/"separating into equal groups" and partitive/"sharing" situations.

Level of understanding: Concrete/receptive

Materials:

- Concrete examples of solutions to various division equations with and without remainders
- "Choice" cards (three for each concrete example) that represent possible solutions to each concrete example. One card includes the appropriate solution. Appropriate language is used to represent the solutions (e.g., "four groups of five with two left over" would represent the solution to "$22 \div 5 =$ ___").
- Response sheet with correct solutions for answer key
- Response sheet numbered according to number of examples provided
- Appropriate accommodations for students with significant writing problems include those that allow them to tape-record their responses or have a letter written at the top of each choice card. Students can write the letter of the card that they choose instead of writing the phrase.
- An appropriate accommodation for students with reading difficulties is to pair them with a classmate who has the ability to read the language choice cards.

Description of activity:

Students work at a center where there are a variety of concrete examples showing solutions to division equations and matching written descriptions.

For example:

The concrete solution to the division equation $16 \div 5 =$ ___ would be three groups of five counting objects and one counting object left over.

It is important to group the counting objects in a distinct manner so that the remainder can be identified clearly.

Above each concrete example are three cards with possible solutions written on them (e.g., "three groups of five with two left over," "three groups of five with one left over," "three groups of five with zero left over"). One card is the correct solution (with remainder). Students select which solution is appropriate and write it down beside the appropriate number on their response sheet.

Activity steps:

1. Review directions for completing structured language experiences and relevant classroom rules.
2. Model how to perform the skill(s) within the context of the activity *before* students begin the activity. Model how to make a choice and how to write the solution on the response sheet.
3. Provide time for student questions.
4. Signal students to begin.
5. Monitor students as they work. Provide positive reinforcement for "trying hard," responding appropriately, and using appropriate behavior. Also provide corrective feedback and modeling.
6. Ask students to explain their choices.

Figure 10.2. Structured language experience activity.

Teaching Tips

Important components of structured cooperative learning groups/peer tutoring include the following (Beirne-Smith, 1991; Calhoon & Fuchs, 2003; Goodlad & Hirst, 1989; Greenwood, Terry, Arreaga-Mayer, & Finney, 1992; Lewis & Doorlag, 1999; Mercer & Mercer, 2005; Rivera, 1996; Slavin, 1990; Vaughn, Bos, & Schumm, 1997):

1. Teaching specific procedures that are needed for completing the activity

2. Teaching appropriate behavior expectations

3. Developing materials that clearly identify the mathematics concept or skill

4. Cuing appropriately

5. Providing monitoring and specific feedback/reinforcement

6. Providing closure to the activity by re-modeling the target mathematics concept or skill

Planning and teacher monitoring are essential because peers often leave struggling learners out of the group because of their learning or behavior difficulties. Designating specific roles for students is one important way to structure cooperative learning activities. Sometimes struggling learners are given a role in the group that provides them with little opportunity to actually practice the target mathematics concept or skill, the assumption being that they really cannot do the mathematics. Other times, teachers give these students roles that require minimal involvement because they believe that doing so will ensure that the group will be better able to complete the cooperative learning activity in a timely manner. Teachers must assign roles conscientiously to students and ensure that all students have the opportunity to perform essential roles that are related to the target mathematics concept or skill.

Another helpful planning consideration is how struggling learners are paired within groups. Pairing students who have learning difficulties with students who can serve as productive learning models is effective. To enhance the effectiveness of peer modeling, teachers should plan situations within the cooperative group activity for these students to interact. Research indicates that students with and without learning difficulties benefit when paired together for structured cooperative learning activities (Osguthorpe & Scruggs, 1990).

It is important that the teacher emphasize in explicit terms how the practice activity relates to the target mathematics skill. An easy way to do this is to identify the concept or skill to be practiced (in both visual and auditory ways) and then to demonstrate how to perform the task or activity with a group of volunteer students (i.e., demonstrate how to perform the skill in the context of the selected cooperative group activity). This step is important because, as a result of characteristics such as attention difficulties, memory difficulties, and cognitive processing difficulties, struggling learners may not make the explicit connection between the activity and the learning objective. Cuing students by providing an example of the concept or skill (e.g., steps to a needed mathematics strategy) on the board or on a cue sheet that is taped to group tables also can be helpful. These cuing tools also provide the teacher the opportunity to emphasize important ideas or procedures with which students are having difficulty as he or she monitors student groups. Students also need opportunities to respond to learning tasks multiple times. Without real opportunities to do so, practice will not be helpful for these students.

When developing practice activities in which students work in peer-tutoring pairs, it can be helpful to designate one student as "coach" and one student as "player" and to structure their practice session in ways that promote specific corrective feedback and their use of metacognitive thinking. For example, the coach presents a problem to be solved, and the player solves the problem. The coach checks the player's response using a prompt sheet provided by the teacher. Providing a prompt sheet or answer key can be an effective way to structure peer-tutoring activities. It provides the coach cuing for asking questions and providing feedback. Prompt sheets could include the problems to be solved and the answers to the problems, an example or a drawing of the target mathematics concept (e.g., fraction circles shaded to represent specific fractions), important features of the problems (e.g., arrows pointing to the base and one side of a rectangle when students are practicing determining the area of geometric figures), or an example of a correctly solved equation (e.g., the steps to solving one-variable algebra equations). Teachers should discuss and model for students how to provide feedback in a supportive and effective way and may provide cue sheets for expected behavior to both the coach and the player. After a period of time, teachers signal students to switch roles; the coach becomes the player and the player becomes the coach.

Example

VIDEO FOCUS
Structured Cooperative Learning

See a teacher implementing structured cooperative learning to provide her students practice with solving division story problems by drawing their solutions (representational level) on the MathVIDS web site.

Using these techniques provides students with supported practice for using metacognitive thinking when they are the coaches and receiving feedback about their mathematical thinking when they are the players. Incorporating points that are assigned by coaches on the basis of the accuracy or the quality of the players' responses can increase motivation for some students. Structures such as these, often referred to in the literature as classwide peer tutoring, are highly effective, peer-mediated, instructional practice for struggling learners (Greenwood, 1991; Harper, Mallette, Maheady, & Brennan, 1993; Maheady, Harper, & Mallette, 1991; Mathes, Fuchs, Fuchs, Henley, & Sanders, 1994). Figure 10.3 shows an example of a structured cooperative learning/peer-tutoring practice activity using the FAST DRAW technique that incorporates the techniques emphasized for this instructional practice.

STRATEGY 3: MATHEMATICS INSTRUCTIONAL GAMES/SELF-CORRECTING MATERIALS

Purpose

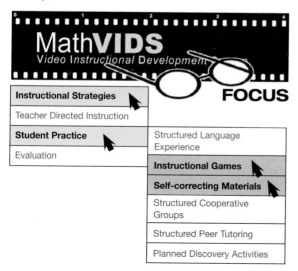

Instructional materials and self-correcting materials are appropriate when students are working at all three levels of understanding: concrete, representational, and abstract. At the concrete level, concrete objects can be provided to students to use as they respond. At the representational level, students can draw as a means for deciding what the correct answer is. Polaroid/ digital pictures or drawings of concrete objects that

Structured Cooperative Learning/Peer-Tutoring Practice Activity

Objective: Use the FAST DRAW strategy to solve story problems and equations that involve addition of fractions with mixed numbers by drawing solutions.

✓ **F**ind what you are solving for.

✓ **A**sk yourself, "what is the important information?" (circle it).

✓ **S**et up the equation.

✓ **T**ake the equation and solve it.

✓ **D**etermine the sign and what it means.

✓ **R**ead the equation (problem).

✓ **A**nswer the equation, or draw and check.

✓ **W**rite the answer and check.

Develop a master learning sheet.

✓ Each learning sheet has multiple story problems with the prompts FAST and DRAW beneath each story problem.

✓ Appropriate space is provided under FAST for students to write the equation and solve it. If students can't solve the equation, the appropriate space is provided under "DRAW" for students to draw their solutions and write the answer. (Students highlight important information and set up the equation for FAST, whereas they draw the solution and write the answer for DRAW.) *Advanced students can assist in making up story problems that reflect addition of fractions with mixed numbers.*

✓ Develop a master answer key for the learning sheet.

✓ Make an appropriate number of copies for the learning sheet and answer key. *These can be laminated, and students can use dry-erase pens to save copying time/expense if you use this activity multiple times.*

✓ Make a FAST DRAW strategy poster or master cue sheet that lists the steps of the FAST DRAW strategy. *An example of how to apply the strategy to story problems that involve addition of fractions with mixed numbers can be included as a cue for students; show story problem with important information highlighted appropriately, the equation written, drawings, and the answer written.*

Materials:

• Each student receives one learning sheet.

• Each student pair receives one answer key.

• Each student has one sheet of notebook paper for recording points and pencils for writing and drawing.

• Each student receives FAST DRAW cue sheets (see Appendix A for example).

Description of activity:

Students work in pairs by responding to learning sheets. The learning sheet has multiple story problems that involve adding fractions with mixed numbers. For each problem, students have to do two things. First, they must use FAST to find the important information in the story problem and set up the equation. Second, they must use DRAW to solve the equation and answer the story problem. The period is divided into two equal time frames. One student in each pair is the "coach" for the first period, and the other student is the "player." Students switch roles for the second time period.

The coach reads the story problem and prompts the player to use FAST to find/highlight the important information and set up an equation. Then, the coach prompts the player to use DRAW to solve the equation and answer the story problem. The coach checks the player's responses using the answer key after the player completes each example, providing positive reinforcement and specific corrective feedback. *The coach also can award points on the basis of the player's response: 2 points for getting each part of the example (FAST and DRAW) correct; 1 point for reworking the example on the basis of feedback and solving it correctly.* Tallies can be made on a sheet of notebook paper that serves as a scoring sheet.

Signal when students are to switch roles and monitor students' social and academic behavior as they work, providing positive reinforcement and specific corrective feedback and answering questions as appropriate. Have students turn in their individual learning sheets and point sheets at the end of the activity. Review individual student learning sheets and point sheets to evaluate their understanding.

Figure 10.3.   Structured cooperative learning/peer-tutoring practice activity.

depict the solution or correct answer can be used for students to check their answers.

Instructional games, when used appropriately, are a creative and motivational way to provide struggling learners with multiple practice opportunities (Mercer & Mercer, 2005). Examples of instructional game formats include game boards (old commercial game boards can be used, or simple game boards can be made), checkers and checker boards, spinners, dice, and cards. Instructional games include prompts that require students to perform a target mathematics skill (e.g., equations, word problems, questions that ask students to represent a particular concept in some way), as well as a process for students to check the accuracy of their responses (e.g., answer key, solution on the opposite side of a card). Instructional games can be individualized such that students work in pairs or in small groups, or they can be used with large groups or the whole class. The opportunity for success is an important variable to consider when using instructional games. Lavoie (1993) noted that for struggling learners to engage fully in any instructional game they need to believe that they have a good chance for success. This means that students must be able to perform the target mathematics skill with an adequate level of accuracy (i.e., advanced acquisition stage of learning) before engaging in an instructional game for that skill.

Like instructional games, self-correcting materials are effective for providing students with many practice opportunities when they incorporate features that meet the learning needs of students. In contrast to instructional games in which students practice with others, students typically work alone when interacting with self-correcting materials. Self-correcting materials provide students with a format for responding to a mathematical prompt or task and then with immediate feedback on their response. One example of a self-correcting material is a laminated manila folder with multiplication facts written on one side and possible solutions written underneath. Holes are punched beneath or beside each choice. On the opposite side, the hole that represents the correct solution has a star beside it. Students read a multiplication fact with several choices for the product or examine different geometric figures when prompted to identify a particular shape, insert their pencil into the hole beside their choice, and then look on the opposite side to see whether they are correct. Figure 10.4 shows an example of this type of self-correcting material.

Teaching Tips

When used as student practice activities, instructional games and self-correcting materials must include only math processes that students can perform independently with at least moderate success. To be most effective, the game or self-correcting context and format should be age and interest appropriate. Because struggling learners often have difficulty with memory, attention, and processing, it is important to model the math skills that are to be used in the game or the self-correcting material and to model how to play the game or complete the self-correcting activity. Behavioral expectations should be stated explicitly and, when appropriate, modeled by the teacher. For strengthening student engagement, a relatively lively pace should be maintained, and materials should be changed regularly. Finally, the teacher needs to monitor students' performance and continually provide corrective feedback and positive reinforcement.

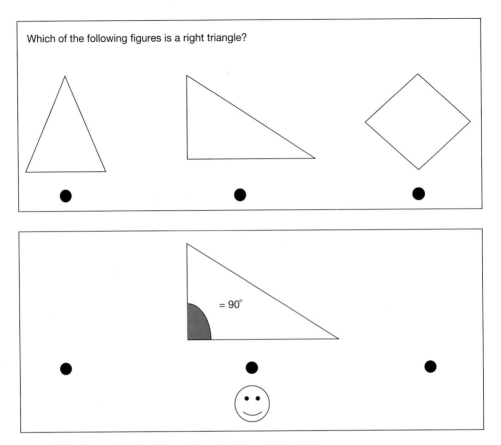

Figure 10.4. An example of a self-correcting material (punch-hole card).

Over time, teachers can develop an inventory of pictures/drawings that depict various mathematics concepts or problems. These pictures or drawings then could be stored in containers on the basis of type of mathematics concept. They could be used either as response prompts or as examples of correct solutions to problems for various instructional games or self-correcting materials. For example, students may play a board game in which they are practicing how to represent place value for three-digit numbers (e.g., 245). Pictures of base-10 materials depicting various three-digit numbers can be retrieved from the "place value" container and taped to the back of cards with the corresponding number on the other side. Students can be prompted by a card to represent the number 245 with base-10 materials. They represent the number using their concrete objects and then compare their concrete objects with the picture taped to the back of the card. If they are correct, then they move the designated number of spaces.

Pictures also can be used as mathematics self-correcting materials. The perimeter of the picture may be drawn on the inside cover of a manila folder

- Use existing game formats (old/discarded game boards such as "Monopoly" or "Life"; traditional sports such as baseball, football, and basketball; card games; checkers; dominoes).

- Individualize group and whole-class instructional games by making packs of cards for individual students that contain math skills/learning tasks that are appropriate for the particular student.

- Use group response cards (each student has a stack of cards with potential answers on each card, or an individual dry-erase/chalkboard on which to write answers). When playing games in which multiple students respond to the same question or problem, provide students who process information at a less rapid pace with equal opportunities to respond by teaching all students not to hold up their response card until you give a signal.

- Make generic game boards that have a "start" and an "end," which can be used for multiple purposes. Include "chance" factors that make the game even more intriguing (e.g., some spaces say "Go ahead 3 spaces").

- Develop decks of cards that have collections of response tasks for specific math skills that are pertinent to the learning objectives of the students whom you teach.

- Use manila folders; they make good game boards because of their sturdiness, manageable size, tabs for easy reference, and easy storage.

- Laminate game boards so that they can be used many times.

- Write rules on the back of the folder for easy reference.

- Put game pieces in clear plastic storage bags for easy storage/organization.

- Consider using cooperative games initially (games that do not stress a "winner" and a "loser") until students demonstrate maturity to handle competitive games.

Figure 10.5. Tips for making instructional games. (*Source:* Mercer & Mercer, [2005]).

and then divided into multiple same-size squares. In this activity, each square contains a written problem, question, or other prompt. The laminated picture is placed face down and also is cut into squares. On the back of each square is

VIDEO FOCUS
Instructional Games and Self-Correcting Materials

See a teacher model the use of instructional games and self-correcting materials on the MathVIDS web site.

a potential solution to each problem that is written on the manila folder. Students place their solutions in the appropriate spaces. After responding to all problems, students flip over the picture to discover what it is. They then can determine which problems they got correct or incorrect on the basis of whether the picture is complete. Figure 10.5 provides some additional tips for developing instructional games.

Table 10.1.   Examples of instructional games and self-correcting materials

Instructional games	Self-correcting materials
Board games	Flip cards
Checker board/Checkers	Flip cards with scaffolding cues
Spinners	"Punch-hole" cards/folders
Dice	Puzzles
Cards	Versatiles

Examples

Table 10.1 and Figures 10.6 and 10.7 provide examples of games and self-correcting activities.

STRATEGY 4: CONTINUOUSLY MONITORING AND CHARTING STUDENTS' MATHEMATICAL UNDERSTANDINGS

Purpose

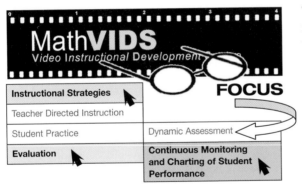

The primary purpose of this instructional practice is threefold: 1) It provides students with tangible and immediate feedback about their learning, 2) it provides teachers with continuous data to make immediate instructional decisions (i.e., continue with current instructions, or change them), and 3) it provides students with a concrete process for developing goal-setting skills and enhancing their metacognition or thinking about what and how they are learning.

Continuous monitoring and charting of student performance is an instructional strategy that has strong research support in terms of promoting positive learning outcomes (Allinder et al., 2000; Calhoon & Fuchs, 2003; Fuchs, Fuchs, Hamlett, Phillips, & Bentz, 1994; Howell et al., 1993; Mercer & Mercer, 2005; Miller & Mercer, 1993; Shafer, 1998; Woodward & Howard, 1994), and it should be integrated within any effective teaching plan for students with learning difficulties. Teachers must plan ways to evaluate student learning throughout the teaching cycle. This practice might be done more informally during initial introduction of a new mathematical concept or skill. For example, a teacher can evaluate students' initial acquisition of a concept by observing their verbal and nonverbal reactions as he or she engages in modeling. Asking receptive- and expressive-type questions and prompting students' thinking about important features of the concept can help teachers ascertain what students understand and at which level they understand (receptive versus expressive; and concrete, representational, or abstract).

Figure 10.6. Example of a bulletin board self-correcting material. (*Source:* Ambrose [2006]). This bulletin board was used for individual student practice. The bulletin board actually is a big review game. Each student has his or her own game piece or card that attaches to the squares by a clothespin or paperclip. Students roll a die, answer a review card, check their answers on the back of the card, and, if they are correct, move the given number of spaces on the game board.

Algebraic Thinking Board Game

Concept/skill: Plotting Ordered Pairs on a Plane

Directions: Students are provided with a laminated football field "grid" where each intersect represents five yards on a football field. Students use ordered pairs (e.g., 5 yards, 10 yards) written on flash cards to move their cardboard football.

- Football game
- Flash cards with ordered pairs
- Students take turns moving their football based on each ordered pair they draw; ball is moved from the coordinates of previous ball—e.g., (10,5)—football moves 10 yards up field and 5 yards toward sideline
- Touchdown scores when football crosses goal line

	1	0	2	0	3	0	4	0	5	0	4	0	3	0	2	0	1	0	

	1	0	2	0	3	0	4	0	5	0	4	0	3	0	2	0	1	0	

Ordered pairs: (0,5), (15,10), (10,0), (20,5)

Starting point

Figure 10.7. Example of an instructional game.

As students move from initial acquisition to advanced acquisition and then to the proficiency, maintenance, generalization, and adaptation stages, it is critical that teachers provide students and themselves with tangible ways to continually show what students are learning. This practice is essential for helping students visualize their learning, and it is essential for helping teachers evaluate the effectiveness of their instruction. Struggling learners experience high levels of math anxiety and often do not believe that their efforts will have an impact on their performance (learned helplessness, passive learning). When teachers provide students with visual representations of their performance over time, students have a tangible way to gain immediate and consistent feedback, which can help to alleviate their anxiety and ameliorate the effects of learned helplessness. Moreover, this practice provides teachers an easy but effective way to determine whether their instruction is effective. Because performance can be evaluated on a continual basis (e.g., daily, every other day), changes in instruction can be made before too much time has passed and the teacher and students have moved to the next concept in the curriculum guide.

Teachers use the data collected to evaluate the effectiveness of their teaching and make changes as needed immediately. The use of simple charts and graphs on which student performance is plotted can be an effective way to provide this visual feedback. Connecting data points across several days provides teachers and students with an easy-to-interpret learning picture that is based on trend lines that are created by connecting each day's data point. Figure 10.8 shows an example of a chart depicting a learning picture.

Teaching Tips and Examples

Continual monitoring and charting of students' mathematical understandings does not need to be unwieldy or time-consuming. In fact, if some time is devoted to teaching students how to monitor and chart their own performance, then the teacher's time can be spent in other ways. Doing this gives students some control over and investment in their learning, and it frees up some of the teacher's time from data keeping.

Unit tests are a common method of evaluating student learning. However, tests often occur infrequently, and when problems are apparent, too much time has passed to alter instruction or to re-teach missed concepts or skills. To monitor and chart students' mathematical understandings continuously, follow several steps:

1. Evaluate student understanding continually (e.g., daily, every other day). Think about how brief "learning probes" can be incorporated into mathematics instruction on a frequent basis (at least 2–3 days per week). Learning probes are sets of prompts, problems, or questions that engage students in a target mathematical concept or skill. The format of a learning probe is flexible and depends on the type of mathematics concept or skill being evaluated and the level of understanding at which students currently are operating (CRA and receptive versus expressive). The format could be a set of equations on a piece of paper that students solve with a pencil, a set of oral or written questions that students respond to by manipulating concrete objects at their seats, or a teacher holding up sets of cards that represent a particular concept and students choose the card that

Level of understanding: Abstract-receptive

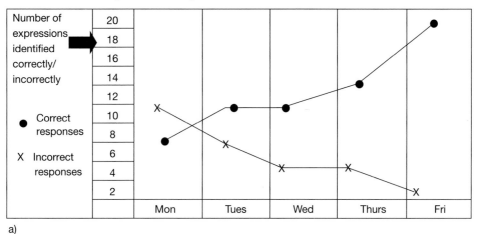

a)

Concept/skill: Identifies expressions that show the commutative property (1 minute)

Level of understanding: Abstract-receptive

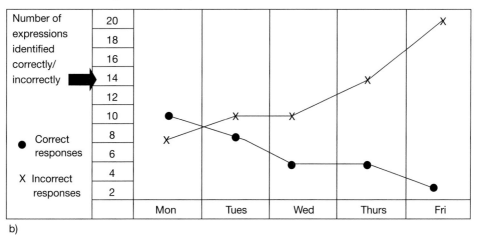

b)

Figure 10.8. Continuous monitoring chart showing learning pictures including a) successful learning picture and b) unsuccessful learning picture. (Note: Chart A shows a "successful" learning picture because the number of correct responses steadily increases and the number of incorrect responses steadily decreases. Chart B shows an "unsuccessful" learning picture because the number of correct responses steadily decreases and the number of incorrect responses steadily increases.

represents the best answer. These mini-evaluations should take no more than 5 to 10 minutes of class time and should be easy to score (e.g., number correct/number incorrect; percentage correct). Figure 10.9 shows examples of learning probes for evaluating students' mathematical understandings at the concrete and representational levels. Figure 10.10 shows an already completed learning probe at the abstract level.

2. Collect performance data and represent them in a visual format (e.g., chart, graph). Determine a method for charting students' understandings in a way that is meaningful for them. This could be a simple line graph

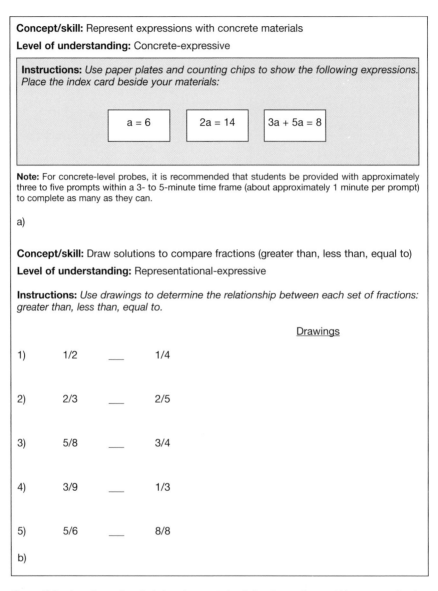

Concept/skill: Represent expressions with concrete materials

Level of understanding: Concrete-expressive

Instructions: *Use paper plates and counting chips to show the following expressions. Place the index card beside your materials:*

| a = 6 | 2a = 14 | 3a + 5a = 8 |

Note: For concrete-level probes, it is recommended that students be provided with approximately three to five prompts within a 3- to 5-minute time frame (about approximately 1 minute per prompt) to complete as many as they can.

a)

Concept/skill: Draw solutions to compare fractions (greater than, less than, equal to)

Level of understanding: Representational-expressive

Instructions: *Use drawings to determine the relationship between each set of fractions: greater than, less than, equal to.*

Drawings

1)   1/2   ___   1/4

2)   2/3   ___   2/5

3)   5/8   ___   3/4

4)   3/9   ___   1/3

5)   5/6   ___   8/8

b)

Figure 10.9.   Learning probes depicting a) concrete-level of understanding, and b) representational-expressive level of understanding.

that depicts the number of correct and incorrect responses or a bar graph that contains stickers indicating how many items a student got correct. Figure 10.11 depicts examples of several different charting techniques for different age or developmental levels.

3.   Teach students to represent their daily performance data visually (e.g., plot data points on a graph). Such visual representations of student learning are powerful motivators for students. The opportunity for students to see their own learning can be a new experience for struggling learners. Because of their lack of metacognitive awareness, memory difficulties, attention difficulties, and cognitive processing difficulties, self-evaluation

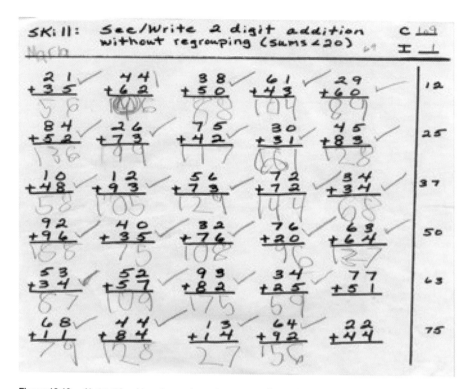

Figure 10.10. Abstract level learning probe and accompanying performance monitoring chart.

of learning is a difficult task for many of these students. Some students do not really know what it feels like to learn because they have never before had their progress in learning made explicit. For these students, failure rather than success is a more common experience.

4. Review progress with the students and assist them in setting learning goals (e.g., "Next time, I want to solve three more problems; tomorrow I'm going to concentrate on checking my answer before moving to the next problem. This will help me not miss so many"). These visual representations of learning teach and support students to set mathematical learning goals. Such charts, or learning pictures, allow students to see where they currently are and to determine where they want to be in 1-, 2-, or 3-days' time. They can even mark their goal on their chart with a line or star (see Figure 10.12 for an example of a goal line depicted on a monitoring chart). Providing this opportunity supports metacognitive development, an area that typically is not well-developed in struggling learners.

5. Track student performance on a regular basis to make effective instructional decisions about how to assist students' learning before it is too late to do so. Teachers can note what they did or did not do instructionally on certain days when student performance increases or decreases and use that information to inform them about what to do tomorrow. Continuous monitoring and charting of students' mathematics performance engages both students and teachers in the learning and teaching process. Figure 10.12 shows an example of a learning probe (shown previously in Figure

Name: Janice

Concept/skill: Addition strategies

Level of understanding: Expressive/Abstract

Number of different strategies used						
	5					
	4					●
	3			●	●	●
● Successful	2	●	●	●	●	●
● Unsuccessful	1	●	●	●	●	●
		Week 1	Week 2	Week 3	Week 4	Week 5
Strategies used		*Count*	*Count up*	*Count up* *Add tens*	*Add tens*	*Add tens* *Make a ten*
		Make a ten	*Make a ten*	*Use easier number*	*Use easier number*	*Use easier number*

Note: Visual display or learning picture: Number of different two-digit addition strategies attempted.

a)

Name: Tandria

Concept/skill: Subtraction facts solved in 3 minutes using concrete objects

Level of understanding: Concrete-expressive

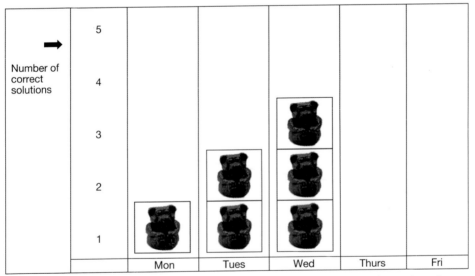

Note: Each teddy bear sticker represents one correct solution. Student solves as many problems as he or she can in 3 minutes using concrete objects.

b)

Figure 10.11. Charting techniques at various grade/developmental levels. a) Elementary mathematics: Student use of various problem-solving strategies. (From Lovin, L., Allsopp, D.A., and Kyger, M. [2004]; adapted by permission). b) Early-grade mathematics: Student use of teddy bear stickers. c) Secondary-grade mathematics: application of algebraic word problem strategy.

Figure 10.11. *(continued)*

Name: Joseph

Concept/skill: Applying problem-solving strategy (FAST DRAW) to algebraic word problems

FAST DRAW Strategy

Find important information
Ask what important information is
Set up the equation
Tie down the sign

Discover the variable
Read the equation
Answer, or draw and check
Write the answer

Level of understanding: Abstract/expressive

Steps Applied Accurately ➡	FAS	FAST	FAST-D	FAST-DRA	
8					
7				●	
6					
5			●		
4	X	●			
3	●				
2		X			
1			X	X	
	Mon	Tues	Wed	Thurs	Fri
Steps Applied Incorrectly ➡	T-DRA	DRA	RA	W	

● - Number of strategy steps applied accurately

X - Number of strategy steps applied incorrectly

Note: Student responds to one word problem within a 3-minute time limit. Shows his work for each step.

c)

10.10) and associated chart. After viewing the learning probe and chart, reflect on the following questions:

- Does the learning picture depicted on the chart show success or lack of success on the part of the student?

- Why are two sets of data plotted on the chart?

- Which data did the teacher and the student plot from the completed learning probe? (Hint: think of number of digits per answer.) Why did they choose to plot these data instead of correct number of answers?

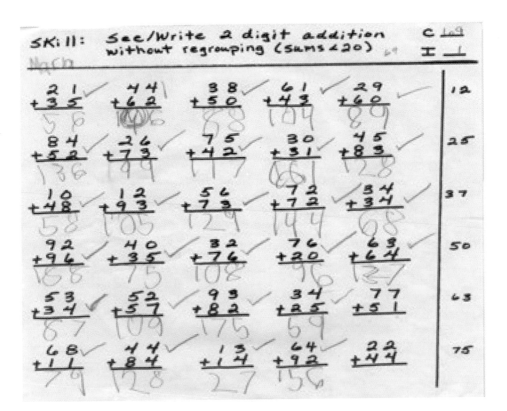

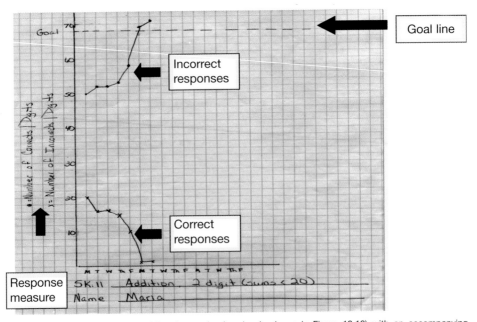

Figure 10.12. Abstract-level timed learning probe (previously shown in Figure 10.10) with an accompanying progress monitoring chart. The monitoring chart shows the student's performance on solving two-digit addition problems in 1 minute for multiple days. The total number of digits that the students got correct and incorrect are plotted.

- Do you believe that the teacher's instruction was effective for this student? Why?

- Did the student reach the goal that he or she set for him- or herself? How do you know?

STRATEGY 5: MAINTENANCE OF MASTERED CONCEPTS AND SKILLS

Purpose

Struggling learners need periodic opportunities to practice using mathematical concepts and skills that they have mastered, but this important instructional approach often is underemphasized. It is important to remember that the learning characteristics of struggling learners can affect their recall of mathematics even after they have demonstrated mastery. Learning characteristics such as memory retrieval (and storage) difficulties, attention difficulties, and metacognitive deficits singularly or in combination can make it difficult for students to use previously learned mathematical knowledge effectively. Therefore, teachers need to engage students periodically in simple yet efficient learning activities to maintain their mathematical understandings as well as their ability to apply their existing understandings in meaningful ways.

Teaching Tips

Maintenance activities should emphasize both conceptual and procedural understandings. Although an entire class period could be used for maintenance work every so often, it is done most efficiently by scheduling a 5- to 10-minute "maintenance" time every day or at least 3 days a week. A convenient way to accomplish this is to develop a routine so that students expect to engage in maintenance learning at a certain time during the period. Many teachers prefer scheduling maintenance at the beginning of the class period. They prepare a prompt (e.g., an equation or a word problem written on the board, a visual display of concrete objects, a drawing representing a mathematics concept), and students respond to the prompt as they enter the room and are seated. For struggling learners in particular, it is important to teach the purpose of maintenance activities explicitly and to remind them periodically why they are doing the maintenance activities and how it can help them.

Following are four important tips for effectively implementing mathematical maintenance activities for struggling learners:

1. Choose mathematics concepts/skills your students have already mastered, of which your students have previously demonstrated mastery (95%–100% accuracy) or with which they already have become proficient (80%+ accuracy).

2. Emphasize both procedurally (e.g., solving equations) and conceptually oriented activities (e.g., writing/telling/drawing a story or word problem that represents a mathematical situation or equation).

3. Emphasize prerequisite concepts/skills for mathematics that students will be learning soon (e.g., the next unit, chapter, state standard).

4. Encourage students to express their understandings in multiple ways, particularly in ways that accommodate their particular disabilities (e.g., verbalizing or drawing pictures versus writing for students with significant fine motor difficulties) (Allsopp, in press).

Maintenance activities can range in type, but it is important to use a variety of formats so that students will find them engaging. Having students respond to a mathematical concept or skill in a variety of ways also assists them in generalizing their mathematical understandings. Although using a variety of formats is important, teachers must always remember to accommodate an individual student's disability-related input and output processing strengths and weaknesses. That is, teachers must ensure that *how* a maintenance learning task is presented and *how* they expect students to respond to the task are commensurate with any sensory or processing needs that students may have (e.g., visual or auditory processing difficulties, sight or hearing deficits, visual-motor integration deficits, physical/motor deficits). Following are tips for accommodating disability-related needs when implementing maintenance activities:

1. When considering maintenance activities, think of individual student needs and plan a way to accommodate their related receptive (input) or expressive (output) need areas.

2. Use prompts that are appropriate for the level of understanding with which students have demonstrated proficiency or mastery (CRA; receptive versus expressive).

3. Use a mixture of concrete-, representational-, and abstract-level tasks when students have demonstrated mastery at each level of understanding.

4. Have students respond independently as well as in cooperative groups.

5. Use a variety of response formats. These may include saying, writing, or drawing what mathematics concept a particular prompt represents; replicating a solved equation using concrete objects or by drawing; developing a word problem for a particular mathematics equation or situation; choosing natural representations in the room of specific mathematics concepts or operations; ordering steps of a mathematics strategy using sentence strips.

6. Have students develop future maintenance activities for specific mathematics concepts/skills independently or in groups, and then have them lead the class in completing the maintenance activity (Allsopp, in press).

Examples

Problem of the Day   At a preset time during the day or period, the teacher presents or displays a relevant prompt that requires students to use a previously mastered mathematics concept or skill. Often, the problem of the day is displayed as students begin the period or day. Students quickly learn

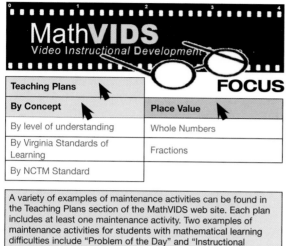

Teaching Plans		FOCUS
By Concept	Place Value	
By level of understanding	Whole Numbers	
By Virginia Standards of Learning	Fractions	
By NCTM Standard		

A variety of examples of maintenance activities can be found in the Teaching Plans section of the MathVIDS web site. Each plan includes at least one maintenance activity. Two examples of maintenance activities for students with mathematical learning difficulties include "Problem of the Day" and "Instructional Games/Self-Correcting Materials."

that they are to respond to the problem as soon as they arrive and get settled. The problem of the day could be an equation or a word problem to be solved, or it could be some type of task that requires students to demonstrate their understanding of a particular mathematics concept or strategy (e.g., by describing the meaning of the denominator in a fraction by writing, by explaining it to the teacher or learning partner, by drawing a picture that represents the concept or strategy). Problems of the day can be at any of the three levels of understanding (concrete, representational, or abstract). With any problem of the day, it is important that the teacher spend 1 or 2 minutes discussing the solution before moving on. Also, any problem should not take more than a few minutes for students to complete.

Instructional Games/Self-Correcting Materials Instructional games and self-correcting materials that previously were used for practice when students were developing proficiency with a concept or skill also can be used for maintenance of the same concepts or skills once students have mastered them. A popular way to structure instructional games and self-correcting materials for maintenance is in the form of centers or individual folders. As students arrive, they can pick up their folder that specifies the instructional game/self-correcting material or center that they are to use. Each instructional game or self-correcting material can be marked (e.g., by a letter, number, picture) and stored so that its corresponding number is clearly visible to students. Clear storage bags or clear plastic tubs that have labels indicating the numbered instructional games/self-correcting materials that they contain are good for storing materials. Students can be taught a routine for reviewing their folders, gaining access to the needed materials, and using the materials appropriately. Students can make simple tallies on a sheet of notebook paper and record the number of responses that they got correct and incorrect. The teacher can review student tally sheets to determine whether particular students demonstrated difficulty with the concept or skill that they were practicing. It is important that the teacher always circulate around the room as students work so that he or she can note when a particular student has difficulty. Providing corrective feedback and modeling are also appropriate ways for teachers to work with students who are having difficulty.

REVIEWING WHAT YOU LEARNED

For the want of a nail, the shoe was lost; for the want of a shoe, the horse was lost; and for the want of a horse the rider was lost, being overtaken and slain by the enemy, all for the want of care about a horseshoe nail.
—Benjamin Franklin

Practice, monitoring, and maintenance activities help students to become proficient with the mathematics concepts and skills that they have worked so hard to acquire during the initial stage of instruction. When students engage in these activities, they are less apt to lose what they have learned. Without multiple planned opportunities to practice at different levels of mathematical understanding, to respond receptively and expressively, to see their learning, and to review the mathematical understandings with which they have become proficient, students with disabilities will fall behind their peers without learning difficulties and have great difficulty finding success in mathematics.

11

Planning Effective Mathematics Instruction in a Variety of Educational Environments

C hapters 8 through 10 described a variety of research-supported, effective mathematics assessment and instructional practices and strategies. The purpose of this chapter is to provide a framework for planning effective mathematics instruction that integrates these practices for struggling learners. A variety of practical yet effective examples of differentiated mathematics instruction plans for diverse classrooms and instructional contexts are described that show the versatility of this planning framework. In addition, this chapter describes how teachers and families can work together to support students' understanding of and abilities to apply mathematics in their daily lives.

RESPONSIVE TEACHING FRAMEWORK

Understanding the learning difficulties of students and recognizing the teaching strategies that best facilitate their learning are important, but how does a teacher integrate these strategies into a particular classroom context? Instructional planning that is based on students' learning needs, the mathematical concept that is being taught, and the structure of the class are critical considerations for answering this important question. This section describes a framework for planning mathematics instruction that helps teachers to accomplish this important task.

The responsive teaching framework poses 10 important questions that should be considered when planning instruction that is responsive to the mathematical learning needs of struggling learners:

1. What is the target mathematics concept?

2. What did I learn from my mathematics dynamic assessment?

3. What is my instructional hypothesis?

4. How do students think about these ideas differently from adults and how can I use this information to inform instruction?

5. How will I differentiate the instructional needs of my students?

6. What authentic context(s) will I use?

7. How will I introduce/model the target concept to the whole class?

8. How will I differentiate the instructional scaffolding/extension (generalization and adaption) needs of my students?

9. How will I provide practice opportunities that promote proficiency/maintenance?

10. How will I evaluate my students' learning and determine the effectiveness of my instruction?

Refer to the example of Mrs. Carlson's class in Chapter 8. The information Mrs. Carlson learned about her students that was presented in the discussion in that chapter will be used as the context to learn more about the Responsive Instructional Planning Framework and how to use it to meet the needs of struggling learners.

Think about Mrs. Carlson and the results of the Mathematics Dynamic Assessment (MDA) that she completed with her middle school students on comparing fractions (see Figure 11.1). Planning should be based on data that guide thinking about what and how to teach. On the basis of the MDA results from her students, Mrs. Carlson was able to learn valuable information about her students in several important areas, including level of understanding (concrete-to-representational-to-abstract; Figure 11.1a), response level (expressive/receptive; Figure 11.1a), and error patterns that illustrate inaccurate or incomplete mathematical thinking (Figure 11.1b). This information allowed Mrs. Carlson to accomplish two important steps related to planning: 1) She was able to identify the needs of individual students and use this information to group students for differentiated instruction, and 2) she was able to develop an informed instructional hypothesis about her students' understanding and misconceptions to guide her instruction so that it targets their particular learning needs (Figure 11.1c).

Summarize Students' Current Understandings About the Target Mathematical Concept

Summarizing students' current understandings about the target mathematical concept and developing an instructional hypothesis are the first two components of the responsive instructional planning framework. Mrs. Carlson addressed these components in the responsive instructional planning framework (Figure 11.2) based on completion of the MDA. Figure 11.2 shows the Responsive Instructional Planning Framework Form with Mrs. Carlson's notes in the right-hand column. This planning form provides teachers with a structure for addressing important considerations for each question of the planning framework. Mrs. Carlson's Responsive Instructional Planning form will serve as a model during the remaining discussion. Review Mrs. Carlson's notes in response to the first three questions of the planning form to refresh your memory about the MDA results for her students. Based on these results, Mrs. Carlson was able

Name	Concrete		Representational		Abstract	
	Expressive	Receptive	Expressive	Receptive	Expressive	Receptive
SA	I	M	I	M	F	I
ZD	I	M	I	M	F	I
JD	I	M	I	M	F	I
AD	M	M	I	M	M	M
RF	M	M	M	M	I	M
FJ	M	M	I	M	M	M
RJ	M	M	I	M	M	M
SK	I	M	I	M	F	I
NM	M	M	M	M	I	M
JM	M	M	M	M	I	M
XM	M	M	M	M	I	M
TR	I	M	I	I	F	I7
JT	M	M	I	M	F	M
TW	M	M	I	M	M	M

a)

—Difficulty representing fractions that are greater than, less than, equal to using unlike denominators (abstract and representational)

—Difficulty determining greater than, less than, equal to using symbols between fractions with unlike denominators (abstract and representational)

—Have some ability to do this with fractions that have natural relationships—2/4 and 1/2; 4/6 and 2/3 (abstract)

—Difficulty relating written fractions to drawings; "meaning" of what a fraction actually represents may be lacking

—Concept of "equivalent area" of whole to part when drawing not evident

b)

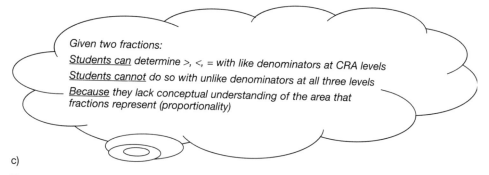

Given two fractions:
Students can determine >, <, = with like denominators at CRA levels
Students cannot do so with unlike denominators at all three levels
Because they lack conceptual understanding of the area that fractions represent (proportionality)

c)

Figure 11.1. Mrs. Carlson's class results from the Mathematics Dynamic Assessment (MDA): a) Level of understanding and instructional phase, b) Mrs. Carlson's conclusions about student mathematical thinking from error pattern analysis and flexible mathematics interviews, and c) Mrs. Carlson's instructional hypothesis.

to develop an instructional hypothesis about her students' understanding of comparing fractions from the Concrete-Representational-Abstract (CRA) assessment, observations made during error pattern analysis, and the several flexible

Questions to aid in planning	Notes
What is the target mathematics concept? **What do my students understand?**	Compare fractions (>, <, =) Instructional level: 3 groups:
Level of understanding (CRA) Receptive or expressive ability Stage of learning	1. Representational/expressive/instructional 2. Abstract/receptive/instructional 3. Abstract/expressive/instructional
Conclusions	Students do not understand proportion as it relates to what fraction represents. Have difficulty with unlike denominators. Need work at concrete level to emphasize proportionality!
What is my instructional hypothesis?	Given two fractions:
What students can do	Students can determine >, <, = with like denominators at CRA levels
What students can't do	Students cannot do so with unlike denominators at all three levels
Why?	Because they lack conceptual understanding of the area that fractions represent
How will I differentiate the instructional needs of my students?	
Within whole-class instruction?	Whole class for initial instruction
By grouping students?	Three groups for scaffolding and practice
What authentic context(s) will I use? To build meaningful student connections	Build meaningful student connections: football game/fractional yards gained
To provide explicit modeling	Explicit modeling: friends sharing fractional parts of a candy bar
How will I introduce/model the target concept to the whole class?	
To build meaningful student connections	Build meaningful student connections: Start with same story problem used during MDA. Use same fraction bars to model comparison. Prompt students to help me. Write learning objective on board and review with students. Say going to learn more with candy bars!
To provide explicit modeling	Explicit modeling: Invite several students up and model comparison using real candy bar. Prompt students to think how to compare and how to decide which portion of a candy bar represents each fraction. Break candy into appropriate pieces. Participating students get to eat the pieces! Repeat two more times with different students. Then model the same comparison using fraction bars.
How will I differentiate the instructional scaffolding/extension (generalization and adaption) needs of my students?	
For whole class (if not using student groups) For groups	For groups after initial modeling: ALL group: I will continue with modeling and then scaffold.

Figure 11.2. Example of a Responsive Instructional Planning Framework Form: Mrs. Carlson's notes.

Figure 11.2. *(continued)*

What is the target mathematics concept?	Compare fractions (>, <, =)
	MOST group: Independent practice with fraction bars (need to provide learning sheet with fractions they are to compare)
	SOME group: In pairs, 1) brainstorm ways to draw fractions, 2) bring examples to me to check, 3) use "approved" drawing approach to compare fractions (same learning sheet as MOST group)
How will I provide practice opportunities that promote proficiency/maintenance (receptive and/or expressive phase)?	
For whole class (if not using student groups)	ALL group: Practice will occur with my support at expressive level (additional scaffolding/guided practice)
For groups	MOST group: Independent practice using learning sheet and fraction bars (expressive level)
	SOME: Peer-mediated; brainstorm at least three ways to draw fractions so that they can be compared; practice using selected drawing technique to solve learning sheet at expressive level (same learning sheet as MOST group)
	ALL: Note individual and overall student successes and difficulties on notepad as conducting scaffolding/guided practice (all students should demonstrate little to no difficulties at end of session)

interviews that she completed with individual students. A blank copy of the Responsive Instructional Planning Framework form appears in Appendix A.

Determine Differentiated Instructional Needs

Determining the differentiated instructional needs of students is the next component of the responsive planning framework. Two primary decisions need to be made at this point. First, will whole class instruction be provided? Second, will students be grouped for differentiated instruction purposes? Mrs. Carlson was able to see from the MDA results that her students basically were at three different levels of understanding, meaning that she could differentiate her instruction according to three groups. Using the planning pyramid (shown in the Responsive Teaching Plan Form, Figure 11.3), she placed students into the ALL group (students who had the least understanding), the MOST group (students who had the next level of understanding), or the SOME group (students who had the greatest level of understanding). Further explanation about the meaning of the terms "ALL," "MOST," and "SOME" and their relationship to instruction is provided later. Figure 11.2 shows Mrs. Carlson's planning notes for this responsive instructional planning component. Mrs. Carlson plans to provide initial instruction on comparing fractions to the whole class and then provide differentiated instruction through the three groups.

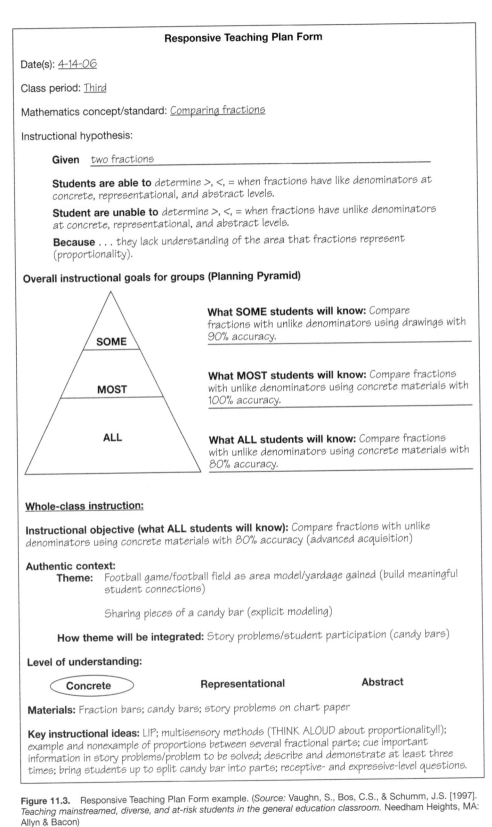

Responsive Teaching Plan Form

Date(s): _4-14-06_

Class period: _Third_

Mathematics concept/standard: _Comparing fractions_

Instructional hypothesis:

Given   _two fractions_

Students are able to _determine >, <, = when fractions have like denominators at concrete, representational, and abstract levels._

Student are unable to _determine >, <, = when fractions have unlike denominators at concrete, representational, and abstract levels._

Because . . . _they lack understanding of the area that fractions represent (proportionality)._

Overall instructional goals for groups (Planning Pyramid)

SOME

MOST

ALL

What SOME students will know: _Compare fractions with unlike denominators using drawings with 90% accuracy._

What MOST students will know: _Compare fractions with unlike denominators using concrete materials with 100% accuracy._

What ALL students will know: _Compare fractions with unlike denominators using concrete materials with 80% accuracy._

<u>**Whole-class instruction:**</u>

Instructional objective (what ALL students will know): _Compare fractions with unlike denominators using concrete materials with 80% accuracy (advanced acquisition)_

Authentic context:
   Theme: _Football game/football field as area model/yardage gained (build meaningful student connections)_

   Sharing pieces of a candy bar (explicit modeling)

   How theme will be integrated: _Story problems/student participation (candy bars)_

Level of understanding:

   (**Concrete**)   **Representational**   **Abstract**

Materials: _Fraction bars; candy bars; story problems on chart paper_

Key instructional ideas: _LIP; multisensory methods (THINK ALOUD about proportionality!!); example and nonexample of proportions between several fractional parts; cue important information in story problems/problem to be solved; describe and demonstrate at least three times; bring students up to split candy bar into parts; receptive- and expressive-level questions._

Figure 11.3.   Responsive Teaching Plan Form example. (*Source:* Vaughn, S., Bos, C.S., & Schumm, J.S. [1997]. *Teaching mainstreamed, diverse, and at-risk students in the general education classroom.* Needham Heights, MA: Allyn & Bacon)

Figure 11.3. *(continued)*

Whole class					
Differentiated group instruction strategies/techniques					
			Important teaching ideas		
			CRA Multisensory modeling Think aloud Examples/ nonexamples Scaffold instruction	CRA Receptive/ expressive Many response chances Monitor/provide corrective feedback Positive reinforcement	Adapt/relate to other concepts Generalize to other environments Develop new strategies
			↓	↓	↓
Whole class/group/ individual	Level of teacher support	Beginning stage of learning	Teacher instruction notes	Student practice notes	Extension notes
All	(Higher support) Lower support	(Acquisition) Proficiency Maintenance Generalization Adaption	—Use additional football-related problems —Model a scaffold (high, medium, low) —Think aloud/ have students think aloud about proportion —Prompt and question		
Most	Higher support (Lower support)	Acquisition (Proficiency) Maintenance Generalization Adaption		—Concrete level with fraction bars —Learning sheets with unlike fractions to compare —Check/monitor periodically!!	
Some	Higher support (Lower support)	Acquisition Proficiency Maintenance (Generalization Adaption)			—Assign peer-mediated partners —Pairs develop three different ways to draw fractions (bring to me to evaluate) —Use MOST learning sheet to draw solutions

Figure 11.3.   *(continued)*

Evaluation of Student Progress:
ALL group: Visual observation/take notes/check off problems solved correctly on my master
MOST group: Percentage correct from learning sheet
SOME group: Percentage correct from learning sheet; percentage of drawings with appropriate proportionality

Maintenance (e.g., problem of the day, centers):
Use versatiles with activity sheet; when completed with practice

---

Grouping Information

Circle which of the following applies:

Whole class (no groups/names not necessary)

Group/individual student (write names below as appropriate)

Write names of group members:

Group 1: ALL	Observation/evaluation notes:
SA	
ZD	
SD	
TR	

Group 2: MOST	
RF	
NM	
JM	
XM	
JD	

Group 3: SOME	
RJ	
AD	
FJ	
JT	
TW	

Select Authentic Contexts

The next component of the Responsive Instructional Planning Framework is to select the authentic context within which the target concept initially will be taught (i.e., when participating in building meaningful student connections and when providing explicit teacher modeling). Several different approaches for determining authentic contexts for students were described in Chapter 8 (e.g., Mathematics Student Interest Inventory). Mrs. Carlson chose to use two authentic contexts for her initial instruction. She decided to use a college football game as a context to build meaningful student connections and to use sharing candy bars among friends as the context for explicit teacher modeling (Figure 11.2).

Plan Whole-Class Instruction

The next planning decision and component of the Responsive Planning Framework is to decide how to provide whole-class instruction, if appropriate, so that everyone is provided an explicit introduction to the target concept. Within this component, two decisions are made: 1) deciding how to build meaningful student connections between what students already know and what they are going to learn (see Chapters 2 and 9) determining how to provide explicit teacher modeling/scaffolding (see Chapter 9). Whole-class instruction should be planned to address what a teacher wants *all* students to learn. This means ensuring that all students are provided with explicit instruction for the learning objective that has been identified as the one that all students in the class will reach for that day's or week's instruction. When instruction is differentiated according to student groups, decisions regarding building meaningful connections and providing explicit teacher modeling/scaffolding for each group, should be commensurate with the areas the teacher wants the students in the ALL group (students with the least understanding) to demonstrate proficiency in by the close of the lesson or unit. Figure 11.2 shows how Mrs. Carlson decided to implement whole-class instruction using these two effective instructional practices.

Plan Differentiated Instruction

Once whole-class instruction has been planned, teachers must determine how instruction will be differentiated for students. Differentiated instruction can be implemented in at least two ways: 1) within whole-class instruction in which instructional strategies or techniques that accommodate the learning needs of all students in the class are used, and 2) by grouping students according to what is known about their understandings from the MDA and on the basis of their need for a higher or lower level of teacher support. Vaughn and colleagues (1997) suggested that students can be grouped according to their instructional goals. For example, groups can be organized according to what all students are expected to know (ALL group), what most students are expected to know (MOST group), and what some students are expected to know (SOME group). For one group of students (e.g., ALL group), the instructional focus may be additional scaffolding (high level of teacher support) of the concept or skill that was introduced or modeled by the teacher during whole-group instruction. The intended outcome for these students might be increasing their stage of learning from initial acquisition to advanced acquisition. For another group of students, it may mean providing them with independent learning experiences (lower level of teacher support) that can help them to build their proficiency (e.g., MOST group). For yet another group, this may mean providing extension-type learning experiences whereby students generalize their concrete-level understandings to the representational level of understanding with a lower level of teacher support (e.g., SOME group). Each group will need more or less teacher direction on the basis of their current level of understanding of the target concept. All activities should be structured so that students understand the purpose of the activity and how to complete it and can identify what they are learning when completing the activity. In addition, a procedure for collecting performance data should be included for individual students whether in a whole-class or differentiated group context. Figure 11.2 shows how Mrs. Carlson planned for this important instructional component.

Plan Practice Opportunities

Next, one has to determine how to provide practice for students so that they become proficient with using the target concept or skill. Again, providing students with opportunities for practice means providing them with multiple opportunities to use their developing understanding of mathematical concepts in meaningful ways. Generally, practice should occur at the level of understanding that matches the level of understanding at which modeling/scaffolding occurred. For whole-class differentiation contexts (no grouping), practice would occur at the same level at which the teacher provided explicit modeling. For differentiated group contexts, practice would occur at the level toward which each group is working. For example, students who are in the ALL group in Mrs. Carlson's class would be provided guided practice (continued scaffolding) at the concrete level of understanding for the purpose of building understanding. Students in the MOST group would be provided independent practice at the concrete level of understanding for the purpose of building proficiency. Students in the SOME group would be provided practice at the representational level for the purpose of generalizing or adapting their concrete understandings to the representational level (see Figure 11.2).

Evaluate Learning and Instruction

Evaluation of student learning is the final component of the responsive instructional planning framework. Whereas evaluation of learning should occur at each level of instruction (modeling, scaffolding, and practice), a tangible way to evaluate student progress (i.e., observable and measurable) must be implemented during student practice. It is important that accuracy of understanding be the focus at the concrete and representational levels and that both the accuracy and the rate (i.e., fluency) be emphasized at the abstract level. Concrete- and representational-level experiences support conceptual understanding; therefore, accuracy of understanding is an important goal. At the abstract level, students need to be able to respond with accuracy and at a rate that allows them to use the concept in practical ways. Accuracy can be evaluated on the basis of the format used by students as they respond during practice (e.g., number of problems solved correctly, number of problem-solving steps used correctly). Accuracy and rate during the proficiency and maintenance stages can be evaluated by implementing timed learning probes such as those described in Chapter 10. Figure 11.2 shows Mrs. Carlson's thoughts about how she will evaluate her students' learning related to comparing fractions.

LESSON PLAN EXAMPLES

With a framework for planning instruction that is responsive to students' needs, this section shows several examples of lesson plans that derive from this planning framework but that are adapted for different instructional contexts. Notes that a teacher makes in response to the nine questions in the planning framework can be used when developing such lesson plans.

Differentiated Instruction Plan: Responsive Teaching Plan for Differentiated Groups

Mrs. Carlson decided to use the Responsive Teaching Plan Form to structure her lesson. The responsive teaching plan provides teachers with a way to integrate into a usable lesson plan the ideas that are generated by the responsive instructional planning framework. This lesson plan format helps teachers to plan instruction on the basis of their instructional hypothesis about student understanding. It incorporates the useful planning pyramid technique suggested by Vaughn and colleagues (1997) for differentiating instructional goals. In addition, it prompts teachers to think about how they will incorporate important assessment information (e.g., levels of understanding, stage of learning) and effective instructional practices into their instruction (e.g., explicit teacher modeling, scaffolding, CRA instruction, continuous evaluation of student learning). Last, it provides teachers with a way to identify which students are in each differentiated instruction group and provides space for noting observations about each group and individual student. Figure 11.3 shows Mrs. Carlson's responsive teaching plan. A blank copy of the Responsive Teaching Plan Form appears in Appendix A.

Differentiated Instruction Plan: Integration of Effective Practices in Whole-Class Instruction

The following lesson demonstrates how a teacher can integrate the effective instructional practices discussed in this book for inclusive whole-class instruction when grouping of students is not used. The teaching methods described would benefit all children yet are targeted at providing support to struggling learners. The instructional modifications illustrated would enhance the learning outcomes for struggling learners within an inclusive mathematics classroom. In fact, this lesson would provide all students in the classroom the opportunity to learn mathematics in a responsive and supportive environment.

The lesson, geared toward a second- or third-grade classroom, encourages students to build on their number sense to find alternative ways to add two-digit numbers. The lesson describes *how* a teacher can integrate effective inclusionary practices in mathematics. The specific differentiation strategies that are designed to support struggling learners are indicated with *italics*.

1. **Review key ideas.** Help students *connect their previous knowledge and experiences* by displaying several problems and having students indicate whether the problem is an addition problem by using response cards. An example is shown next. To help students focus on relevant information,

the teacher (or a student) can *underline the important information as well as the question that he or she is answering.*

Myra has put 14 cupcakes in a box. Her mother gives her 4 more cupcakes to put in the box. How many cupcakes will Myra have in the box?

Have students *hold up response cards* that have either an addition sign or a subtraction sign with the corresponding word to indicate which operation they think should be used to solve each problem that is displayed. *Color code the written words and symbols on the response cards.* Evaluate student understanding by checking students' responses. After students have shown their cards, a volunteer can be asked to explain why the situation does or does not require addition. Add these color-coded vocabulary words and symbols to a *math wall* in the class for students to reference when needed. Have students develop *math talk notebooks* for individual reference. (Help students organize their notebooks by math concept, problem-solving strategy, or other scheme so that students will have a meaningful reference to mathematical language *using their own words.*)

2. **Establishing Expectations.** The focus of the lesson is to encourage students to find alternative ways to add two two-digit numbers. Make the expectations for doing this task clear, *using simpler problems that are familiar.* Display two or three basic facts and ask students to work silently on this task:

    "If you did not know these already, then show two ways you could figure them out."

    8 + 5   5 + 6   8 + 9

Use a structured cuing form such as the one referenced in Chapter 9. Show students how to write the addition statement on the form and where they can illustrate, with pictures or words, the strategy that they used. Explain to students that this recording can be any kind of representation that will help them to explain their reasoning to classmates later. *Give students additional opportunities to use language and to have structured opportunities for movement by having them partner and share their solutions.* While students are working, walk around so that you can monitor students' responses and so that you can capitalize later on various students' approaches.

   After students have discussed their answers in pairs, ask for volunteers to share one way to solve the problem. During the whole-class discussion, *provide a visual organization for the students by drawing a chart or Cue Sheet* (Figure 11.4) to categorize the various ways to add. *Provide structured opportunities for movement* by having students come up and illustrate various ways to add. The headings should be added as students share the strategies that they used.

   As students share their approaches, make sure to *model asking questions if students are not asking questions* (e.g., "How did you do ____?" "How did

Ways we know to add			
Counting up	**Make a 10**	**Near Doubles**	**Other**

Count up from 9. Count 10, 11, 12 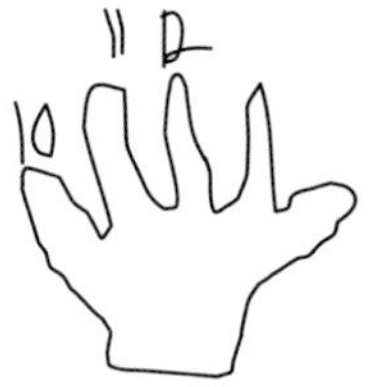	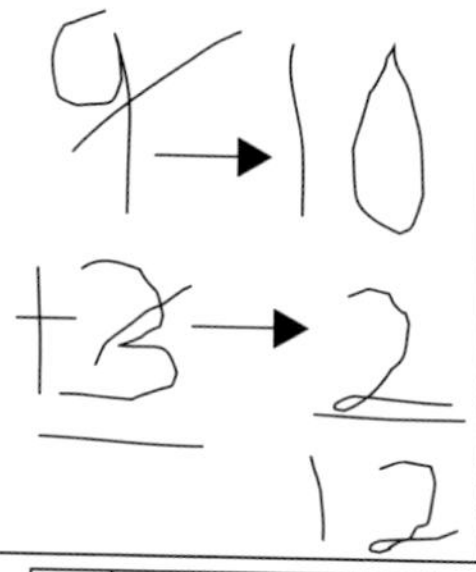	5 5
		+8 +5
		     10 + 3 = 13
			9 9
			+4 +9
			     18 − 5 = 13

	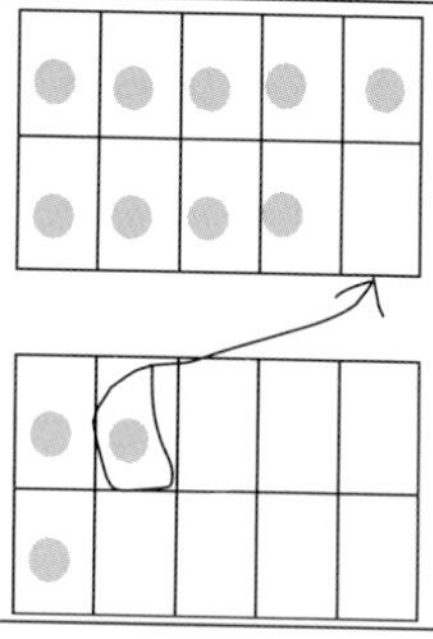		

Figure 11.4. Differentiation example: Cue Sheet for using different addition strategies. (*Source:* Lovin, L., Kyger, M., and Allsopp, D.H. [2004]. Differentiation for special needs learners, *Teaching Children Mathematics* (11), 164.

you know to do _____ first?"). Point out ways for students to make their reasoning explicit to others (e.g., different representations: pictures, drawings, written explanations, symbols). Students need to understand that there can be different purposes for using different materials and representations in mathematics. One student may need to use manipulatives or a picture to reason through a particular mathematical problem. Another student may choose to use the manipulatives or picture to communicate his or her reasoning about the problem. Making these purposes explicit can circumvent students' resistance to using materials that they have perceived as being used only by the "slower" students. Continue asking for volunteers until the various approaches are exhausted. Facilitate understanding for students with learning difficulties by asking the class to *look for and discuss similarities and differences between responses.*

3. **Focus of lesson.** After the class has discussed this process of using alternative ways to add single-digit numbers, move to the focus of the lesson: finding alternative ways to add two-digit numbers. Display a problem such as the one given next and ask students to think (silently!) about how they could solve this problem. Suggest that they might be able to use some of the strategies that were used with the basic facts. Suggest that there might be other ways to solve the problem. Students with learning difficulties may find success more easily by first *choosing their "favorite" strategy* (from their previous work with facts). From this initial success,

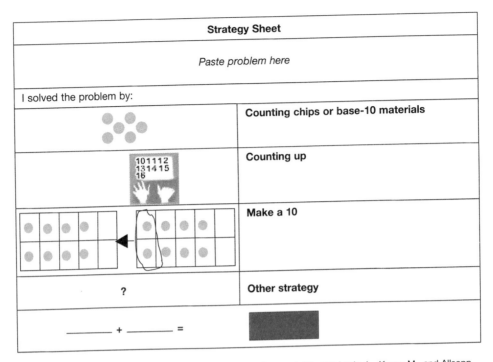

Figure 11.5.   Initial strategy sheet to record different strategies used. (*Source:* Lovin, L., Kyger, M., and Allsopp, D.A. [2004]. Differentiation for special needs learners, *Teaching Children Mathematics* (11), 165.

students with learning difficulties will be more apt to take a risk and explore other strategies.

> Find two different ways to solve this problem: There were 37 boy scouts and 61 girl scouts at the park on Saturday. How many scouts were at the park on Saturday?

To help students organize the information and provide visual structure, give students strategy sheets (Figure 11.5 shows an initial strategy sheet) and a copy of the problem. Show them how to paste the problem to the top of the sheet, to use the left-hand column to record the strategy that they used to solve the problem (remind students of illustrations used with the basic facts), and to write the numbers that they added and their answer at the bottom. The key to the strategy sheet is to provide enough structure and cuing to allow students to make progress independently without doing the reasoning for them.

This type of sheet is beneficial for both students and the teacher. For special needs learners, the sheet provides a structure that allows them to proceed without constant direct guidance from the teacher. It also makes explicit for students the notion of using a strategy to tackle a mathematical task. For the teacher, the sheet provides insights into the level of sophistication in the strategies used: who is using a less sophisticated strategy, such as counting all or counting up; and who is using a more sophisticated strategy, such as compensating or making a 10. Use this information to inform subsequent instruction, which may include providing additional, individualized support for some learners.

Lead a class discussion following the same structure as before, beginning with an opportunity to partner and share before the whole-class discussion. As students generate new strategies (e.g., add the tens first), these strategies can be added to the strategy sheet and posted to the strategies listed on the math wall. If a particular strategy does not emerge, then the teacher can pose a problem that exhibits the strategy. Consider the following problem:

$$
\begin{array}{r}
48 \\
+36 \\
\hline
70 \\
+14 \\
\hline
84
\end{array}
$$

Think about this student's work. Is the student correct?
What do you think the student did to get 84?
Write down what you think about the student's work.

After responses have been discussed, struggling learners greatly benefit from having the teacher *review by re-modeling* pertinent approaches. Use *cuing techniques such as color coding and arrows* to facilitate understanding for these students. Consider the same problem with such cuing integrated. In the following problem, bolding highlights the major steps of the "add tens first" strategy, and arrows emphasize the relationship between the numbers.

4. *Closure.* To bring closure to the day's activities, the class can *review key vocabulary and summarize the different strategies used.* As part of the summary, the class may want to compare the different strategies for differences and similarities as well as efficiency (e.g., Let's compare Jason's approach with Maria's approach. What similarities/differences do you notice?). New strategies can be added to the strategies on the math wall and math talk notebooks. Students also can create a visual display of their learning using a simple chart, such as the one depicted in Figure 10.8. Share these with students, other teachers, and parents to provide concrete but powerful ways to see learning progress, especially when particular mathematics concepts and skills are practiced over several days or weeks.

Planning for the Purpose of Accommodating Specific Learning Barriers

Whether you are teaching math in a general education classroom or a special education environment, you will have learners who are at different levels and who experience different learning difficulties. The Learning Barriers Planning Form can be used to help with planning specific ways to address the learning needs of students at different points in the teaching cycle. Four important components of most mathematics lessons are addressed: lesson objective, teaching procedures, student responses, and evaluation of learning.

This planning form is not meant to be a lesson plan but rather a way to frame planning while taking into consideration the unique learning needs of students. Proactively identifying the barriers to learning for students and then devising appropriate modifications in these four areas will lead to more effective instruction. It is important not to confuse differentiation with watering down the curriculum. Identifying and modifying lesson delivery does not mean changing the purpose and the objectives of a lesson. High expectations can and should be maintained, but struggling learners can realize them only when effective instruction that addresses their learning needs is provided. Figure 11.6 shows how the form can be used to address the learning needs of students as they learn about number sense. A blank copy of the Learning Barriers Planning Form appears in Appendix A.

Planning Format/Tips for Co-Teaching/Collaborative Teaching Contexts

To plan effective differentiated lessons, both special education and general education teachers need to engage in a purposeful decision-making process. In planning differentiated math lessons, the following decision-making structure has proved helpful. The prompts are not meant to be all-encompassing; rather, they provide a framework on which to build.

1. What is the lesson objective?

    a. Is it appropriate for all, some, most of the students?

    b. Is it on the students' level of understanding (CRA)?

    c. Does it link to big ideas in mathematics?

2. How are you going to teach the objective(s)?

    a. How do students think about these ideas differently from adults and how can I use this information to inform instruction?

    b. Which types of instructional strategies will you use? Is there specialized strategy instruction needed? If so, who will be responsible for this?

    c. How will you explain/show/model the task or activity? What will the role/responsibility of each teacher?

    d. Which materials are you going to use, and are they multisensory? Who is going to supply/create the materials (or adapt existing materials)?

3. When and where do you want students to respond?

    a. How do you expect students will respond?

    b. How are students going to practice (e.g., C, R, or A level of understanding? Providing receptive or expressive responses? Working inde-

Mathematical concept: Number sense, a flexible understanding of numbers and their relationships to other numbers

Lesson plan Lesson objectives	Possible barriers	Possible modifications
Use different ways to arrange a set of objects, such as rectangular arrays and equal-sized groups. Analyze visual images (i.e., look for patterns or groupings). Describe position of and spatial relationships among objects.	Language problems interfere with describing. Visual perception problems interfere with spatial relationships. Attention problems interfere with seeing patterns. Students are unfamiliar with use of arrays.	Add vocabulary and representations (e.g., symbols, pictures) to math wall and math talk notebooks. Focus on relevant information and key features of lesson with color cuing, providing arrays to feel and manipulate. Place in authentic problem-solving contexts.
Instructional procedures Give students sectioned paper Teacher explanation.	Explanation is too language based, does not link students' previous knowledge. Students with attention and memory problems have no cues to remember, key into information. There is no mention of authentic context to assist with meaning.	Use previously mastered problems to introduce lesson. Focus on relevant information and key features of lesson.
Student responses Students draw. Students explain drawing. Students comment/question. Students continue to group dots by drawing.	Students are using only one level of understanding.	Use guided questioning. Use a checklist to complete activity (based on steps of the task). Provide partner games.
Evaluation of learning Give students dot pattern. Have them find two ways to describe image.	Students with language problems, auditory processing problems may have difficulty with explanations and questions.	Use CRA levels for responses. Use flexible interviews.

Figure 11.6.   Learning Barriers Planning Form example: Number sense.

pendently or in collaborative groups)? Who is responsible for creating and monitoring practice opportunities?

c.   Which types of home–school connections will you provide (see section on home-school connections for suggestions)?

4.   How are you going to assess student understanding?

a.   Is your evaluation meaningful (i.e., does it let you know both what students do and do not understand)?

b.   Can you and the student learn from the evaluation? How will you and your teaching partner use the evaluation data to inform future instruction?

Other Lesson Plan Examples

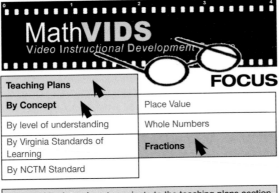

Teaching Plans	FOCUS
By Concept	Place Value
By level of understanding	Whole Numbers
By Virginia Standards of Learning	**Fractions**
By NCTM Standard	

This graphic shows how to navigate to the teaching plans section of the MathVIDS web site. After selecting *"Teaching Plans"* on the top menu, you can view plans according to mathematical concept, by level of understanding, and by standard (Virginia Standards of Learning or NCTM). Once you have selected an area of interest (e.g., by concept, such as fractions), you can then access the relevant teaching plan(s).

Additional lesson plan examples can be found in Appendix B. These lesson plans demonstrate how the effective instructional practices that are described in Chapters 9 and 10 can be integrated to teach a variety of mathematical concepts and skills at different levels of understanding (concrete, representational, and abstract). Additional plans can be found on the MathVIDS web site by clicking on the "Teaching Plans" link on the top menu bar.

Home–School Connections

Effective planning and teaching are vital to the mathematical learning success of struggling learners. However, this in and of itself is not enough for many students; struggling learners need wrap-around supports. They need to have connections made to the mathematics that are used in their home environments and to practice their skills in authentic, relevant contexts. These connections should be planned and should *not* be worksheets or rote drills; rather, home connections should help students learn to use their mathematical understanding to make meaning of their world. For example, students who are working on recognizing patterns could construct a pattern portfolio to help them focus on the relevant features of the patterns that they are exploring. This portfolio can be used to extend students' recognition of patterns across contexts and can be in a paper or a digital format. The portfolio then can grow as students move from using pictures to line drawings and finally symbols to represent various patterns. The portfolio in Figure 11.7 shows a student's representation of patterns with letters and words for two patterns that he observed. As the student continues to find patterns, he will continue to complete his portfolio.

It is important to provide generalization opportunities to allow students to extend their understandings. One way to facilitate generalization is to have activities at school that can lead to generalization outside the classroom (e.g., having students sort utensils in the cafeteria can lead to a generalization activity at home). Older students can sort video games, DVDs, or trading cards.

Having students bring information gained from their community or home environment also is important for effective generalization. For example, when teaching students about changes to the slope, or *y* intercept, the teacher could use the context of organizing a concert with local musical bands. Using the

My patterns	My class	My school	My home
Pattern 1: **ABAB**	*How boys and girls are lined up for lunch:* *Boy, girl, boy, girl (BGBGB)*	*First four stripes on the American flag that flies at my school:* *red, white, red, white (RWRW)*	*Order of knives and forks set around the dinner table:* *Knife, fork, knife, fork, (FKFKF)*
Pattern 2: **ABABCABABC**	*Days each week we have PE, music, or Art during third period:* *PE, Music, PE, Music, Art, PE, Music, PE, Music, Art*		

Figure 11.7. Student portfolio showing real-life applications of patterns.

notion of slope and the *y* intercept, have students consider different scenarios with the length of the concert versus admission price. For example, for longer concerts, students could charge more for admission. If students charged $3 for every 15 minutes of music, they would make a table of values showing concert time versus ticket price for four or five possible scenarios, then plot these values and examine the graph (Figure 11.8). Model with students how to determine the equation for this linear function (*y* = 1/5*x*). Graph a second line onto the same coordinate plane and guide students to examine how this second graph is related to the first one (the second line is steeper and above the first line) (Figure 11.9). Again, work with the students to determine the equation for this linear function (*y* = 1/3*x*). Finally, discuss with students what the graphs mean in the context of concert length and ticket price and why that might occur (e.g., "The second line represents a situation where the ticket prices are higher than in the first situation. If more popular bands play at the

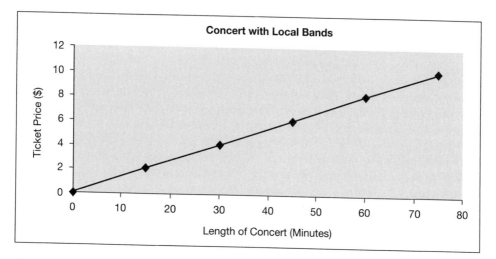

Figure 11.8. Graph depicting use of a meaningful context to explore slope and *y*-intercept.

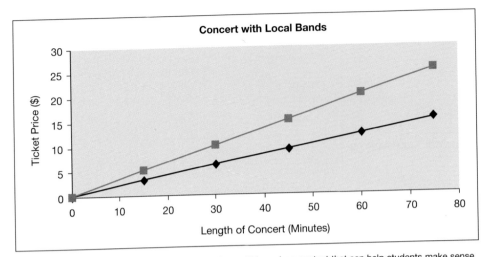

Figure 11.9. Graph comparing the slopes of the lines within a given context that can help students make sense of slope.

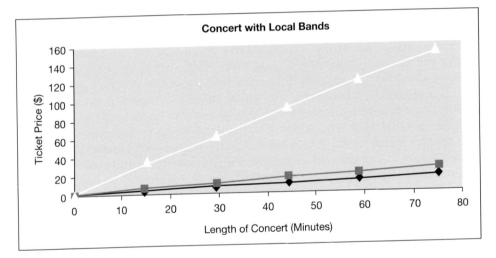

Figure 11.10. Graphs showing length of concert versus ticket price.

concert, then students may be able to charge higher ticket prices"). During this discussion, make explicit the connections between the graphs and the equations. Have students predict what the line would look like if the equation was $y = 2x$ (it should be even steeper than the second line). Graph it and discuss with students how this graph makes sense given this context (Figure 11.10). Ask students to consider what the graph in Figure 11.11 might mean within the given context (e.g., ticket prices started at a higher price than in the first situation). Comparing the slopes and intercepts of the lines within meaningful contexts can help students make sense of these mathematical ideas. Van de Walle and Lovin (2006c) offer several ideas about using real-world contexts to help make functions and other mathematical ideas more meaningful to students.

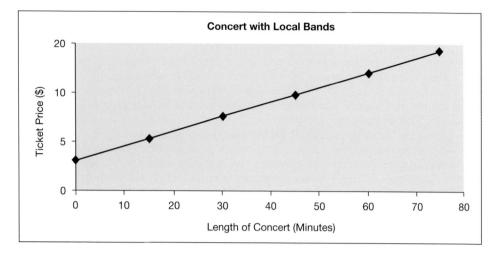

Figure 11.11.   Considering a graph with a different *y*-intercept to make sense of the *y*-intercept.

Combining Reality with Practice

Finally, it is important for teachers to use all of their resources and to look beyond the walls of the school to make mathematics real. Consider the following story:

A ninth grade math teacher at her local high school, Mrs. A had increasingly been frustrated with her ability to reach her students with learning disabilities. Although they spent a significant amount of time on mathematics, her students appeared to be falling further behind. Mrs. A was sharing her frustration with a friend when Buddy Ross, a local homebuilder and fellow parishioner, overheard her concerns.

Buddy knew Mrs. A for almost two decades. Most summers, he would actually hire one or two of Mrs. A's students to help on construction projects and house painting. Buddy approached Mrs. A about her concerns. He wasn't sure how he could help but wanted to see if there might be some way to reduce her frustration. Mrs. A shared her concerns and Buddy listened. Having gone right to work after high school, Buddy preferred work over the classroom. However, as he listened to her concerns, he realized many of the difficulties in math coincided with the skills his employees had to have to be successful. As they left the church, Buddy offered his assistance and his willingness to do whatever would be helpful. Mrs. A thanked Buddy for his concern but realized that this was a classroom challenge and not something Buddy could address at his work sites. Or could he?

As the school year continued, Mrs. A became increasingly frazzled over her students' inability to understand the concepts. At her wits end, she looked for possible solutions and immediately agreed to attend a Saturday workshop being offered at the local college. The workshop focused on middle and secondary content and how authentic instruction could be a vehicle to connecting learners to the standards-based curriculum. With problem-based learning a critical feature, the workshop instructor shared ways teachers could connect students to the curriculum and support the learning process through instruction that focused on concept comprehension and application instead of rote memorization. Not certain of her next steps, Mrs. A left the workshop feeling she had some ideas but still needed additional support.

The following Sunday, Mrs. A waved to Buddy as they left the church parking lot. As her husband drove home, she thought more about Buddy and his willingness to help. She also thought about the recent workshop and its focus on authentic instruction. On her way into work that Monday morning, Mrs. A connected the dots. She realized that Buddy could be of help in her efforts to integrate an authentic instructional approach.

The next day she contacted Buddy and they discussed possible options. Soon, Buddy was sharing various components of his construction projects with Mrs. A and her class. For example, for every home construction, Buddy and his staff had to take a series of measurements to ensure home placement, foundation depth and width, irrigation considerations and the like. With this need in mind, Buddy soon shared with Mrs. A upcoming projects and asked for student assistance in planning the construction. For example, for a new development east of town, Buddy shared his plans and asked teams of students to use their linear measurements skills to review and check the measurements of the foundation and the related floor plans (e.g., scale of measurement).

Within a week students were completing problems designed to determine the total number of square yards of carpet and vinyl needed by the builder. Mrs. A was able to compare the students' answers to the estimates provided by Buddy. By the end of the month, Buddy asked students to assist in solving problems related to measuring for and choosing window coverings, determining the amount of materials needed to fence a yard, and to solve complex geometric problems such as measuring for the construction of shutters of an octagonal window. Buddy and Mrs. A loved the interaction and the students responded to the assignments and felt an ownership to Buddy's needs and application to the math problems.

As the end of the school year approached Mrs. A decided to engage students in a number of classroom-based activities using technology. Using the home building related activities as anchors for her classroom activities, Mrs. A had students solving additional problems related to measurement and basic geometry using a student version of Computer Assisted Drawing (CAD) program. Besides working on Buddy's needs, Mrs. A's students began developing plans for their own homes. To ensure they were able to apply these skills to local and state assessment requirements, Mrs. A also integrated web-based activities developed by the NCTM (http://standards.nctm.org/document/eexamples/chap6/6.3/index.htm).

By the last week of school, Mrs. A was ecstatic. Her class was engaged in math for a purpose and their willingness to work and equally important, their ability to comprehend the complex concepts had progressed significantly. As a reward, Buddy arranged for the students to visit the housing development. There, students were able to walk through several of the homes they helped to measure, talk with some of the architects, and even meet one of the families who had just purchased a completed home. With summer upon her, Mrs. A wasn't certain what next year would bring but knew that Buddy and his ongoing construction projects would be a key component to her math instruction. (From Allsopp, in press; reprinted by permission of Prentice Hall/Pearson Education.)

Consider the components that were critical to Mrs. A's students' interest, comprehension, and subsequent success. Mrs. Alvarez was able to reach her students; for some, however, this approach may not be enough. Which other components do you believe would be critical for students' successful understanding and application?

In pondering these questions and reflecting on Mrs. A's experiences, teachers will begin the journey of decision making that is so crucial to providing effective mathematics instruction to struggling learners. Identifying the big ideas of mathematics and exploring them in authentic, relevant contexts; providing a mixture of teacher guidance and modeling with student practice; and continual assessment of student progress were key to Mrs. A's success.

THINKING ABOUT YOUR CLASSROOM

How do you envision yourself as a teacher of mathematics? Which types of learning experiences do you want to provide for your students? This chapter provides a framework to guide you in planning and implementing responsive teaching and also provides several different examples to help you engage in effective teaching of mathematics across a number of different environments. Additional lesson plan examples can be found in Appendix B and in the MathVIDS web site. Although no two environments are alike, it is hoped that you will be able to apply some, if not all, of this chapter's content as you develop lessons for your students.

12

Using Technology to Promote Access to Mathematics

"Should I use technology?" This is a question that teachers might face or have already faced in instructional planning. This question, as it is posed, seems to omit the most significant piece of the puzzle. The question can be more helpful if rephrased as, "Will technology enhance my students' understanding?" To answer this question, teachers must consider 1) whether technology that enhances students' understanding of mathematics is available and, 2) how teachers and students should use the technology to enhance the students' understanding (e.g., for exploration, for support during more complex work, for modeling). The learning objective(s), the needs of students, and the availability of appropriate technology should drive decisions about the integration of technology into mathematics instruction. Teachers should not use technology simply to be able to say that they are using it; rather, they should determine whether technology can facilitate their students' mathematical understandings, particularly as they relate to the big ideas.

This chapter describes ways to integrate technology into teaching mathematics so as to promote access for struggling learners. Therefore, the emphasis is on instructional technology applications that facilitate mathematical understanding. Assistive technology—technology that assists students with disabilities to circumvent sensory and motor impairments—is an important area of innovation for students with disabilities but is not a point of emphasis in this chapter. This chapter begins with an overview of a variety of general mathematics education–related technologies that are commonly available, then discusses the benefits of these technologies with examples of their use, and finally, summarizes teaching strategies that educators can use when using technology to facilitate mathematical learning outcomes for struggling learners.

TYPES OF COMMON MATHEMATICS-RELATED TECHNOLOGY AND GUIDELINES FOR SELECTION

People often think of technology as something that makes tasks more efficient and easier to accomplish. Technology is often used at the workplace to facilitate accomplishing one's job duties in a timely and cost-effective way (e.g., use of spreadsheets to assist with tracking inventory, use of word processing to communicate, use of e-mail and videoconferencing to avoid the expense of travel). Technology can be helpful in a mathematics class as well. However, when technology is used to engage students in the learning of mathematics, it should not be seen simply as a tool to complete a task or as a replacement for understanding. Technology should be viewed as a way to enhance students' learning. The focus should be on helping students to better understand a given mathematics learning objective.

A variety of technologies can support student learning in the five mathematical content areas identified in Chapter 3. The technologies discussed in this chapter are not exhaustive but rather are meant to be illustrative. Table 12.1 identifies some technologies that address the five content areas.

Several types of selected technologies are discussed further in the next section, which provides a good summary of a variety of technology applications found within mathematics classrooms that can be used effectively with struggling learners. Each description is meant to provide an overview of the technology and how it is applied to the mathematics curriculum. The final section of this chapter provides teaching suggestions for adapting the use of such technologies to the learning needs of struggling learners.

Mathematics Software: How to Select Appropriate Software for Students

The technologies identified in Table 12.1 are mostly general in nature and do not include a wide selection of computer software that is available. Kerrigan (2002) evaluated several software packages that are available on the market and categorized them according to the skills or concepts taught. The categories included programs that

- Promote higher order thinking

- Teach children how to use sophisticated spreadsheets to play what-if games with numbers

- Help students to develop and maintain mathematical skills

- Introduce students to collecting and analyzing data

- Introduce algebraic and geometric thinking

- Show the role of mathematics in an interdisciplinary environment

As a teacher, one must keep in mind that not all software packages are equal in quality. Many software packages at first glance seem to provide students with real-life contexts and are colorful and engaging, but at second glance, there is not much substance behind the glitter and flashing lights. Many issues must be considered when deciding whether to use a particular software package. Following are some questions to guide evaluation of computer programs. These questions, in part, are suggestions from Kerrigan, 2002, and Van de Walle, 2005.

- Is the mathematics depicted done so accurately?

- What is the content likely to be learned? (Try to get past the glitter, bells, and whistles.) Does this meet with my learning objectives?

Table 12.1. Examples of technologies that address the five big idea content areas

Content area	Technology	Sample learning outcome
Number and operations	Calculators	Number sense Computation
	Spreadsheets	Number sense Computation
Algebra	Calculators (with calculator-based rangers and probes)	Behavior of graphs Connecting slope to rate of change Data collection
	Spreadsheets	Behavior of graphs Data collection Creating functions, making generalizations
Probability and statistics	Spreadsheets	Data collection and analysis Changing data to understand how various statistics (e.g., mean, median, standard deviation) are affected Simulations
	Java scripts	Simulations
Geometry	Dynamic geometry program (e.g., Geometer's Sketchpad)	Through generating several examples, investigate properties of shapes through exploration Through generating several examples, investigate relationships between properties through exploration Making and testing conjectures Making generalizations
	Java scripts (e.g., tangram puzzles)	Visualization
Measurement	Dynamic geometry program (e.g., Geometer's Sketchpad)	Through generating several examples, investigate relationships, such as how area changes if dimensions change, the measures of angles formed by a transversal crossing two parallel lines, the sum of the angles in a triangle
	Spreadsheets	Investigating relationships such as how volume changes if dimensions change
	Java scripts (e.g., electronic geoboard)	Exploring area and perimeter and the relationship between area and perimeter

- Is the program easy to use? Does it meet the learning needs of my students (e.g., is it disability accessible? Do my students have the requisite technology skills to use the program)?

- Does the package do what its documentation says that it will do?

- Is it appropriate for the academic (grade) and developmental (age/disability-related) level of my students?

- How are students likely to be engaged with the mathematics? Does the program offer a high level of interactive experience? Does the package engage the student in higher order thinking? Are there opportunities for reflective thought? If not, then can I add these opportunities without a great deal of additional work on my part?

- With "computation skill practice" packages, how are incorrect answers handled (to provide opportunities for self-correction and corrective feedback)? Will the approach help facilitate students' understanding?

- How does the software package enhance learning beyond what typically would be done?

- Is there a way to keep records of students' activity to monitor progress?

- Are there built-in controls so that I can turn off sound, add color, or modify the level of difficulty or the kinds of feedback? In other words, can the program be differentiated on the basis of the individual learning needs of my students?

Teachers can use the criteria embedded in these questions to identify appropriate computer programs for enriching students' mathematical understanding. In fact, these criteria can be used more globally to evaluate other kinds of technology, such as spreadsheets and java scripts. However, the most important question that should be asked is "Does the technology application enhance my students' understanding of the target mathematical concept?" Understanding the mathematical ideas has to remain the focus. A word of caution regarding commercial software is that there is a noticeable absence in the literature regarding their actual effectiveness on mathematics learning outcomes for struggling learners (Maccini & Gagnon, 2005). However, Bottge, Heinrichs, Chan, Mehta, and Watson (2003) have found that students with learning disabilities demonstrate positive mathematical learning outcomes with technology that situates learning in meaningful contexts (e.g., video). Hence, it would seem to reason that commercial software that simulates learning in meaningful contexts has the potential of being helpful.

Wireless Technology

The integration of wireless technology in K–12 schools is increasing. "One-to-one" laptop/personal digital assistant (PDA) classrooms (i.e., where there is one laptop/PDA for every student in the class) and "shared access" classrooms (i.e., where students share several computers) are becoming more and more common. Such arrangements provide exciting possibilities for teaching and student learning. Teachers are learning how wireless technology and the powerful applications that can be downloaded onto these computers can transform traditional instruction across curricular areas, mathematics included. For example, by coupling digital media (e.g., digital photography, digital audio/music) with laptop computers, students are able to develop their own movies to describe the mathematics that they are learning and to demonstrate deeper levels of understanding, something that certainly complements the instructional practice of integrating language experiences in mathematics (see Strategy 1: Structured Language Experiences in Chapter 10). Students can make movies that depict particular problem-solving situations (e.g., three friends have pooled money to purchase video games at the video store and they need to know how much each needs to spend: $3x = \$120$) and then show how they would solve the problem (e.g., depict dividing the money evenly on the basis of different numbers of video games that each buys: each buys two games; each buys three games). Students share their movies, learning from each other about different strategies to solve the task.

Students also can use educational software applications such as *Inspiration* and *Kidspiration* to create structure for their mathematical thinking by developing semantic maps and flow charts that describe relationships between and among mathematical concepts. They also can create simple mathematics instructional games using basic interactive features such as graphics, text talk, and hyperlink (i.e., linking a graphic or word in their Inspiration document to web sites, video, pictures, and other files) capabilities. For example, students can pose a problem and have it appear in one graphic, then show three different solutions using three other graphics. To play the game, a student uses the "connect" feature (an arrow appears from one graphic to the other). To check whether his or her answer is correct, the student clicks the "note" feature on the graphic depicting the problem (the note feature allows text to be written in a box that can be hidden until the note icon is clicked). The note then appears and shows the correct solution. The student or teacher can hide the note by simply clicking the note icon again. Figure 12.1 shows an example.

An engaging, interactive way to help students develop and use mathematical metacognitive skills using computers and digital media involves their making simple stop-animation videos. An important skill related to place value is identifying the relative values of digits based on where they are in a number (e.g., in 435, the value of the digit 4 is four-hundred, the value of the digit 3 is thirty, the value of the digit 5 is five). An activity that students might engage in to build on their knowledge of place value is to have students use a place value mat and ask them to place or write digits in the appropriate columns when given a number verbally (i.e., "Use your place value mats to show four-hundred thirty-five."). The teacher could then ask students about why they placed digits as they did or he or she could ask them to say the value of selected digits as represented on students' place value mats. Using digital technology, students can extend this teacher-directed activity and further build their reasoning skills by developing stop-frame movies showing their understanding of place value and their use of thinking/reasoning skills, and by providing other students with an interactive medium to practice using their developing knowledge independently. For example, students can randomly place four single-digit manipulative numbers on a white background, like a whiteboard, that also has written on it a place value mat that identifies "hundreds, ones, tenths, and hundredths." Students decide what number they want to represent on the place value mat. Then they move each single-digit number in incremental steps to each place value starting with the "hundreds" place, taking a digital picture each time until all four numbers are in their place value position. Students download the digital pictures and order them in the timeline using a video-editing program (e.g., iMovie, Windows Movie Maker 2.0). Students record audio where they say what number will be represented. They also decide what place value reasoning questions they want to include that will

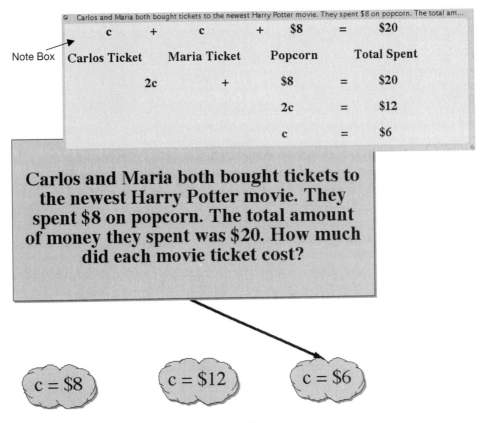

Note Box

Carlos and Maria both bought tickets to the newest Harry Potter movie. They spent $8 on popcorn. The total am...

c	+	c	+	$8	=	$20
Carlos Ticket		Maria Ticket		Popcorn		Total Spent
		$2c$	+	$8	=	$20
				$2c$	=	$12
				c	=	$6

Carlos and Maria both bought tickets to the newest Harry Potter movie. They spent $8 on popcorn. The total amount of money they spent was $20. How much did each movie ticket cost?

$c = \$8$ $c = \$12$ $c = \$6$

Figure 12.1.   Example of math game using Inspiration software.

stimulate thinking about place value for other students who will view their movie later on: "In which place value will the 8 end up? What value does the 8 represent? Students then save the movie that they have made. The end product is a short stop-frame movie in which each number moves toward its "assigned" place value, interspersed with questions that prompt thinking about what is occurring and its relation to place value. The movie ends when all four digits are in the appropriate place value on the place value mat. Then the movie can be used to engage other students in thinking about place value and what that means in terms of the value of each of the digits. Providing struggling learners ways to show and practice metacognitive thinking is important because this is an area that is underdeveloped by many students with learning difficulties. Technology offers many engaging ways to do this through multimedia. A wide variety of innovative approaches to integrating wireless technology in K–12 mathematics classrooms can be found at the Florida Center for Instructional Technology (FCIT) web site (http://fcit.usf.edu); specifically, "No Strings Attached!" a program for wireless laptops in education, can be found within the "Publications" section of the FCIT web site at the following URL: http://etc.usf.edu/plans/default.htm. This site provides video examples of students integrating wireless technology in various curricular areas, including lesson plans that concisely describe the learning objective and associated subject area and technology standards, materials needed, and procedures for implementing the lesson. Explore this site to see firsthand the possibilities for integrating wireless technology in the classroom.

On-Line Resources

The following list of additional on-line resources can be useful for learning more about how to use and implement interactive technology for teaching purposes. The resources offer a range of support in the form of lesson plans, virtual manipulatives (i.e., interactive manipulatives, many of which are similar to physical manipulatives, such as geoboards, pattern blocks, base-10 materials), and java scripts (another form of interactive program):

- E-Examples from the NCTM (http://standards.nctm.org/document/ eexamples/index.htm). These are virtual (interactive) manipulatives and graphing tools that provide activities and sites for exploring in all five mathematical content areas (number and operations, algebra, geometry, measurement, and data analysis and probability) across grades pre-K through 12. These tools warrant a look from any teacher who is interested in offering students quality explorations with technology.

- The National Library of Virtual Manipulatives (http://nlvm.usu.edu/en/ nav/vlibrary.html). Provides access to on-line activities using virtual manipulatives for application across the pre-K–12 mathematics curriculum.

- Educational Technology Clearinghouse in the FCIT web site (http://etc. usf.edu/math/index.htm). A very well-organized collection of various web sites that provide instructional ideas and support for a wide range of mathematics topics.

- InterMath (http://www.intermath-uga.gatech.edu). Produced in collaboration by the University of Georgia and the Georgia Institute of Technology, it supports the professional development of teachers by enhancing their mathematics content knowledge through mathematical investigations using technology. The web site includes a variety of activities and lesson plans that are geared toward middle-grade mathematics.

- The Math Portal (http://fcit.usf.edu/math/default.htm). Contains links to many different on-line resources both for teachers and for students. The site also allows for users to submit lesson plans that they have found useful.

- The WebQuest Page (http://webquest.sdsu.edu). (WebQuests are Internet-based problem-solving activities that have a defined structure. See more on WebQuests in the next section pertaining to authentic contexts.) Provides already developed WebQuests that are ready for use by teachers and students. Teachers also can learn how to make their own WebQuests using simple-to-use templates that are available for download on-line.

- Texas Instruments (http://education.ti.com/educationportal/sites/US/ homePage/index.html). Click on the "Classroom Activities" link at the top of the page and then "Activities Exchange" to find a variety of calculator activities for use with Texas Instruments calculators. (Click on "Math" in the navigation menu on the left to browse the collection by content area (e.g., algebra, pre-calculus, general math). Even if a school does not use Texas Instruments calculators, there are some outstanding ideas that can be modified easily to other brand-name calculators.

- Casio (http://www.casioeducation.com/activities/lesson_calc.php). Offers a variety of very good calculator activities. As with the Texas Instruments calculator activities, the activities that are offered by Casio can be adapted for use with other brand-name calculators.

- Regional Math and Science Center (http://www.svsu.edu/mathsci-center/hprob.htm). Produced by Saginaw Valley State University, this web site provides interactive probability simulators in which situations are simulated so that students can conduct repeated trials to investigate probability. The activities are based on high school benchmarks, but some activities could be adapted for use in middle grades.

- Coin tossing (http://nlvm.usu.edu/en/nav/frames_asid_305_g_3_t_5.html). There are a number of interactive simulators on the Internet. These offer a way for students to generate several trials very quickly so that they have more time to spend contemplating how probability works. This particular one is from the National Library of Virtual Manipulatives and allows students to change the number of trials as well as change the coin from a "fair" coin (chance of getting heads is one half) to an "unfair" coin (chance of getting heads is not one half).

- Apple Learning Interchange (http://ali.apple.com). Provides tutorials for how to use various multimedia applications (e.g., digital photography, video, audio, music).

The reader should consult Gardner and Wissick (2005) to learn more about web-based resources and on-line instructional considerations for students with learning difficulties.

Special Education–Specific Instructional Technology Resources for Mathematics

Interest in the application of instructional technology in mathematics for struggling learners is growing. The Math Matrix web site (Center for Implementing Technology in Education; http://www.citeducation.org/mathmatrix) provides links to and information about a wide variety of technology applications for mathematics in special education. This site, a cooperative endeavor among the American Institutes for Research, the Center for Applied Special Technology, and the Education Development Center, provides information about technology resources in six mathematical areas: building computational fluency; converting symbols, notations, and text; building conceptual understanding; making calculations and creating mathematical representations; organizing ideas; and building problem solving and reasoning. Math Matrix offers a matrix for each mathematical area that identifies appropriate resources and how each resource integrates elements of nine technology features that are important for the differentiated learning needs of students with disabilities (levels, customizable interface, input, text to speech, feedback, graphics, user profiles, adaptability to different operating systems, and grade level). Links to research articles that address each mathematical area also are provided.

POTENTIAL BENEFITS OF USING TECHNOLOGY
Building Proficiency

Struggling learners require multiple opportunities to respond to mathematics tasks to become proficient (fluent) with using and applying skills and concepts to other areas. To accomplish this, students need to be engaged in ways that are motivating so that they *want* to respond many times. Technology can provide both of these instructional characteristics. Computer software that provides students with multiple practice opportunities while engaging student interest is one example. Although many software applications are available, teachers should use the guidelines already described for selecting software for mathematics instruction. In addition, teachers must evaluate whether the software or other technology application possesses the important characteristics of the student practice strategies described in Chapter 10. The following list summarizes important features that at a minimum should be included:

1. The target mathematics concept or task is the focus of the activity.

2. The technology application is "doable"/accessible by the student (cognitively, sensory-wise, motor-skill wise).

3. Students are provided many response opportunities.

4. The activity is situated in an engaging/motivating context.

5. Students are provided corrective feedback and positive reinforcement.

6. Student performance is measured or can be determined by the teacher.

Creating Authentic Contexts for Problem Solving

Technology can play an important role in developing authentic contexts in which students learn and apply mathematics. A growing body of literature demonstrates the potential for using video and gaming applications to anchor mathematics instruction in meaningful contexts that enhance learning outcomes for students with learning difficulties (e.g., Bottge, Heinrichs, Chan, Mehta, & Watson, 2003; Bottge et al., 2002, 2004). Bottge and his colleagues have found that students with learning difficulties demonstrate positive mathematical learning outcomes when technology is integrated into instruction that situates learning in meaningful contexts (e.g., video). As the integration of wireless technology (e.g., laptop computers, PDAs) in classrooms increases, the opportunities for teachers to use multimedia technology applications, such as digital photography, digital video, and animation, to anchor learning of mathematics in rich, problem-solving contexts will increase.

WebQuests are another excellent way to provide authentic problem-solving contexts in mathematics. Each WebQuest poses a problem to be solved, is developed to address one or more defined learning objectives, describes a set of tasks in which students are to involve themselves (e.g., search for particular information in a specific web site), identifies a product that students are to complete and that provides a solution to the problem, and provides an evaluation rubric (for grading or self-evaluation purposes). Several web site resources contain already developed WebQuests that are ready for immediate use by teachers and students. Teachers also can learn how to make their own

WebQuests using simple-to-use templates that are available for download on-line. Make sure to visit The WebQuest Page, maintained by the Educational Technology Department at San Diego State University (http://webquest.sdsu.edu), an excellent resource for WebQuests. This site also provides information about how to create your own WebQuest, including links to sites that have free WebQuest templates that can be used quickly without having to understand web-based programming.

Testing Conjectures and Modifying Understanding

An important application of technology for mathematical learning is that it can provide ways for students to build mathematical models (e.g., graphs, polygons) to test conjectures or hypotheses about mathematical concepts. With technology, students can change these models easily, playing the what-if game with geometric, numeric, and algebraic ideas, which helps students to modify their understanding of these ideas. Examples of this kind of activity follow.

Examples   Dynamic geometry programs allow students to construct a geometric object and then explore its mathematical properties by manipulating with the computer mouse parts of the object, such as angles and segment lengths. Any mathematical relationship that defines the object will not change (e.g., right angles in a square), which allows the student to begin to notice which parts remain constant and which parts change. In a short amount of time, students are able to generate several examples, something that just is not possible with traditional geometric tools (e.g., compass, protractor) and paper and pencil. By noticing constants in the examples, students are able to develop further hypotheses and test them, working toward generalizations about the mathematical ideas.

Consider the task of investigating the diagonals of quadrilaterals. Students can begin exploring rectangles, because they often are seen as the typical quadrilateral. After constructing a rectangle on the computer screen, students can measure any and all of the attributes of the object (Figure 12.2). In Figure 12.2, the students may notice that the diagonals are equal in length and

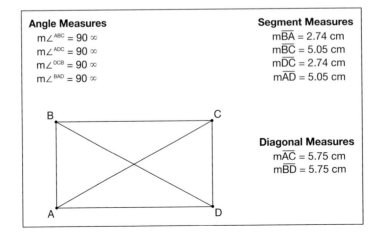

Figure 12.2.   Dynamic geometry program example: rectangle with measurements.

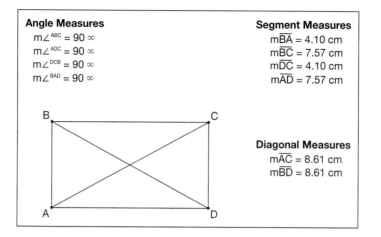

Figure 12.3. Dynamic geometry program example: enlarging rectangle maintains equal-length diagonals.

may wonder whether this relationship remains constant if they change the size of the rectangle. Consequently, they click on and drag one of the vertices and see not only that the angle measures remain at 90 degrees but also that the lengths of the diagonals remain equal to each other (Figure 12.3). They can continue to change the size of the rectangle until they have seen enough examples to be convinced that the diagonals of a rectangle are equal in length. Some students then may look at how the diagonals seem to bisect each other (or cut each other in half). They can measure each of those segments and generate as many examples as needed to become convinced that this also is a characteristic of diagonals of a rectangle.

Because squares are special cases of rectangles, the students may suspect that the diagonals in squares also bisect each other, but they need to see a picture and measure it to be certain. With a dynamic geometry program, they can check whether what they suspect seems to be true. By generating several examples of squares and their diagonals, their suspicions can be confirmed, but as they are exploring this characteristic of a square's diagonals, they notice that the angles where the diagonals intersect seem to be right angles. When they measure the angles, sure enough, their conjecture is verified (Figure 12.4). They go back to check the angles formed by the diagonals in rectangles and see that although the angles are not right angles, pairs of angles are congruent (e.g., in Figure 12.5, angles BEA and CED and angles DEA and CEB are congruent).

Now that they have generated several examples and seen the measures of the diagonals in rectangles (which includes squares), they begin to develop the generalizations that diagonals in rectangles bisect each other and that at least pairs of angles are congruent. They can continue their exploration of diagonals in other kinds of quadrilaterals (e.g., rhombus, trapezoid, kite) and compare their findings, continuing to develop more generalizations.

One of the biggest benefits of dynamic geometry programs is that they allow students to generate several examples easily and quickly. All of these examples can increase students' confidence in the validity of their conjectures, but it does not explain why the conjectures are true. Fortunately, explorations

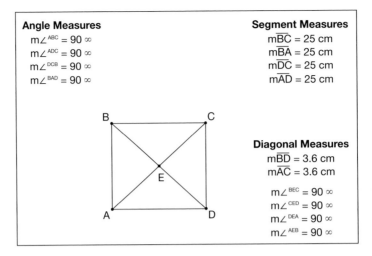

Angle Measures

$m\angle^{ABC} = 90\ \infty$
$m\angle^{ADC} = 90\ \infty$
$m\angle^{DCB} = 90\ \infty$
$m\angle^{BAD} = 90\ \infty$

Segment Measures

$m\overline{BC} = 25$ cm
$m\overline{BA} = 25$ cm
$m\overline{DC} = 25$ cm
$m\overline{AD} = 25$ cm

Diagonal Measures

$m\overline{BD} = 3.6$ cm
$m\overline{AC} = 3.6$ cm

$m\angle^{BEC} = 90\ \infty$
$m\angle^{CED} = 90\ \infty$
$m\angle^{DEA} = 90\ \infty$
$m\angle^{AEB} = 90\ \infty$

Figure 12.4.   A square's diagonals bisect each other at right angles.

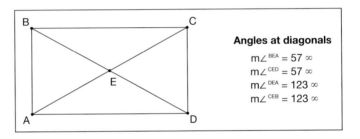

Angles at diagonals

$m\angle^{BEA} = 57\ \infty$
$m\angle^{CED} = 57\ \infty$
$m\angle^{DEA} = 123\ \infty$
$m\angle^{CEB} = 123\ \infty$

Figure 12.5.   The angles formed by a rectangle's diagonals form pairs of congruent angles.

with dynamic geometry programs also can generate ideas that may be useful in creating formal proofs (a deductive argument—not based on specific examples or numbers—using ideas whose absolute truth has already been established to be certain that a particular outcome holds for all cases).

Consider an example to illustrate this point. Most students after a certain age know that the sum of the angles in a triangle is 180 degrees, but many are not able to explain why this always holds. Using a dynamic geometry program, they can create several different triangles, noticing what happens to the sum of the angles (the sum does not change). At some point, by at least high school, students need to realize that on the basis of several examples, it seems that the sum of the angles is always 180 degrees, but they do not know this with absolute certainty because they cannot check every possible triangle; that is, they cannot be sure that the pattern will not break. Because checking every possible triangle is impossible, there is a need to look for other ways to be certain that this outcome holds for all cases. At this point, the teacher can encourage students to develop a deductive argument using ideas that they know are true (e.g., alternate interior angles are equivalent; supplemental angles are 180 degrees). The teacher might provide Figure 12.6 (without the measurements) as a point of exploration.

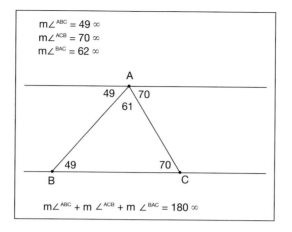

Figure 12.6. Using alternate interior angles, prove that the sum of the angles in a triangle is 180 degrees.

After measuring various parts of the figure (e.g., angles, segment lengths), students should recognize that there are two pairs of angles that are congruent. Why is this so? What relationship do these angles have to each other? They are alternate interior angles that they know are congruent to each other when formed between two parallel lines. Using these reasons, students can develop a deductive argument that does not rely on particular examples or numbers but rather is general in nature and so covers all possible cases.

Students also can use technology with graphing capabilities to explore algebraic ideas. When students graph equations, they are creating a visual representation or model of an algebraic idea, which provides them with a different perspective on what the equation means. For instance, consider how students can use graphing technology to investigate linear equations (y = mx + b). With graphing calculators, students are able to generate graphs quickly, which leaves more time for them to spend on what-if questions, such as, "What if the b value equals 0?" or, "What if the coefficient with the x is a fraction between 0 and 1?" With graphing technology, students can keep one of the coefficients in y = mx + b constant as they explore how changes in the other constant affect the graph. As an example, they could explore the equation y = 3x + b by using different values for b. In the various graphs that they produce, they can recognize that the b simply moves the graph of the line up and down on the y axis (Figure 12.7). When students learn that the b is called the y intercept, it all makes sense! Similarly, students can use technology to explore the behavior of other kinds of equations, such as quadratic and cubic functions.

Some dynamic geometry programs, such as Key Curriculum Press's Geometer's Sketchpad (see http://www.keypress.com/sketchpad for more information), also offer graphing capabilities. An added bonus with dynamic geometry programs such as Geometer's Sketchpad is that the sketches allow one to change colors as well as the type of lines and line segments (thin, heavy, or dotted). The line-width and color options with many technologies allow the teacher and the students to change parts of their sketches to highlight the parts that they want to emphasize.

	Number of baskets made	Number of baskets missed
Day 1	20	30
Day 2	18	32
Day 3	25	25
Day 4	23	27
Day 5	29	21
Day 6	32	18
Day 7	33	17
Day 8	40	10
Day 9	35	15
Mean	28.3	21.7
Median	29.0	21.0

Figure 12.7. Spread sheet example: free-throw data.

Spreadsheets also are useful tools that can help students to modify their understanding of particular mathematical ideas, such as mean and median. They provide students with a way to organize and analyze their own data sets, making it personally interesting for them. For example, consider the free-throw data that were collected and entered into a spreadsheet by a middle school student in Figure 12.7. The student wondered how the mean and the median would be affected if, on day 4, he had an "off" day and did not hit any free throws. When he changed the data, he noticed that the mean fluctuated while the median remained constant (see Figure 12.8). This made him wonder whether means were more sensitive to outliers (data that are either relatively smaller or larger than the rest of the data) than medians. Further exploration of this data set and other data sets convinced him that this is indeed true.

	Number of baskets made	Number of baskets missed
Day 1	20	30
Day 2	18	32
Day 3	25	25
Day 4	0	50
Day 5	29	21
Day 6	32	18
Day 7	33	17
Day 8	40	10
Day 9	35	15
Mean	25.8	24.2
Median	29.0	21.0

Figure 12.8. Spread sheet example: modified free-throw data.

Spreadsheets also provide opportunities for students to look for ways to use generalizations. For example, as this student was entering his data, he realized that the second column (number of baskets missed) was simply 50 minus the number of baskets that he made. He created the formula 50 − M, where M was the number of baskets that he made. Then, when he manipulated his data, he did not have to re-enter the data for the second column because it was updated automatically. Situations such as this also provide students with a purposeful use of variables and equations, making algebra more meaningful to them.

Facilitating Higher Order Thinking by Circumventing Basic Skill Difficulties

Some educators might believe that students should never be allowed to use calculators until they have mastered their basic facts and computational algorithms. One perspective is to evaluate the purpose of the activity. If the purpose is to develop computational proficiency, then calculators may not be suitable. However, if the purpose is to engage students in using basic facts to learn about and do higher order mathematics, then the use of calculators is suitable. For example, calculators are excellent tools for pattern seeking and problem solving. Calculators can be used to create and extend patterns such as in skip-counting. When students are first learning to skip-count, using the calculator to skip-count say by fives allows students to see that the numbers alternatingly end in 0 and 5. Calculators can be used for problem solving, as when students are investigating the behavior of linear or quadratic graphs in general. For these uses, the calculator is supportive or compensatory in nature because it frees the students to focus on higher order reasoning without having to be concerned with remembering basic facts or algorithmic procedures. This is an especially important consideration with students who have difficulties with memory, processing, and attention.

Activities with calculators can be motivating for students when they are incorporated into an instructional game format (see Chapter 9). Consider a game called Wipe Out. This calculator game can either reinforce or further a student's understanding of place value. In the game of Wipe Out, the students are asked to enter into a calculator a multidigit number, such as 384. In this example the students' task would be to subtract one number so that the 8 is wiped out, or becomes 0. Although simple in nature, this game can be both challenging to students and can provide teachers with insight into students' understanding of place value. When working with a group of second and third graders in a particular school district, some teachers were convinced that their students would find this game too simple because they already "understood" place value. Consequently, they were surprised at how the activity revealed their students' superficial understanding of place value. They were equally surprised at how the technology (the calculator) enabled students to achieve a more complete understanding of place value. The use of the calculator allowed something to happen that the students were not expecting: When they subtracted an 8, the 8 in the tens place did not become 0! The students were intrigued by this unexpected result and began making hypotheses and testing those hypotheses with the calculator until they were successful in wiping out the target digit.

TEACHING STRATEGIES FOR INCORPORATING THE USE OF TECHNOLOGY

Technology offers the benefits of providing different representations of various mathematical ideas (e.g., graphs, equation), providing ways to organize and analyze data efficiently as well as ways to compute efficiently and accurately to free students for more complex tasks so that they can focus on the conceptual ideas and reasoning rather than solely on the procedures. However great the benefits of technology, technology can be frustrating to use if one is not aware of strategies that can facilitate how struggling learners interact with the technology and, consequently, the mathematics.

Guidelines for Deciding When and How to Use Technology

Because people assume that technology makes tasks easier, some students will always reach for the technology before thinking whether technology in fact will make a given task easier or more understandable. Ball and Stacey (2005) described four teaching strategies for facilitating judicious use of technology by students. These suggestions have been adapted here to address the needs of struggling learners:

1. Promote careful decision making about technology use.

    *   The teacher and the students should share, on a regular basis, reasons for using various approaches (e.g., mental, paper and pencil, technology) for particular situations (e.g., think-alouds). Always review with struggling learners how technology will help them achieve the learning objective before beginning its use in a lesson.

    *   Students should track their use of technology to determine whether they are overusing or underusing technology. Self-evaluation strategy cue sheets, such as those described in Chapters 9 through 11, can help struggling learners to evaluate their use of technology independently, what they used particular technology applications to do, and whether these applications worked.

2. Integrate technology into the curriculum. The teacher should

    *   Plan to show examples and nonexamples of when technology is a good way to illustrate or think about a particular mathematical concept or to perform a particular mathematical skill. This can engage students in thinking critically about technology use and the important features of the target mathematics

    *   Encourage students to make their own choices of approaches in doing mathematics (e.g., mental, paper and pencil, technology) and to justify their choices

    *   Maintain a focus on learning the mathematics, not on learning the technology

3. Tactically restrict the use of technology for a limited time to meet specific learning objectives

    • Restrict the use of technology for part of a lesson when the goal is to enhance mathematical insight (e.g., students are given a number such as 144 and are asked to estimate the square root, then are prompted to ask, "Is my estimate, answer, or result reasonable?"). Then technology can be used to check/verify (e.g., calculator can be used to determine the square root of the number 144 after students have developed their own estimates and rationales for their estimate).

    • Do not use technology during lessons when other approaches best help students to develop understanding of a particular concept (e.g., concrete objects) or of necessary paper-and-pencil skills (e.g., computations, drawing graphs).

    • Restrict the use of technology to enhance students' appreciation of what technology can do for enhancing their learning of and doing mathematics. Guide students to engage in a mathematics task using a nontechnological approach, and then complete the same task using the appropriate technology application. Brainstorm with students why one or the other was more efficient.

4. Promote habits of using "mathematical insight" for overview and monitoring. The teacher and the students model mathematical insight by using information in each problem to make an educated guess (estimate) of the result and continuing to monitor results that are produced by technology ("Does the result make sense given what I know?"). Students with learning difficulties benefit from teachers who make modeling these habits a priority and who support them as they use technology to check/monitor their developing insights. The teacher can be the one who does the modeling of these habits, or a student can be the one who models these habits. The important idea is that these habits be modeled explicitly and made apparent to all of the students in the classroom.

Techniques and Strategies to Incorporate When Integrating Technology in Mathematics Instruction for Struggling Learners

As in most tasks, struggling learners should be provided with an appropriate level of structure and guidance with the integration of technology and mathematics in order to increase the likelihood that they will develop valid mathematical ideas and connect these ideas to their existing knowledge base. The instructional practices described in Chapters 8 through 11 should be applied when using technology in mathematics instruction, just as they should when technology is not integrated. Four additional ideas to remember are as follows:

1. *Model metacognitive thinking and technology use.* Once students understand how to use the technology (e.g., calculator, computer program), using an inquiry mode is just as important as when the teacher is not teaching

with technology. Because students may have trouble remembering which keys to use on a calculator or which tools to use in a software program, teachers can model explicitly the types of questions that they ask themselves and the trial-and-error approach that they might take in exploring the technology as well as the mathematics. For example, to explore a graphing calculator, a teacher might think aloud about which keys to use when a graph does not appear in the graphing window: "Hmmm . . . I typed in x^2 + 13 and hit "graph," but it did not graph it. Okay, I see the coordinate plane, but the graph is not showing in the window. I know that I entered the equation correctly. Maybe the graph is somewhere else on the coordinate plane than right around (0,0). I'll try to change the scale on the x and y axes. The "window" key might work. Yes, I'll change it so that the window shows between –20 and 20 on both the x and y axes. Now hit "graph." There it is! And no wonder! That 13 makes it go up the y axis 13 spaces."

2. Model the use of any technology before using it to learn mathematics or provide opportunities for practice. Always model the use of any technology that is incorporated into the classroom and provide students with opportunities to practice using it before expecting them to use it to learn a new mathematical concept. Remember that the purpose of integrating technology in mathematics instruction is to enhance students' learning of mathematics. For struggling learners, adding the frustration of not knowing how to use technology to the mix is not helpful, particularly given the barriers that these students already experience.

3. Provide visual cues or directions for manipulating technology. Create posters or displays that cue students about how to use particular technology applications, and post them close to areas where technology is used by students. Cue sheets that highlight the steps for using technology for particular purposes (e.g., which buttons on a graphing calculator perform certain functions and in which order they should be pressed to perform a certain operation). Color-code paper examples of a spreadsheet so that students can visualize where certain information should be entered and which formulas might relate to certain cells.

4. Ensure that the technology is accessible to all students. Teachers who have students with disabilities must ensure that the appropriate assistive adaptations are made available so that each student can use and learn through technology as appropriate to that student (e.g., screen readers for students with visual impairments, switches for students with motor/physical impairments). See the Council for Exceptional Children Technology and Media Division (http://www.tamcec.org) and Center for Applied Special Technology (http://www.cast.org) web sites for more information about accessibility and use of technology.

The same theme that runs through the other chapters in this book also should be observed here: Mathematics must be made meaningful for students. Technology offers an efficient way for students both to self-check and to modify their mathematical understanding so that the mathematics makes sense.

References

Allinder, R.M., Bolling, R.M., Oats, R.G., & Gagnon, W.A. (2000). Effects of teacher self-monitoring on implementation of curriculum-based measurement and mathematics computation achievement of students with disabilities. *Remedial and Special Education, 21,* 219–226.

Allsopp, D.H. (1997). Using classwide peer tutoring to teach beginning algebra problem solving skills in heterogeneous classrooms. *Remedial and Special Education, 18,* 367–380.

Allsopp, D.H. (1999). Using modeling, manipulatives, and mnemonics with eighth grade students. *Teaching Exceptional Children, 32*(2), 74–81.

Allsopp, D.H. (2001). *Building algebra skills: A beginning algebra program for students who have difficulty learning mathematics.* Unpublished manuscript.

Allsopp, D.H. (in press). Meaningful mathematics instruction. In J. Langone & S. Smith (Eds.), *Instructional strategies for students with mild disabilities.* Upper Saddle River, NJ: Prentice Hall.

Allsopp, D.H., Ingram, R.E., & Kyger, M.M. (2001). *MathVIDS: Mathematics Video Instructional Development Series.* Retrieved February 27, 2006, from http://coe.jmu.edu/mathvidsr.

Allsopp, D.H., Lovin, L., Green, G.W., & Savage-Davis, E. (2003). Why students with high incidence disabilities have difficulty learning mathematics and what teachers can do to help. *Mathematics Teaching in the Middle School, 8,* 308–314.

Allsopp, D.H., Minskoff, E.H., & Bolt, L. (2005). Individualized course-specific strategy instruction for college students with learning disabilities and ADHD: Lessons from a model demonstration project. *Learning Disabilities Research & Practice, 20,* 103–118.

Ball, L. & Stacey, K. (2005). Teaching strategies for developing judicious technology use. In W. Masalski (Ed.), *Technology-Supported Mathematics Learning Environments* (pp. 3–16). Reston, VA: NCTM.

Baroody, A. (1987). *Children's mathematical thinking: A developmental framework for preschool, primary, and special education teachers.* New York: Teachers College Press.

Baxter, J.A., Woodward, J., & Olson, D. (2005). Writing in mathematics: An alternative form of communication for academically low-achieving students. *Learning Disabilities Research & Practice, 20,* 119–135.

Begle, E. (1979). *Critical variables in mathematics education: Findings from a survey of the empirical literature.* Washington, D.C.: Mathematical Association of America and National Council of Teachers of Mathematics.

Beirne-Smith, M. (1991). Peer tutoring in arithmetic for children with learning disabilities. *Exceptional Children, 57,* 330–337.

Black, P., & Dylan Williams, D. (1998). Assessment and classroom learning. *Assessment in Education, 5*(1), 7–74.

Bley N.S., & Thornton, C.A.(1995). *Teaching mathematics to students with learning disabilities* (3rd ed.). Austin, TX: PRO-ED.

Borkowski, J.G. (1992). Metacognitive theory: A framework for teaching literacy, writing, and math skills. *Journal of Learning Disabilities, 25,* 253–257.

Bottge, B.A. (1999). Effects of contextualized math instruction on problem solving of average and below-average achieving students. *The Journal of Special Education, 33,* 81–92.

Bottge, B.A., Heinrichs, M., Chan, S., Mehta, Z.D., & Watson, E. (2003). Effects of video-based and applied problems on the procedural math skills of average- and low-achieving adolescents. *Journal of Special Education Technology, 18*(2), 5–22.

Bottge, B.A., Heinrichs, M., Chan, S., & Serlin, R. (2001). Anchoring adolescents' understanding of math concepts in rich problem solving environments. *Remedial and Special Education, 22,* 299–314.

Bottge, B.A., Heinrichs, M., Mehta, Z.D., Rueda, E., Hung, Y., & Danneker, J. (2004). Teaching mathematical problem solving to middle school students in math, technology education, and special education classrooms. *Research in Middle Level Education On-line, 27*(1). Retrieved August 1, 2006, from http://www.nmsa.org/research/rmle/winter_03/27_1_article_1.htm.

Brophy, J., & Good, T.L. (1986). Teacher behavior and student achievement. In M.C. Wittrock (Ed.), *Handbook of research on teaching* (3rd ed., pp. 328–375). Upper Saddle River, NJ: Prentice Hall.

Bryant, B.R. (1996). Using alternative assessment techniques to plan and evaluate mathematics instruction. *LD Forum, 21* (2), 24–33.

Burns, M. (1996, April). How to make the most of math manipulatives. *Instructor,* 45–50.

Butler, D.L., Beckingham, B., & Novak-Lauscher, H.J. (2005). Promoting strategic learning by eighth-grade students struggling in mathematics: A report of three case studies. *Learning Disabilities Research & Practice, 20,* 156–174.

Butler, F.M., Miller, S.P., Crehan, K., Babbitt, B., & Pierce, T. (2003). *Learning Disabilities: Research & Practice, 18,* 99–111.

Calhoon, B., & Fuchs, L. (2003). The effects of peer-assisted learning strategies and curriculum-based measurement on the mathematics performance of secondary students with disabilities. *Remedial and Special Education, 24,* 235–245.

Carnine, D.W., Dixon, R.C., & Silbert, J. (1998). Effective strategies for teaching mathematics. In E. Kameenui & D. Carnine (Eds.), *Effective teaching strategies that accommodate diverse learners.* Upper Saddle River, NJ: Prentice Hall.

Carpenter, T.P., Fennema, E., Franke, M.L., Levi, L., & Empson, S.B. (1999). *Children's mathematics: Cognitively guided instruction.* Reston, VA: National Council of Teachers of Mathematics, 1999.

Cawley, J. (2002). Mathematics interventions and students with high incidence disabilities. *Remedial and Special Education, 23,* 2–6.

Cawley, J., Parmar, R., Foley, T.E., Salmon, S., & Roy, S. (2001). Arithmetic performance of students: Implications for standards and programming. *Exceptional Children, 67,* 311–328.

Cawley, J.F., Parmar, R.S., Yan, W., & Miller, J.H. (1998). Arithmetic computation performance of students with learning disabilities: Implication for curriculum. *Learning Disabilities Research & Practice, 13,* 68–74.

Chard, D., & Gersten, R. (1999). Number sense: Rethinking arithmetic instruction for students with mathematical disabilities. *Journal of Special Education, 33,* 18–28.

Cobb, P., Yackel, E., & Wood, T. (1992). A constructivist alternative to the representational view of mind in mathematics education. *Journal for Research in Mathematics Education, 23,* 2–33.

Darling-Hammond, L. (2000). Teacher quality and student achievement: A review of state policy evidence. *Educational Policy Analysis Archives, 8*(1), 1–51.

Deshler, D.D., & Schumaker, J.B. (1986). Learning strategies: An instructional alternative for low-achieving adolescents. *Exceptional Children, 52,* 583–590.

Ed.gov. (2004). *Key policy letters signed by the education secretary or deputy secretary.* Washington, DC: U.S. Department of Education. Retrieved February 10, 2006, from http://www.ed.gov/policy/elsec/guid/secletter/040331.html.

Englert, C.S., Garmon, A., Mariage, T., Rozendal, M., Tarrant, K., & Urba, J. (1995). The early literacy project: Connecting across the literacy curriculum. *Learning Disability Quarterly, 18,* 253–275.

Englert, C.S., & Mariage, T.V. (1991). Shared understandings: Structuring the writing experience through dialogue. *Journal of Learning Disabilities, 24,* 330–342.

Educational Resources Information Center/Office of Special Education Programs Special Project. (2002). Strengthening the third "R": Helping students with disabilities achieve in mathematics. *Research Connections in Special Education, 11,* 1–7.

Florida Department of Education State Board of Education Administrative Rules. (2003). Retrieved July 31, 2006 from http://www.firn.edu/doe/rules/6a-5.htm#6A-5.066.

Fuchs, L.S., & Fuchs, D. (2001). Principles for the prevention and intervention of mathematics difficulties. *Learning Disabilities Research & Practice, 16,* 85–95.

Fuchs, L.S., Fuchs, D., Hamlett, C.L., Phillips, N.B., & Bentz, J. (1994). Classwide curriculum-based measurement: Helping general educators meet the challenge of student diversity. *Exceptional Children, 60,* 518–537.

Gagnon, J.C., & Maccini, P. (2001). Preparing students with disabilities for algebra. *Teaching Exceptional Children, 34*(1), 8–15.

Gardner, J.E., & Wissick, C.A., (2005). Web-based resources and instructional considerations for students with mild cognitive disabilities. Eds. Edyburn, D., Higgins, K., & Boone, R. *The handbook of special education technology: Research and practice* (pp. 683–718). Whitefish Bay, WI: Knowledge by Design.

Geary, D.C. (1993). Mathematical disabilities: Cognitive, neuropsychological, and genetic components. *Psychological Bulletin, 114,* 345–362.

Gersten, R. (1998). Recent advances in instructional research for students with learning disabilities: An overview. *Learning Disabilities Research and Practice, 13,* 162–170.

Gersten, R., Baker, S., & Edwards, L. (1999). Teaching expressive writing to students with learning disabilities. ERIC Digest #E590. ERIC Clearinghouse on Disabilities and Gifted Education (ERIC EC). Arlington, VA: The Council for Exceptional Children.

Ginsburg, H.P. (1987). How to assess number facts, calculation, and understanding. In D.D. Hammill (Ed.), *Assessing the abilities and instructional needs of students* (pp. 483–503). Austin, TX: PRO-ED.

Ginsburg, H.P. (1997). Mathematics learning disabilities: A view from developmental psychology. *Journal of Learning Disabilities, 30,* 20–33.

Goodlad, S., & Hirst, B. (1989). *Peer tutoring. A guide to learning by teaching.* New York: Nichols Publishing.

Graham, S., & Harris, K.R. (1989). Improving learning disabled students' skills at composing essays: Self-instructional strategy training. *Exceptional Children, 56,* 201–214.

Graham, S., Harris, K.R., & Larsen, L. (2001). Prevention and intervention of writing difficulties with students with learning problems. *Learning Disabilities Research & Practice, 16,* 74–84.

Greenwood, C.R. (1991). Classwide peer tutoring: Longitudinal effects on the reading, language, and mathematics achievement of at risk students. *Reading, Writing, and Learning Disabilities International, 7,* 105–123.

Greenwood, C.R., Terry, B., Arreaga-Mayer, C., & Finney, R. (1992). The classwide peer tutoring program: Implementation factors moderating students' achievement. *Journal of Applied Behavior Analysis, 25*, 101–116.

Harper, G.F., Mallette, B., Maheady, L., & Brennan, G. (1993). Classwide student tutoring teams and direct instruction as a combined instructional program to teach generalizeable strategies for mathematics word problems. *Education and Treatment of Children, 16*, 115–134.

Harris, C.A., Miller, S.P., & Mercer, C.D. (1995). Teaching initial multiplication skills to students with disabilities in general education classrooms. *Learning Disabilities Research & Practice, 10*, 180–195.

Hecht, S.A., Torgesen, J.K., Wagner, R.K., & Rashotte, C.A. (2001). The relations between phonological processing abilities and emerging individual differences in mathematical computation skills: A longitudinal study from second to fourth grade. *Journal of Experimental Child Psychology, 79*, 192–227.

Howell, K.W., Fox, S.L., & Morehead, M.K. (1993). *Curriculum-based evaluation: Teaching and decision-making* (2nd ed.). Pacific Grove, CA: Brooks/Cole.

Hughes, C.A., & Maccini, P. (2000). Effects of a problem-solving strategy on the introductory algebra performance of secondary students with learning disabilities. *Learning Disabilities Research & Practice, 15*, 10–21.

iMovie HD. © 1999–2006 Apple Computer Inc. All rights reserved.

Inspiration, Kidspiration. 1988–2006 Inspiration Software, Inc. All rights reserved.

Jitendra, A., Hoff, K., & Beck, M. (1999). Teaching middle school students with learning disabilities to solve word problems using a schema-based approach. *Remedial and Special Education, 20*, 50–64.

Johnson, D.W., & Johnson, R.T. (1986). Mainstreaming and cooperative learning strategies. *Exceptional Children, 52*, 553–561.

Kami, C. (1985). *Young children reinvent arithmetic*. New York: Teachers College Press.

Kami, C. (1989). *Young children continue to reinvent arithmetic: 2nd grade*. New York: Teachers College Press.

Kami, C. (2000). *Young children reinvent arithmetic: Implications of Piaget's theory*. New York: Teachers College Press.

Kennedy, L.M., & Tipps, S. (1994). *Guiding children's learning of mathematics* (7th ed.). Belmont, CA: Wadsworth.

Kennedy, L.M., & Tipps, S. (1998). *Guiding children's learning of mathematics* (8th ed.). Belmont, CA: Wadsworth.

Kerrigan, J. (2002). Powerful software to enhance the elementary schools mathematics program. *Teaching Children Mathematics, 8*(6), 364–370.

Kroesbergen, E., & van Luit, J. (2002). Teaching multiplication to low math performers: Guided versus structured instruction. *Instructional Science, 30*, 361–378.

Kroesbergen, E.H., & van Luit, J.E.H. (2003). Mathematics interventions for children with special educational needs. *Remedial and Special Education, 24*, 97–114.

Lamon, S. (1996). Ratio and proportion: Connecting content and children's thinking. *Journal for Research in Mathematics Education, 24*, 41–61.

Lamon, S. (1999). *Teaching fractions and ratios for understanding: Essential content knowledge and instructional strategies for teachers*. Mahwah, NJ: Lawrence Erlbaum & Associates.

Lavoie, R.D. (1993, March). *Batteries are not included: Motivating the reluctant learner*. Paper presented at the Learning Disabilities Association International Conference, Washington, DC.

Lenz, B.K., Ellis, E.S., & Scanlon, D. (1996). *Teaching learning strategies to adolescents and adults with learning disabilities*. Austin, TX: PRO-ED.

Lewis, R.B., & Doorlag, D.H. (1999). *Teaching special students in general education classrooms* (5th ed.). Upper Saddle River, NJ: Prentice Hall.

Liedtke, W. (1988, November). Diagnosis in mathematics: The advantages of an inter-view. *Arithmetic Teacher*, 181–184.

Lock, R.H. (1996, Winter). Adapting mathematics instruction in the general education classroom for students with mathematics disabilities. *LD Forum 21*(4), 1–9.

Lovin, L., Kyger, M., & Allsopp, D. (2004). Differentiation for special needs learners, *Teaching Children Mathematics* (11), p. 158–167.

Maccini, P., & Gagnon, J.C. (2000). Best practices for teaching mathematics to second-ary students with special needs. *Focus on Exceptional Children, 32*, 1–22.

Maccini, P., & Gagnon, J.C. (2002). Perceptions and applications of NCTM standards by special and general education teachers. *Exceptional Children, 68*, 325–344.

Maccini, P., & Gagnon, J. C. (2005). Mathematics and technology-based interventions for secondary students with learning disabilities. In D. Edyburn, K. Higgins, & R. Boone, *The handbook of special education technology research and practice* (pp. 599–622). Winston-Salem, NC: Knowledge By Design, Inc.

Maheady, L., Harper, G.F., & Mallette, B. (1991). Peer-mediated instruction: A review of potential applications for special education. *Reading, Writing, and Learning Dis-abilities, 7*, 75–103.

Mason, L.H., Harris, K.R., & Graham, S. (2002). Every child has a story to tell: Self-regulated strategy development for story writing. *Educational Treatment of Chil-dren, 25*(4), 496–506.

Mathematics Video Development Source (MathVIDS). (2001). Virginia Department of Education/James Madison University. Available at: http://coe.jmu.edu/mathvidsr.

Mathes, P.G., Fuchs, D., Fuchs, L.S., Henley, A.M., & Sanders, A. (1994). Increasing strategic reading practice with Peabody classwide peer tutoring. *Learning Disabili-ties Research & Practice, 9*, 44–48.

Mercer, C., Harris, C., & Miller, P. (1993). First invited response: Reforming reforms in mathematics. *Remedial and Special Education, 14*, 14–19.

Mercer, C.D., Jordan, L., & Miller, S.P. (1996). Constructivistic math instruction for di-verse learners. *Learning Disabilities Research & Practice, 11*, 147–156.

Mercer, C.D., Lane, H.B., Jordan, L, Allsopp, D.H., & Eisele, M.R. (1996). Empowering teachers and students with instructional choices in inclusive settings. *Remedial and Special Education, 17*, 226–236.

Mercer, C.D., & Mercer, A.R. (2005). *Teaching students with learning problems* (7th ed.). Upper Saddle River, NJ: Prentice Hall.

Miller, S., & Mercer, C. (1993). Mnemonics: Enhancing the math performance of stu-dents with learning difficulties. *Intervention in School and Clinic, 29*, 78–82.

Miller, S., Strawser, S., & Mercer, C. (1996). Promoting strategic math performance among students with learning disabilities. *LD Forum, 21*, 34–40.

Miller, S.P., Butler, F.M., & Lee, K. (1998). Validated practices for teaching mathemat-ics to students with learning disabilities: A review of the literature. *Focus on Excep-tional Children, 31*, 1–24.

Miller, S.P., & Mercer, C.D. (1993). Using data to learn about concrete-semiconcrete-abstract instruction for students with math disabilities. *Learning Disabilities Re-search & Practice, 8*, 89–96.

Miller, S.P., & Mercer, C.D. (1997). Educational aspects of mathematics disabilities. *Journal of Learning Disabilities, 30*, 47–56.

Miller, S.P., Mercer, C.D., & Dillon, A.S. (1992). CSA: Acquiring and attaining math skills—A systematic and practical approach to teaching basic math skills at the con-crete, semi-concrete, and abstract levels. *Intervention in School and Clinic, 28*, 105–110.

Minskoff, E.H. (1998). Sam Kirk: The man who made special education special. *Learn-ing Disabilities Research and Practice, 13*(1), 15–21.

Minskoff, E., & Allsopp, D. (2003). *Academic success strategies for adolescents with learning disabilities and ADHD.* Baltimore: Paul H. Brookes Publishing Co.

Monk, D. (1994). Subject area preparation of secondary mathematics and science teachers and student achievement. *Economics of Education Review, 13*(2), 125–145.

Montague, M. (1992). The effects of cognitive and metacognitive strategy instruction on the mathematical problem solving of middle school students with learning disabilities. *Journal of Learning Disabilities, 25,* 230–248.

Montague, M., Morgan, T.H., & Warger, C. (2000). Solve it! Strategy instruction to improve mathematical problem solving. *Learning Disabilities Research & Practice, 15,* 110–116.

National Council of Teachers of Mathematics. (2000). *Principles and standards for school mathematics.* Reston, VA: National Council of Teachers of Mathematics.

No Child Left Behind Act of 2001, PL 107-110, 115 Stat. 1425, 20 U.S.C. §§ 6301 *et seq.*

Osguthorpe, R.T., & Scruggs, T.E. (1990). Special education students as tutors: A review and analysis. In S. Goodlad & B. Hirst (Eds.), *Peer tutoring: A guide to learning by teaching* (pp. 176–193). New York: Nichols Publishing.

Owen, R.L., & Fuchs, L.S. (2002). Mathematical problem-solving strategy instruction for third-grade students with learning disabilities. *Remedial and Special Education, 34,* 268–278.

Paris, S.G., & Winograd, P. (1990). Promoting metacognition and motivation of exceptional children. *Remedial and Special Education, 11,* 7–15.

Parmar, R.S., & Cawley, J.F. (1991). Challenging the routines and passivity that characterize arithmetic instruction for children with mild handicaps. *Remedial and Special Education, 12,* 23–32.

Peterson, S.K., Mercer, C.D., & O'Shea, L. (1988). Teaching learning disabled children place value using the concrete to abstract sequence. *Learning Disabilities Research, 4,* 52–56.

Polloway, E.A., & Patton, J.R. (1993). *Strategies for teaching learners with high incidence disabilities* (5th ed.). New York: Merrill.

Reed, V. (2005). *An introduction to children with language disorders* (2nd Ed). New York: Merrill.

Rivera, D.P. (1996, Spring). Using cooperative learning to teach mathematics to students with learning disabilities. *LD Forum, 21*(3), 1–9.

Ross, S. (1989). Parts, wholes, and place value: A developmental view. *Arithmetic Teacher,* 47–51.

Schumm, J.S., Vaughn, S., Haager, D., McDowell, J., Rothlein, L., & Saumell, L. (1995). General education teacher planning: What can students with learning disabilities expect? *Exceptional Children, 61*(4), 335–352.

Shafer, P. (1998). Three ways to improve math scores. *Principal, 78,* 26–27.

Skemp, R. (1978). Relational understanding and instrumental understanding. *Arithmetic Teacher, 26*(3), 9–15.

Slavin, R.E. (1990). *Cooperative learning theory, research, and practice.* Upper Saddle River, NJ: Prentice Hall.

Strichart, S.S., Mangrum, C.T., & Iannuzzi, P. (1998). Teaching study skills and strategies to students with learning disabilities: Support for a combined strategy and direct instruction model. *Learning Disabilities Research & Practice, 14,* 129–140.

Sullivan, P. & Lilburn, P. (2002). *Good questions for math teaching: Why ask them and what to ask, Grades K–6.* Sausalito, CA: Math Solutions Publications.

Sutherland, K.S., & Wehby, J.H. (2001). Exploring the relationship between increased opportunities to respond to academic requests and the academic and behavioral outcomes of students with EBD. *Remedial and Special Education, 22,* 113–121.

Swanson, H.L. (1999). Instructional components that predict treatment outcomes for students with learning disabilities: Support for a combined strategy and direct instruction model. *Learning Disabilities Research & Practice, 14*(3), 129–140.

Tomey, H.A. (1998, March). *Mathematics, it's elementary Dr. Watson.* Paper presented at the Learning Disabilities Association International Conference, Washington, DC.

Van de Walle, J.A. (1994). *Elementary school mathematics: Teaching developmentally* (2nd ed.). White Plains, NY: Longman Publishing Group.

Van de Walle, J.A. (2005). *Elementary school mathematics: Teaching developmentally* (5th ed.). White Plains, NY: Longman Publishing Group.

Van de Walle, J., & Lovin, L. (2006a). *Teaching student-centered mathematics: Grades K–3.* Needham Heights, MA: Allyn & Bacon.

Van de Walle, J. & Lovin, L. (2006b). *Teaching student-centered mathematics: Grades 3–5.* Needham Heights, MA: Allyn & Bacon.

Van de Walle, J., & Lovin, L. (2006c). *Teaching student-centered mathematics: Grades 5–8.* Needham Heights, MA: Allyn & Bacon.

van Hiele, P. M. (1986). *Structure and insight: A theory of mathematics education.* Orlando, FL: Academic Press, Inc.

Vaughn, S., Bos, C.S., & Schumm, J.S. (1997). *Teaching mainstreamed, diverse, and at-risk students in the general education classroom.* Needham Heights, MA: Allyn & Bacon.

Vaughn, S., Gersten, R., & Chard, D.J. (2000). The underlying message in LD intervention research: Findings from research syntheses. *Exceptional Children, 67,* 98–114.

Wehmeyer, M.L., Palmer, S., & Agran, M. (1998). Promoting causal agency: The self-determined learning model of instruction. *Exceptional Children, 66*(4), 439–453.

Windows Movie Maker 2.0. © 2006 Microsoft Corporation. All rights reserved.

Witzel, B., Mercer, C.D., & Miller, D. (2003). Teaching algebra to students with learning difficulties: An investigation of an explicit instruction model. *Learning Disabilities Research & Practice, 18,* 121–131.

Woodward, J., & Howard, L. (1994). The misconceptions of youth: Errors and their mathematical meaning. *Exceptional Children, 61,* 126–136.

Zigmond, N., Vallecorsa, A., & Silverman, R. (1981). *Assessment for instructional planning in special education.* Upper Saddle River, NJ: Prentice Hall.

Appendix A

Blank Forms and Charts

CONTENTS

Brainstorming Chart Showing How Mathematics Is Important in the Lives of Struggling Learners Form

Life skills		Graduation/ diploma	Success in other subject areas	Other
Current	Future			

Teacher Self-Reflection Inventory

Instructions: *Briefly respond to each of the following items in a genuine and thoughtful manner.*

1. When I was in school, my experiences with learning mathematics could be described as . . .

2. I tend to teach mathematics differently from how I was taught or from how I learned it (as a pre-K–12 student).

1	2	3	4	5	6	7	8	9	10

    strongly disagree   strongly agree

3. For struggling learners, I believe that successfully learning mathematics is as important as successfully learning to read.

1	2	3	4	5	6	7	8	9	10

    strongly disagree   strongly agree

4. I enjoy teaching mathematics to struggling learners.

1	2	3	4	5	6	7	8	9	10

    strongly disagree   strongly agree

5. I believe that struggling learners can excel and find meaning in mathematics.

1	2	3	4	5	6	7	8	9	10

    strongly disagree   strongly agree

6. Circle the number on the following scale that best represents your confidence/level of comfort with the mathematics content that you teach.

1	2	3	4	5	6	7	8	9	10

    not confident   very confident

7. I fully understand both the National Council of Teachers of Mathematics (NCTM) content standards (what students should learn) and process standards (how students should use and do mathematics) for grade-level mathematics that I teach.

1	2	3	4	5	6	7	8	9	10

    strongly disagree   strongly agree

(continued)

8. My primary focus when I evaluate student progress in mathematics is how accurate students are in arriving at the correct solution.

1	2	3	4	5	6	7	8	9	10

strongly disagree   strongly agree

9. My primary focus when I evaluate student progress in mathematics is the extent to which students communicate their reasoning for how they approached a problem.

1	2	3	4	5	6	7	8	9	10

strongly disagree   strongly agree

10. I am aware of how students think differently from adults about many mathematical ideas and I use this information to inform my teaching.

1	2	3	4	5	6	7	8	9	10

strongly disagree   strongly agree

11. Circle the number that best represents your ability to identify (i.e., knowledge of) specific research-supported learning characteristics that make learning mathematics difficult for struggling learners.

1	2	3	4	5	6	7	8	9	10

I cannot identify any research-supported learning characteristics.   I can identify many research-supported learning characteristics.

12. Circle the number that best represents your knowledge of research-supported curriculum/instructional practices that present mathematical learning barriers for struggling learners.

1	2	3	4	5	6	7	8	9	10

I cannot identify any research-supported curriculum/instructional practices.   I can identify many research-supported curriculum/instructional practices.

13. Circle the number that best represents your knowledge of research-supported effective mathematics instructional strategies that support struggling learners' initial understanding of mathematical concepts/skills.

1	2	3	4	5	6	7	8	9	10

I can't name any.   I can name many.

(continued)

14. Circle the number that best represents your knowledge of research-supported effective mathematics instructional strategies that support struggling learners' development of proficiency in mathematics.

1	2	3	4	5	6	7	8	9	10

I can't name any.   I can name many.

15. Circle the number that best represents your ability to implement research-supported effective mathematics instructional strategies for struggling learners, such that it results in positive student learning outcomes.

1	2	3	4	5	6	7	8	9	10

not very effective   very effective

Self-Evaluation and Scoring Your Responses

Self-Evaluation

Instructions: Once you have completed the Teacher Self-Reflection Inventory, take a few minutes to review your responses. What do your responses tell you about your readiness to be an effective teacher of mathematics for struggling learners in each of the four professional development areas described next (a–d)? Write down your thoughts in the spaces provided after each. Related question numbers are identified in parentheses next to each professional development area listed below.

a. *Valuing mathematics instruction for students with learning difficulties.* Describe your beliefs about the ability of struggling learners to learn mathematics (**questions 1–5**):

b. *Mathematics content knowledge for teaching.* Describe your knowledge of mathematics, the different processes for doing mathematics, and how students make sense of the mathematical content (**questions 6–10**):

c. *Understanding of why students with learning difficulties struggle to learn mathematics.* Describe your understanding of why struggling learners have difficulty learning mathematics (**questions 11–12**):

d. *Research-supported instructional practices for students with learning difficulties.* Describe your understanding of and ability to implement effective mathematics instructional strategies that address the learning needs of struggling learners (**questions 13–15**):

(continued)

Scoring Your Responses

Use the following Individual Professional Development Need Rating Chart to determine your numbered ratings for each question and then find out the level of need that you have for each professional development area.

Individual Professional Development Need Rating Chart

Instructions: *For each set of questions listed below, sum the total rating number. Then consult the rating scale below to determine the level of need suggested for your professional development related to effective mathematics instruction for students with learning difficulties.*

Professional development area	Related questions from the Teacher Self-Reflection Inventory	Score
Valuing mathematics instruction for students with learning difficulties	2–5	_____
Mathematics content knowledge for teaching (content and methods)	6–10	_____
Understanding why students with learning difficulties have difficulty learning mathematics	11–12	_____
Research-supported instructional practices for students with learning difficulties	13–15	_____

Rating Scale

Scoring:

Professional development area	Level of need		
	High need	Medium need	Low need
Valuing mathematics instruction for struggling students	4–16	17–29	30–40
Mathematics content knowledge for teaching (content and methods)	4–16	17–29	30–40
Understanding why struggling learners have difficulty learning mathematics	2–8	9–14	15–20
Research-supported instructional practices for struggling students	3–2	13–22	23–30

Planning for Professional Development

Your responses to the Teacher Self-Reflection Inventory are intended to reveal some insights about your professional development needs. Your total rating score for each professional development area suggests levels of need for professional development in those areas, as well. Now, use both sources of information to plan how best to use this book and *other appropriate resources** to meet your own professional development needs, which you can map out using the Professional Development Planning Form given here. First, compare your self-evaluation of each professional development area with the level of need suggested using the Individual Professional Development Need Rating Chart. For one or more areas, your self-evaluation and the rating scale may be similar. For example, you may have noted in your self-reflection that you are not knowledgeable about research-supported student learning characteristics that make learning mathematics difficult. Perhaps you were not even aware that such information was available. Your rating for this professional development area may show this as an area of high need. Such a situation would mean that this should be a priority for you. In another professional development area, your self-evaluation may differ from the level of need suggested by the rating scale. In such a case, you should evaluate critically what you really understand and what you truly are able to do in that professional development area. Use your best judgment to decide how to prioritize that area in relation to other areas.

Professional Development Planning Form

Priority level	Professional development area	Chapters from *Teaching Mathematics Meaningfully* that address this need	Other sources of information
High			
Medium			
Low			

* For excellent information about mathematical knowledge for teachers and general mathematics education methods we suggest Van de Walle and Lovin (2006a; 2006b; 2006c) and the Navigation Series from NCTM (www.NCTM.org).

Textbook Curriculum Chart

Grade __	Grade __	Similarities and differences
		Similarities: **Differences:**

(Mathematics Student Interest Inventory)

Individual Mathematics Student Interest Inventory Form

Student name: _____

Age/grade level: _____

Period/class: _____

Things I like to do on my own	Special hobbies that I have	Things I like to learn about	Things I like to do with my friends	Fun things my family does together

(Mathematics Student Interest Inventory)

Class Mathematics Student Interest Inventory Form

Period/class: _____

School year: _____

Interests	Relevant mathematics concepts/skills I teach that match interest	Ideas for creating authentic contexts
Individual interests/activities (Columns 1–3 on Individual Mathematics Student Interest Inventory)		
1.		
2.		
Peer-related interests/activities (Column 4 on Individual Mathematics Student Interest Inventory)		
1.		
2.		
Family-related interests/activities (Column 5 on Individual Mathematics Student Student Interest Inventory)		
1.		
2.		

MATHEMATICS INSTRUCTION DECISION-MAKING INVENTORY FOR DIVERSE LEARNERS

The following are part of the Mathematics Instruction Decision-Making Inventory for Diverse Learners (MIDMIDL): Whole-Class Student Characteristics Inventory Form, Individual and Small-Group Student Characteristics Inventory Form, Student Characteristics Rating Guide, Mathematics Curriculum/Content Characteristics Form, and the Mathematics Instructional Planning Guide.

(Mathematics Instruction Decision-Making Inventory for Diverse Learners)

Whole-Class Student Characteristics Inventory Form

Student learning characteristics	Rating scale			Score
1. Number of students receiving special education services.	**Zero** 0	**One to three** 5	**Four or more** 10	
2. Number of students receiving Title I services and/or who are at risk for school failure.	**Zero** 0	**One to three** 5	**Four or more** 10	
3. Number of students receiving free or reduced-cost lunches.	**Zero** 0	**One to three** 5	**Four or more** 10	
4. Number of students whose previous math grades are less than satisfactory (e.g., below a C or S level).	**Zero to two** 0	**Three to five** 5	**Five or more** 10	
5. General achievement level of your class considering all students.	**High** The majority of students maintain a B+ to A average 0	**Average** The majority of students maintain a C or B average. 5	**Low** The majority of students maintain grades below average 10	
6. Number of students with a history of behavior/discipline problems.	**Zero** 0	**One to three** 5	**Four or more** 10	
7. Level of absenteeism for students in your class.	**Low** There are very few absences in my class. 0	**Medium** There are more absences in my class than I would like. 5	**High** The number of absences in my class is a significant problem. 10	
8. General degree of intrinsic/internal motivation of students in your class toward math.	**High** A majority of students express that they like math and that they value math as something relevant to their lives. 0	**Medium** An equal mix of students do and do not like math and do and do not value math as something relevant to their lives. 5	**Low** A majority of students do not like math and do not value math as something relevant to their lives. 10	
Total score				
Appropriate level of teacher support				

(Mathematics Instruction Decision-Making Inventory for Diverse Learners)

Individual and Small-Group Student Characteristics Inventory Form

Student learning characteristics	Rating scale			Score
1. Student/significant percentage of students in group receive(s) special education services.	**Yes** 10	**No** 0		
2. Student/significant percentage of students in group receive(s) Title I services and/or who are at risk for school failure.	**Yes** 10	**No** 0		
3. Student/significant percentage of students in group receive(s) free or reduced lunches.	**Yes** 5	**One to three** 0		
4. Student/significant percentage of students has/have previous math grades that are less than satisfactory (e.g., below a C or S level).	**Yes** 5	**No** 0		
5. General achievement level of student/significant percentage of students in group.	**High** The majority of students maintain a B+ to A average. 0	**Average** The majority of students maintain a C or B average. 5	**Low** The majority of students maintain grades below average. 10	
6. Student/significant percentage of students in group has/have a history of behavior/discipline problems.	**Yes** 10	**No** 0		
7. Level of absenteeism for student/significant percentage of students in group.	**Low** There are very few absences in my class. 0	**Medium** There are more absences in my class than I would like. 5	**High** The number of absences in my class is a significant problem. 10	
8. General degree of intrinsic/internal motivation of student/significant percentage of students in group toward math.	**High** A majority of students express that they like math and that they value math as something relevant to their lives. 0	**Medium** An equal mix of students do and do not like math and do and do not value math as something relevant to their lives. 5	**Low** A majority of students do not like math and do not value math as something relevant to their lives. 10	
Total score				
Appropriate level of teacher support				

(Mathematics Instruction Decision-Making Inventory for Diverse Learners)

Student Characteristics Rating Guide

Level of teacher support	Total score
Student characteristics indicate need for a **higher** level of teacher support	30–80
Student characteristics indicate need for a **lower** level of teacher support	0–29

(Mathematics Instruction Decision-Making Inventory for Diverse Learners)

Mathematics Curriculum/Content Characteristics Form

Curriculum/content characteristics	Rating scale		Score
1. Degree of content complexity	**Simple** The content is well-defined, is primarily conceptual in nature, and does not require multiple steps/complex procedures (e.g., comparing attributes of shapes). 0	**Complex** The content is not well-defined, is factual in nature, and/or requires multiple steps/complex procedures (e.g., algorithms, word problems). 10	
2. Degree of accuracy required	**Low** Procedural accuracy is not relevant; emphasis is not on "getting the right answer;" multiple responses may be appropriate (e.g., estimation, classification). 0	**High** Procedural accuracy is expected (e.g., solving equations using a specific algorithm, solving word problems that have one solution). 5	
3. Amount of instructional time available	**Unrestricted** Time allows for students to extend their understandings of a concept/skill; students have ample time to learn and practice essential skills but also have time for extending their acquired knowledge through games, "brain teasers," and other extension activities. 0	**Limited** Time constraints dictate that students acquire concept/skill in an efficient and timely manner. 5	
4. Foundational nature of content	**Not foundational** Content is not foundational to understanding future math concepts/skills; primarily relies on students' using concepts/skills already acquired (e.g., commutative property of addition and multiplication). 0	**Foundational** Content is foundational to understanding future math concepts/skills (e.g., concept of order/seriation, conservation, place value); primarily relies on new concepts/skills or concepts/skills that are complex in nature (e.g., long division, regrouping with $+, -, \times, \div$, computation). 10	
Total score			
Appropriate level of teacher support			

(Mathematics Instruction Decision-Making Inventory for Diverse Learners)

Mathematics Curriculum/Content Characteristics Rating Guide

Level of teacher support	Total score
Math curriculum/content characteristics indicate need for a higher level of teacher support	15–30
Math curriculum/content characteristics indicate need for a lower level of teacher support	0–14

Mathematics Instructional Planning Guide

Instructions: *Use the following table to decide the level of teacher support that is appropriate for your students (whole class, small group, or individual student) on the basis of both their student learning characteristics rating and the mathematics curriculum/content characteristics rating. Examine the first and second columns of the table and find the row that matches both the student learning characteristics rating and the mathematics curriculum/content rating for your student(s). The third and fourth columns indicate the level of teacher support needed by your students for both teacher instruction and student practice.*

Student learning characteristics rating	Mathematics curriculum/content rating	Level of teacher support: Teacher instruction	Level of teacher support: Student practice
HIGHER LEVEL	HIGHER LEVEL	HIGHER LEVEL	HIGHER LEVEL
HIGHER LEVEL	LOWER LEVEL	HIGHER LEVEL	LOWER LEVEL
LOWER LEVEL	HIGHER LEVEL	HIGHER LEVEL	LOWER LEVEL
LOWER LEVEL	LOWER LEVEL	LOWER LEVEL	LOWER LEVEL

Concrete-Representational-Abstract (CRA) Assessment Planning Form

Authentic context (from Class Mathematics Student Interest Inventory)	
Relevant standard(s)	
Identified big ideas	
Key problem (based on identified authentic context)	
Target objective	

		Concrete	Representational	Abstract
CRA Assessment Table	Receptive			
	Task 1			
	Task 2			
	Task 3			
	Expressive			
	Task 1			
	Task 2			
	Task 3			

Instructional Practices Descriptions

Practice	Explanation	Purpose for students	Features	Research support	My ideas
Teach within authentic contexts	Introduction to all new mathematics concepts are embedded within contexts that are authentic and meaningful to the students.	Provides students a meaningful context to • Understand the significance of mathematics that they learn • Enhance memory promotes interest/ engagement	Authentic contexts are selected from use of Mathematics Student Interest Inventory. Target concept or skill is introduced within selected context in tangible way (e.g., story problem, using props, video). Teacher will describe explicitly how target concept relates to selected context.	Baroody (1987); Bottge (1999); Bottge et al. (2001, 2002); Kennedy & Tipps (1998); Mercer, Jordan, et al. (1996); NCTM (2000); Van De Walle (1994)	
Build meaningful student connections	Teacher links students' previous knowledge and experiences to new mathematics concepts and skills.	Provides students with support for using what they already know to help them to learn a new mathematical concept.	Teacher links previous knowledge to new concept; identifies learning objective; provides rationale for the new concept's importance to students' lives.	Baroody (1997); Kennedy & Tipps (1994); Mercer, Jordan, et al. (1996); Mercer, Lane, et al. (1996); Mercer & Mercer (2005); Van De Walle (1994)	
Use explicit Concrete-Representational-Abstract (CRA) instruction	Mathematics concepts are introduced and practiced at the level of understanding that is most appropriate for students (concrete, representational, or abstract). At the concrete level, students engage in use of manipulatives to do mathematics and to demonstrate their understandings. At the representational level, students draw solutions. At the abstract level, students do mathematics using numbers and symbols only.	Provides a process for truly developing conceptual understanding. Students' concrete experiences provide a meaningful foundation for developing more abstract yet still meaningful understandings of a concept.	Depending on the results of the Mathematics Dynamic Assessment (MDA) the teacher will incorporate the appropriate concrete materials, representational strategy, or abstract strategy.	Allsopp (1999); Baroody (1987); Butler et al. (2003); Harris et al. (1993); Kennedy & Tipps (1998); Mercer, Jordan, et al. (1996); Mercer & Mercer (2005); Miller & Mercer, 1993; Peterson et al. (1988); Van De Walle (1994); Witzel et al. (2003) Baroody (1987); Borkowski (1992);	

(continued)

Instructional Practices Descriptions *(continued)*

Practice	Explanation	Purpose for students	Features	Research support	My ideas
Provide modeling/ scaffolding instruction	When students are initially acquiring an understanding of a concept or skill, the teacher takes responsibility for ensuring that the concept or skill is modeled clearly, meaningfully, and accurately using a variety of techniques (e.g., multisensory teaching, cuing essential features of a concept, providing examples and nonexamples, thinking aloud, prompting student thinking). As students demonstrate greater and greater understanding, the teacher fades direction and encourages the students to take on more and more responsibility for demonstrating/doing the mathematics concept.	Allows teacher to be able to meet students "where they are" in terms of their under- standing of a concept, providing them the level of support that is needed for them to demonstrate complete understanding (advanced acquisition) at a beginning level of proficiency. Specific feedback is provided as needed, which prompts students' thinking and promotes understanding.	The teacher supports students' initial and advanced acquisition of the concept at three levels: high teacher support, medium teacher support, and low teacher support. As students demonstrate greater understanding, the teacher moves from high to medium to low levels of support.	Brophy & Good (1986); Carnine et al. (1998); Cobb et al. (1992); Kennedy & Tipps (1994); Mercer, Jordan et al. (1996); Mercer & Mercer (2005); Miller et al. (1998); Montague (1992); Paris & Winograd (1990); Polloway & Patton (1993); Swanson (1999)	
Teach problem- solving strategies	Develop students' metacognitive (thinking) processes by teaching students learnable/memorable strategies that they can apply to particular types of problem-solving situations.	Develops students' metacognitive abilities and allows them to become independent problem solvers.	Teacher explicitly models an appropriate strategy and provides opportunities for students to apply the strategy to relevant problem-solving situations.	Allsopp (1997); Borkowski (1992); Jitendra, Hoff, & Beck (1999); Lenz, Ellis, & Scanlon (1996); Miller & Mercer (1993); Miller, Strawser, & Mercer (1996); Montague (1992); Owen & Fuchs (2002); Paris & Winograd (1990); Strichart, Mangrum, & Iannuzzi (1998); Swanson (1999)	

FAST DRAW Cue Sheet

(for solving story problems that involve adding fractions with mixed numbers)

FAST

Step 1: <u>F</u>ind what you are solving for.
Underline the information that tells you what you are solving for.

Step 2: <u>A</u>sk yourself, "What is the important information?"
Circle the important information.

Step 3: <u>S</u>et up the equation.
Write the equation, making sure all of the important information is represented.

Step 4: <u>T</u>ake the equation and solve it.
If you cannot solve it from memory, use DRAW to solve it.

DRAW

Step 1: <u>D</u>etermine the sign and what it means.

Step 2: <u>R</u>ead the equation.

Step 3: <u>A</u>nswer the equation, or draw and check.
- Draw circles or boxes for whole numbers.
- Divide a circle or box into fractional parts and shade in the correct number of parts for fractions.
- Circle wholes and fractional parts to answer.
- Add the wholes and fractional parts to answer.

Step 4: <u>W</u>rite the answer and check.

Source: Mercer, C.D., & Miller, S.P. (1992). *Multiplication facts 0–81*. Lawrence, KS: Edge Enterprises.

Teaching Mathematics Meaningfully: Solutions for Reaching Struggling Learners by David H. Allsopp, Maggie M. Kyger, & LouAnn H. Lovin. Copyright © 2007 by Paul H. Brookes Publishing Co., Inc. All rights reserved.

FAST DRAW Learning Sheet

1. After a weekend camping trip, the Hartman family members added up the total number of miles hiked by all members. Three members had stayed together and hiked the same number of miles each. Corey went on a different path and hiked 5 miles. If the combined total was 17 miles, then how many miles were hiked by each of the family members who stayed together?

FAST:

DRAW:

2. On a back-to-school shopping trip, Kimberly, Kari, and Jacklyn bought the same number of jeans. When they had finished, there were 12 pairs of jeans in the bag. How many pairs of jeans did each young lady buy?

FAST:

DRAW:

3. Gabriel bought the same CD for each of her three best friends. A store coupon saved her $5. If her final bill was $16, then how much did each CD cost?

FAST:

DRAW:

From Allsopp, D.H. (2001). *Building algebra skills: A beginning algebra program for students who have difficulty learning mathematics.* Unpublished manuscript.

Responsive Instructional Planning Framework Form

Instructions: *Read the following questions in the left-hand column and write notes to help you plan for instruction in the right-hand column.*

Question to aid in planning	Notes
What is the target mathematics concept?_____	
What do my students understand? Level of understanding (CRA) Receptive or expressive ability Stage of learning Conclusions	
What is my instructional hypothesis? What students can do What students cannot do Why?	
How will I differentiate the instructional needs of my students? Within whole-class instruction? By grouping students?	
What authentic context(s) will I use? To build meaningful student connections To provide explicit modeling	
How will I introduce/model the target concept to the whole class? To build meaningful student connections To provide explicit modeling	
How will I differentiate the instructional scaffolding/extension (generalization and adaption) needs of my students? For whole class (if not using student groups) For groups	
How will I provide practice opportunities that promote proficiency/maintenance (receptive and/or expressive phase)? For whole class (if not using student groups) For groups	
How will I evaluate my students' learning and determine the effectiveness of my instruction?	

Responsive Teaching Plan Form

Date(s):

Class period:

Mathematics concept/standard:

Instructional hypothesis:

Given _____

Students are able to

Student are unable to

Because. . . .

Overall instructional goals for groups (Planning Pyramid)

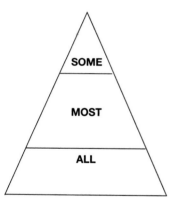

What SOME students will know:

_____

What MOST students will know:

_____

What ALL students will know:

_____

Whole-class instruction:

Instructional objective (what ALL students will know):

Authentic context:
    Theme:
    How theme will be integrated:

Level of understanding:

    Concrete   Representational   Abstract

Materials:

Key instructional ideas:

_____

Source: Vaughn, S., Bos, C.S., and Schumm, J.S. [1997] (Planning Pyramid).

Teaching Mathematics Meaningfully: Solutions for Reaching Struggling Learners by David H. Allsopp, Maggie M. Kyger, & LouAnn H. Lovin. Copyright © 2007 by Paul H. Brookes Publishing Co., Inc. All rights reserved.

Whole class

Differentiated group instruction strategies/techniques

Important teaching ideas

			CRA Multisensory modeling Think aloud Examples/ nonexamples Scaffold instruction	CRA Receptive/ expressive Many response chances Monitor/provide corrective feedback Positive reinforcement	Adapt/relate to other concepts Generalize to other environments Develop new strategies
Whole class/group/ individual	**Level of teacher support**	**Beginning stage of learning**	**Teacher instruction notes**	**Student practice notes**	**Extension notes**
All	Higher support Lower support	Acquisition Proficiency Maintenance Generalization Adaption			
Most	Higher support Lower support	Acquisition Proficiency Maintenance Generalization Adaption			
Some	Higher support Lower support	Acquisition Proficiency Maintenance Generalization Adaption			

Evaluation of Student Progress:
ALL group:
MOST group:
SOME group:

Maintenance (e.g., problem of the day, centers):

Grouping Information

Circle which of the following applies:

   Whole class (no groups/names not necessary)

   Group/individual student (write names below as appropriate)

Write names of group members:

Group 1: ALL   **Observation/evaluation notes:**

_____   _____

_____   _____

_____   _____

_____   _____

_____   _____

Group 2: MOST

_____   _____

_____   _____

_____   _____

_____   _____

_____   _____

Group 3: SOME

_____   _____

_____   _____

_____   _____

_____   _____

_____   _____

Learning Barriers Planning Form

Mathematical concept:		

Lesson plan Lesson objectives	Possible barriers	Possible modifications
Instructional procedures		
Student responses		
Evaluation of learning		

Appendix B

Sample Mathematics Dynamic Assessment Charts and Lesson Plans

This Appendix contains samples of Mathematics Dynamic Assessment Concrete-Representational-Abstract (CRA) charts and accompanying lesson plans. These charts and plans are not meant to be exhaustive but are for your reference and use.

CONTENTS

Probability and Statistics

(Upper Elementary)

CONCRETE-REPRESENTATIONAL-ABSTRACT ASSESSMENT

The following Concrete-Representational-Abstract (CRA) chart and accompanying outline describes how to conduct a CRA assessment in an upper elementary school classroom. Notice that the teacher assesses students at all three levels of mathematical understanding and provides tasks at both the receptive and the expressive levels.

Standard: The student will identify and describe the number of possible arrangements of several objects using tree diagrams or the fundamental (Basic) counting principle (FCP).

Big idea: Have students draw tree diagrams to show all of the possible combinations (outcomes) in a sample space. The counting principle tells how to find the number of outcomes when there is more than one way to put things together.

Authentic context: Summer vacation

Key problem/context: Identify how many possible outfits to pack for a family vacation.

Target objective (for future lessons based on results of assessment): Students will compute the number of possible arrangements of no more than three types of objects by using a tree diagram and by using the fundamental counting principle (FCP).

Directions for Setting Up Stations

Concrete

Receptive: For the first task, display different combinations of clothing. One should include blue jeans with a red shirt, another should include blue

We acknowledge the following teachers who helped us to develop the lesson plans in this appendix: Sarah Anderson, Chelsea Caulfield, Shannon Davies, Kristen Everett, Heather Hemsley, Lisa Prather, Julia Redden, Krissy Schnebel, and Margaret Wasaff.

SAMPLE CRA CHART

Instructions: *This chart can be used to plan and then set up the stations needed for the CRA assessment. Each column of the chart states the task that the students are to complete. More detailed explanations follow.*

		Representational	Abstract

Receptive

Task 1 — Look at the arrangement of clothing on the table. Now look at the descriptions of the arrangement. On your paper, write whether description A, B, or C fits the arrangement.

Circle the tree diagram that only shows every combination once.

Shoes → **Socks**

1. red → orange / white

   blue → orange / white

   green → orange / white

   red → orange / white

2. white → white / black

   black → white / black

For this arrangement, choose the correct computation using the FCP:

Hats → **Glasses**

Yellow → Blue / Red

Purple → Blue / Red

Green → Blue / Red

A. 2(1 × 3)
B. 3 × 2
C. 3 + 2 + 1

Expressive

Task 1 — Given a preexisting tree diagram (without labels, with branches), students will use color-coordinated manipulatives to represent combinations of clothing.

Draw a tree diagram that shows the following combinations:

Blue pants and white shirt
Blue pants and green shirt
Blue pants and red shirt
Brown pants and white shirt
Brown pants and green shirt
Brown pants and red shirt

Use the FCP to write what the tree diagram is representing:

Shorts → **T-shirts**

solid → solid / stripes / dots

stripe → solid / stripes / dots

Task 2 — Use the bags of chips and the cans of soda to make as many food/drink combinations as possible. Tally your results.

Write a word problem based on the following computations (use the FCP):

1. 4 × 3 × 3 = 36
2. 5 × 2 × 1 = 10
3. 6 × 4 × 2 = 48

jeans with a green shirt, and another should include blue jeans with a yellow shirt. Then, provide sheets of paper that have descriptions of the different combinations of clothing:

Description A: There are three combinations on the table. These combinations include blue jeans with a red shirt, blue jeans with a green shirt, and blue jeans with a yellow shirt.

Description B: There are five pieces of clothing on the table.

Description C: There are two pairs of jeans and three shirts on the table.

Ask the students to pick the best description (which is A).

Expressive: For the first task, provide each student with a set of shapes comprised of four different-colored triangles and three different-colored squares and a piece of paper that reads, "Make the triangles and squares into as many arrangements as possible. Each arrangement should have only two shapes, and every arrangement must have only one triangle." Ask the students to record their findings on the piece of paper. For the second task, give each student an identical set of two bags of chips and three sodas, and give them a piece of paper on which to write. Ask students to make food/drink combinations until they believe that they have made *all* possible combinations.

Representational

Receptive: For the first task, provide each student with a sheet of paper that includes the following tree diagrams:

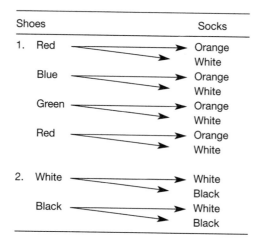

The directions on the paper read, "Circle the tree diagram that shows every combination only once." (Although the first diagram seems to have more choices, it actually is the second diagram that shows every combination only once.)

Expressive: For the first task, ask students to draw a tree diagram that shows the following combinations. The items to use will be pictures of clothing: blue pants and green shirt, blue pants and white shirt, blue pants and red shirt, brown pants and white shirt, brown pants and green shirt, brown pants and red shirt. When completed, it will look like this:

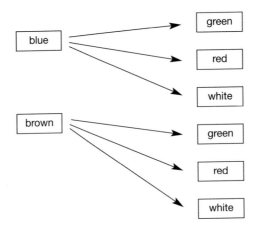

Abstract

Receptive: For this task, provide a tree diagram that illustrates the FCP and show the three choices of computations (see Receptive Abstract Task 1 in the chart). Ask the students to select the best option (B).

Expressive: The first task in this column of the chart requires students to write a correct computation using the FCP based on a tree diagram. The students will have to develop their own answer, which should be 2 × 3 = 6 (2 types of shorts times 3 types of shirts = 6 possible outfits). The second example in this portion of the chart gives three different number sentences that represent the FCP. The students have to describe an example of what each of the number sentences could represent (based on the FCP). An example for the first equation (4 × 3 × 3 = 36) might be the following:

> Anna wanted to make as many paint color combinations as she could. She had 4 bold colors, 3 pastel colors, and 3 primary colors. She could use each type of color only once in each combination. Anna was able to make 36 different new colors!

Both of the tasks should be displayed on pieces of paper and the students should write their answers on the same pieces of paper.

Description of Grouping Considerations

Have each student start at the abstract center for the CRA assessment. Assign the students who are waiting to start the process the maintenance activity (described in the next section) to complete. Put students in groups of three or four. These groups should be relatively heterogeneous in regard to ability, organizational skills, working rate, group work tendencies, and so forth. This is because the assignments are individual, and every student will likely work through the tasks differently, especially with the nature of the questions.

Give each group approximately 6 minutes at each center. Issue a 1-minute warning before the groups are to switch to the next station to allow them to complete their thoughts. When groups are finished, they can return to the maintenance activity, as well.

Maintenance Activity

Groups who are waiting to start the CRA assessment and groups who complete the assessment can play a card game such as SET.

THE GAME: Place 12 cards face up on the table. Each player looks for a "set" of 3 cards. When a player finds a set, he or she puts it in his or her own pile, then 3 new cards are placed on the table to bring the total back to 12. The game continues until all cards are dealt and no more sets can be found. If at any time during the game no sets can be found, 3 more cards are added until a set is found. The player with the most sets at the end of the game wins.

CARDS: Each card can be identified by four attributes, each of which has three values: number (1, 2, or 3), color (red, green, or blue), symbol (diamond, oval, or square), and shading (open, striped, or solid). The deck is made up of one card of each type. Three cards make a set if, for each attribute, the values on the cards are either all the same or all different.

After the assessment is finished, ask the students how the card game that they played reminded them of the different stations in which they participated. Also ask the students, using what they learned in the stations, whether they could figure out how many cards are in a deck (number $\times$ color $\times$ symbol $\times$ shading = total number of cards: $3 \times 3 \times 3 \times 3 = 81$).

Lesson Outline for Using the CRA Assessment

Introduce the Assessment   Introduce the activity by referencing an authentic context, as in the following example.

Link to previous knowledge:

"When you go on vacation, how do you know how much to pack? Do you know any way to use math to figure out how to wear as many combinations of clothing as possible? Today we are going to begin to understand how."

Identify objective:

"Today, we are going to work with the fundamental counting principle and using tree diagrams. I want to find out how much each of you knows about it, and I want you to be able to relate it to your everyday life and interests."

Provide rationale:

"The principle is important to learn and understand because you can solve a lot questions by using probability."

Describe/Model and Check for Understanding   Explain the three stations to the students and expected behavior during the activity.

"Before I teach you about tree diagrams and the fundamental counting principle, I want to find out how much you already know, so, I have set up three stations that have a few tasks."

[Briefly explain the tasks at each station.]

"Each of you will be assigned to a group and will start with station A (abstract). You will have 6 minutes at each station. When you have 1 minute left, I will give you a warning. May I have student volunteers to show examples and nonexamples of the correct way to transition from one station to the other? I understand that some of the tasks may be more difficult than others. I do not expect you to know everything at every station, but I do expect everyone to try his or her best!"

Closure   After all of the students have completed the station, ask the students how the card game might be related to the stations and the tasks. This will be a comprehensive question that clearly has more than one intent and, therefore, more than one answer. Also review your observations of effort and group cooperation and reinforce that there were some aspects of each station that were more difficult than others (Caulfield, 2006).

CONCRETE-LEVEL LESSON PLAN: TREE DIAGRAMS

The following is an example of a lesson plan that might be used after the CRA assessment just described. It is designed for students who need instruction at the concrete level of understanding.

Learning objective: Use concrete objects to make tree diagrams to demonstrate that changing one item in a combination creates an entirely new choice or combination 5 out of 5 times.

Prerequisite: Students need to have an understanding that there is a guess-and-check method to determine probability (which leads to a more systematic approach) to find the number of possible arrangements/combinations of several objects.

PHASE 1: Initial Acquisition of Skill

✏️ Teach Skill within Authentic Context

Description: Provide an authentic problem context such as the following:

"You are on your summer vacation and it's time to stop and eat at a Wendy's fast food restaurant. You already know that you want either a Junior Bacon Cheeseburger or chicken fingers, but you want to figure out the maximum number of entrée/side item/soft-drink combinations that you could create. Each combination should have only one entrée, one side item, and one soft drink choice. You can choose from the following items I have listed on the board."

Entrée	Side items	Soft drinks
Junior Bacon Cheeseburger	Fries	Coke
Chicken fingers	Salad	Orange soda
		Sprite

🏠 Build Meaningful Student Connections

Purpose: To help students make meaningful connections between what they have experienced in their life and how they can apply problem-solving mathematical strategies to their real-life experiences.

Materials: Wendy's menu chart, food item photographs, pencil, paper, overhead projector

Description:

1. **Link to students' previous knowledge:** "To figure out how many possible Wendy's value meal combinations there are, we have to know how to keep track of the total number of entrée/side item/soft-drink combinations. Remember that in our last lesson we used a guess-and-check method to figure out a similar outcome, but now we can use an organized way to figure

out the same information. Let's now look at our Wendy's value meal menus. I know I want a Junior Bacon Cheeseburger [place photo of cheese-burger in students' view]. I also want fries and a Coke [place photos of fries and Coke in students' view]. This makes one meal (line up photos in order], so I'm going to write down that combination. Now I've decided that I want an orange soda instead of a Coke but with the same side item and entrée [take away photo of Coke, replace it with photo of orange soda]. Did I change the combination when I chose a different drink? Yes, I did change the combination, so now we have made a total of 2 combinations. Let's write our second combination. See, we are using an organized method of determine outcomes instead of making random guesses!"

(Students will have previous knowledge of "The student will investigate and describe the difference between the probability of an event found through simulation versus the theoretical probability of that same event," which means that students will "understand that in experimental proba-bility, as the number of trials increases, the experimental probability gets closer to the theoretical probability." This teaches the students that as they make guesses and check them, they come closer to the actual answer of a probability question.)

2. Identify the skill that students will learn: "I've figured out that even if I change one item in the meal, I can completely change the combination, but listing every single combination can take up way too much time, so we are going to learn how to make a diagram—called a tree diagram—to figure out our number of choices instead of making a list. We are going to use food item photographs to take the place of our words."

3. Provide rationale/meaning: "Sometimes it's easier to use a diagram to fig-ure out the total number of choices rather than writing down a list."

Provide Explicit Teacher Modeling

Purpose: To provide students a clear teacher model of how to complete a tree diagram using concrete materials.

Learning objective: Use concrete objects (food item photographs) to com-plete a tree diagram of the total number of combinations of a Wendy's value meal.

Steps for reaching learning objectives:

• Students need to identify how many entrée (2), side item (2), and soft-drink (3) choices there are.

• Students need to place the food item photographs in the appropriate places on the tree diagram template.

• Students tally each time they create a different value meal combination.

• Students add up the tallies to find the total number of combinations possi-ble (total number of 12).

Materials: Tree diagram blank template, list of 12 possible combinations, food item photographs, Wendy's menu, pencil, paper

Description:

"Let's look at this diagram [classroom-size tree diagram template with ti-tles 'entrées,' 'side items,' and 'drinks' in appropriate columns]. I want to be able to fill in this diagram with the same information on the value meal menu and the list of all of the possible combinations. We already picked out two of our combinations. One of our combinations was a Junior Bacon Cheeseburger, fries, and a Coke. [Place photos of food items in front of students.] Now look at the titles above the diagram. Where do you think we should put the Junior Bacon Cheeseburger? Right, under the title 'entrée' because that is where it is located on our menu. [Follow the same steps with fries and a Coke.] We also had another (different) combination, remember? It was a Junior Bacon Cheese-burger, fries, and an orange soda. Let's look at how we changed the combina-tion from one to the other with pictures. The only thing that changed was the soda. So we would show only the change (from Coke to orange soda) on our di-agram here. [Place a picture of orange soda in correct location on diagram.] That is because the soda was the only food item that we changed to make a new combination. [Follow the same steps by changing the soda to Sprite.] From the diagram, we can see that by changing only the type of soda, we made 3 different combinations."

Scaffold Instruction

Materials:

Teacher: Tree diagram blank template, list of 12 possible combinations, food item photographs, Wendy's menu, pencil, paper

Students: Personal tree diagram template with mini food pictures, list of 12 possible combinations, pencil, paper

Description:

1. **Scaffold using a high level of teacher direction/support:** First, instruct the students to place the combinations that have already been completed on their personal tree diagram. Then, to finish the first "set" of combinations (in which only the drink is changed), set out the appropriate pictures (Ju-nior Bacon Cheeseburger, fries, and a Sprite) and ask the students whether, once again, they must show the entire combination on their diagram or just the change. The students will likely respond, "Just the change." Then, together, count how many combinations have been made so far (3) and put tally marks on the board next to the diagram to keep a running total of combinations. Point on the class size tree diagram how you are counting each combination only once. Then, reemphasize two facts: a) even when two of the three variables in a combination stay the same, they are making an entirely new combination; and b) students can look at a tree diagram and be able to count and record the combinations.

    Note: If students can talk about/make sense of what the teacher is doing, then the group would move on to a medium level of scaffolding. If not, then they would go over a new example following the same pattern.

2. **Scaffold using a medium level of teacher direction/support:** Next, model changing from the first side-item choice to the second side-item choice by placing the appropriate photograph in the correct location on the tree dia-

gram. Ask the students why you put the photograph where you did. A simple response would be that you are following the labels on the tree diagram. A more complex response would be that they have exhausted all possibilities with the Junior Bacon Cheeseburger and fries combinations. Then, explain that the same process must occur with the same entrée and a new side item combination when filling in the soft-drink spaces. Give students an opportunity to place the drinks in the correct spaces, and then place the soft drinks on the large diagram for the class to see. This will give the students an opportunity to practice what they learned using the high level of teacher direction. Once every student has placed his or her total of one entrée, two side items, and six drinks in the correct position, ask how many new combinations they have come up with and how they arrived at their answer. Then ask what the total number of combinations is, making sure to reference the tallies already on the board (and wait for the correct response of six and explanation of the response).

Note: If students can talk about/make sense of what you are doing, then the group is ready to move on to a low level of scaffolding. If not, then they should go over a new example following the same pattern.

3. **Scaffold using a low level of teacher direction/support:** Now that you have modeled the steps to finding the total number of combinations with a Junior Bacon Cheeseburger entrée, ask a question such as, *"How would we use the other entrée in the diagram?"* This should allow students to demonstrate their increased understanding of math problem-solving skills using the information on their diagrams. Continue with questions such as, *"What is similar about the process that we are doing now compared with the Junior Bacon Cheeseburger? What is different?"* *"Why do the side items and soft drinks look like they are repeating themselves when we were actually making new combinations?"* Once students have completed the third set of combinations with the class, then have them complete the fourth set of combinations individually at their desks as you work together. While this is happening, allow the students to ask you or the other students questions to enhance the understanding of the material. During this time, have the students use their mini food item manipulatives to complete the tree diagram and to count the total number of combinations that they have created.

PHASE 2: Practice Strategies

💡 Receptive/Recognition Level
Purpose: To provide students with multiple practice opportunities to complete a tree diagram using concrete materials.
Activity: "Lunchtimes" tree diagram activity
Materials: Completed tree diagram, pencil, paper
Description: Students will look at a completed tree diagram of lunchtime objects (1 sandwich, 2 kinds of fruit, and 3 drink choices) and answer questions about the diagram. Here is one example:

1. Which of these tells you how many total combinations for lunch you have?
   a. 12
   b. 3
   c. 6
2. What would your recording look like? (Provide three to four options that show different numbers of tally marks.)
3. What do you need to make one complete combination?
   a. 1 sandwich, 1 fruit, 1 drink
   b. 1 sandwich, 2 pieces of fruit, 2 drinks
   c. 2 sandwiches, 1 drink, 2 pieces of fruit

Expressive Level

Purpose: To provide students with multiple practice opportunities to complete a tree diagram using concrete materials.

Learning objective: Using concrete objects, cooperative learning

Activity: "Favorite Food" tree diagram activity

Materials: Food magazines, scissors, glue, blank tree diagram

Description: Ask students to cut out pictures of one favorite dish, two favorite side dishes, and 2 sets of their favorite drinks. Then, they will glue the pictures onto a blank tree diagram and orally present their favorite foods. You and the other students may ask them questions about their favorite foods or the tree diagram itself.

PHASE 3: Evaluation

Continuously Monitor and Chart Student Performance

Purpose: To obtain continuous data for evaluating student learning and determining whether instruction is effective. It also provides students a way to visualize their learning/progress.

Materials: Various examples of tree diagrams, pencil, paper

Description: Give students five different examples of tree diagrams (similar to the diagrams they have been working with) and ask the students to determine how many possible combinations are shown for each tree diagram.

Assessment

Flexible Math Interview

Purpose: To obtain additional diagnostic information with which to check student understanding and to plan and/or modify instruction accordingly.

Materials: Individual students' "Favorite Food" or "Lunchtime" tree diagram

Description: Using a student's tree diagram, have the student instruct the teacher on how to construct a similar diagram.

PHASE 4: Maintenance

Purpose: To provide periodic student practice activities and teacher-directed review of this skill after students have mastered it.

Activity: Problem of the Day

Materials: "Combination" box of choices, pencil, paper, chalk (for chalkboard)

Description: Ask students to write any combination (limited to three categories and three choices within each category) of information about themselves, their interests, their hobbies, and so forth. Have them put their combinations in the "combination" box of choices. Every day, pick one of the choices and develop a word problem about whatever the students wrote down on the paper. Students will have to solve the word problem by performing the correct calculation of combinations.

Home–school connection: Students can interview family members or friends about ways they have solved (math-related) problems in their everyday life. Then, have them talk about how they solved an everyday life problem with tree diagrams. They may bring in the interview for credit.

Individual accommodations:

1. For students with organization and sequencing problems, provide a short reminder of the steps that they can follow later in developing a tree diagram.

2. For students with math anxiety, help them develop a self-checking strategy to use.

3. For students with lower math achievement levels, reinforce basic calculation skills used in solving combination questions in tree diagrams.

REPRESENTATIONAL-LEVEL MATH LESSON PLAN: TREE DIAGRAMS

Description   This is an example of a lesson plan that might be used following the CRA assessment or after students demonstrate mastery with the concrete lesson plan just described. It is designed for students who need instruction at the representational level of understanding.

Standard: The student will identify and describe the number of possible arrangements of several objects using the tree diagram or the FCP.

Lesson Objectives

1. Students will solve five two-part math word problems involving tree diagrams and the FCP with 80% accuracy.

2. Students will write at least two complete paragraphs using correct sentence structure and word usage that accurately describes using tree diagrams to solve problems.

Steps in Instruction and Teaching Methods
Advanced organizer

1. Link to previous learning by referencing prior lessons.

    "Yesterday, we used food item pictures to create tree diagrams in order to determine the number of possible meal options from a subset Wendy's menu choices. We also answered questions about the completed tree diagram."

2. Identify learning objectives for students:

    "Today, we are going to practice the same skill without the food item pictures. We will continue to use the tree diagram, but we will learn a faster way to figure out all possible combinations."

3. Provide meaning for learning skill:

    "It's important to use different ways to find possible combinations, because not everyone learns the same way, and some ways are easier to understand for some students and some ways work for others."

    Describe/model and check for understanding: Use a class-size copy of the food diagram at the front of the room (on overhead projector) and review the total number of combinations shown by the tree diagram (12). Then use think-alouds to count and put tally marks for the three sections of the tree diagram (2 entrées, 2 side items, 3 drinks) and show students how to find the same number of combinations by multiplying the numbers together:

    "How many entrees do we have? That's right, 2, so I'm going to draw two big circles here using blue to show it's for the entrée column. One circle is for the Junior Bacon Cheeseburger, one is for the chicken fingers. Now, how many side choices do I have for each entrée? Right, 2 again. This time

I'm going to put yellow tally marks in the entrée circles to show how many sides I can get with an entrée. So, I can get fries or a salad with my cheeseburger and I can get fries or a salad with my chicken fingers. How many total combinations do I have now? Well, I have 2 sets of tally marks in this circle, and 2 here, so I have 2 sets of 2 or 4 total combinations. Let's look at the tree diagram; how many boxes are in this column? Right; 4. Hmmm, I wonder why there are 4 boxes here? [Guide students to understanding that the number of boxes shows the total number of combinations as you move across the tree diagram.] "Now, let's add the drinks. I am going to draw a box for each of my combinations for entrées and sides. How many boxes will I draw? Why did I draw my boxes with blue and shade the inside yellow? Right—to help us remember that each box represents a combination of entrées and sides. Now, for each of these boxes, I'm going to draw red tally marks to show how many drinks would go with each combination. How many drinks will I draw in each circle? Right. 3. How many total combinations do I have?" [Have students volunteer answers and explain their reasoning. Through questions and discussions, guide students to see that you have sets of boxes each with 3 tally marks.]

Guided practice: Provide students with colored pencils and at least five individual tree diagrams that have been filled out using pictures. First, count the number of possible combinations together using the same process as previously. As students become more proficient, fade your instruction and have students direct the lesson by telling the teacher what to do as they work through problems together. Ask questions such as, "Does the number we get from our tally marks and circles have any connection to the number of boxes on the tree diagram?" "Why is this the same number?" "Do you think that you will get the same number every time?" If students start to make the connection with multiplication, lead them to explore this connection and provide additional practice to strengthen this connection.

Independent practice: Give students word problems and accompanying tree diagrams with the correct number of blank spaces, with room to write in the choices. Ask the students to solve the problems by drawing circles and tally marks to show the FCP (or by using only multiplication if they have reached that level of understanding). Also provide students with a chart to compare their answers when using the tree diagram and the FCP. Ask students to put a star on the chart when they get the same number for each product/answer. This will indicate that the students are making the connection between the two procedures.

Closure   Summarize the lesson and provide information about subsequent lessons:

"Today we used the tree diagram and the FCP to figure out the number of possible combinations using word problems. Tomorrow, we will learn to solve similar word problems using the FCP."

Evaluation of Student Performance Students will solve five two-part math word problems involving tree diagrams and FCP with 90% accuracy.

Home–School Connection Students will write a two-paragraph essay/response on which way (tree diagram or FCP) they prefer to solve the word problems. The first paragraph should be a reflection using the following questions:

1. Which one did you like better?
2. Why?
3. Which method was faster?
4. Which method used more of your mathematic strengths?

The second paragraph should be a description of how the student would explain the process to someone who does not know how to use the FCP or the tree diagram.

Number and Number Sense

(Middle School)

CONCRETE-REPRESENTATIONAL-ABSTRACT ASSESSMENT

The following chart describes centers needed to conduct a CRA assessment in a middle school classroom. Notice that the chart allows the teacher to assess students at all three levels of mathematical understanding (CRA; concrete, representational, abstract) and provides tasks at both the receptive and the expressive levels.

Authentic context: Shopping

Standard: Compare, order, and determine equivalent relationships among fractions, decimals, and percents, including use of scientific notation for numbers greater than 10.

Big ideas: Fractions, decimals, and percents are three different representations of the same number.

Key problem/context:

"You go to the mall to buy a necklace that originally was $10. You see the necklace on sale at three different stores. You want to buy the necklace at the cheapest price. From which store will you buy it?"

a. At JC Penny, the necklace is 2/5 off the original price.
b. At Belk, the necklace is $3.00 off the original price.
c. At Sears, the necklace is 20% off the original price.

Target objective: Students will compare, order, and use fractions, decimals, and percents interchangeably.

INSTRUCTIONS FOR SETTING UP STATIONS

Instructions for setting up each center are included in the following chart.

SAMPLE CRA CHART

This chart can be used to plan and then set up the stations needed for the CRA assessment. Each block of the chart states the task that the students are to complete. Students will complete the assessment in small groups, with each group taking approximately 8 minutes/center.

	Concrete	Representational	Abstract
Receptive			
Task 1	Look at the object sets. On your paper, match each set (A, B, C) with the equivalent number: 1/6, 80%, 0.1. (Students will be given a piece of paper with the numbers 1/6, 80%, 0.1 There will be three different sets of objects set A, set B, set C).	Look at each of the pictures on your paper. Draw a line to match each picture with the correct percent, fraction, or decimal in the other column on the paper.	Choose all answers that represent the same as 1/3: 33%, 3/10, 2/6, 6/12.
Task 2	Look at the objects on the table (objects can be tiles or blocks). For each row, I want you to write down whether A = B, A < B, A > B.	Look at the pictures (Pictures A, B, C) , and determine which represents the quantity 0.40. Write the letter of the picture next to 0.40 on your paper.	Circle =, >, < for each of the following: 5/10 = > < 0.6 8/10 = > < 1/5 25% = > < 3/4 0.7 = > < 70%
Expressive			
Task 1	Using the given tiles (2 piles of tiles) put aside 3/6 of number "1" pile and put aside 75% of number "2" pile Take a picture of your results.	Draw a picture that represents 30%.	Put the following in order from least to greatest: 1/2, 15/20, 18%, 0.7, 0.08.
Task 2	Use the red and green blocks to represent 50%, 0.75, and 1/3. Take a picture of your block representation for each number.	Draw a picture to show the percent equivalent of each decimal: Make sure you label each picture. 0.7 0.33 0.2 0.5 0.65	Write the following fractions and percents as decimals: 1/6 75% 40% 5/10 1/4
Task 3		Draw and label a picture to represent the quantities 0.2 and 25%, and circle the quantity that is greater.	

Description of Grouping Considerations

Every student will start at the abstract center for the CRA assessment. The students who are waiting to start the process will have a review activity to complete. Students will be put in small groups and will work individually.

	9:00–9:08	9:10–9:18	9:20–9:28	9:30–9:38	9:40–9:48	9:50–9:58	10:00–10:08
Group 1	A	R	C	Maintenance	Maintenance	Maintenance	Maintenance
Group 2	Maintenance	A	R	C	Maintenance	Maintenance	Maintenance
Group 3	Maintenance	Maintenance	A	R	C	Maintenance	Maintenance
Group 4	Maintenance	Maintenance	Maintenance	A	R	C	Maintenance
Group 5	Maintenance	Maintenance	Maintenance	Maintenance	A	R	C

Note: To accommodate larger class sizes, multiple stations can be set up (i.e, two abstract stations, two representational, two concrete) and/or more tasks can be added at each station. The groups should be relatively heterogeneous in regard to ability, organization skills, working rate, group work tendencies, and so forth. This is because the assignments are individual, and every student will likely work through the tasks differently, especially with the nature of the questions.

Each group is given approximately 8 minutes at each center. The teacher gives a 1-minute warning before the groups are to switch to the next station to allow them to complete their thoughts. When groups are finished, they can return to the maintenance activity as well. The chart shown on the previous page is an example of how the students can move through the stations.

Maintenance Activity

Groups who are waiting to start the CRA assessment and groups who complete the assessment can engage in a review activity to reinforce previously covered material. Such reviews could include fraction concentration (matching fractional equivalents), fraction art (making collages/pictures using fraction pieces), and Fraction Tool (see NCTM Illuminations at http://illuminations.nctm.org/tools/fraction/fraction.asp).

Lesson Outline for Using the CRA Assessment

Introduce Assessment   Introduce the activity by referencing an authentic context:

"How often do you go shopping and find the same item at different stores? One store might have it for 20% off, another store might have a $2.00-off sale, and still another might say that everything is one half off. You want to find the best buy. Today we are going to find out what we need to work on to be able to solve problems like this. Here is a word problem using slightly different sales amounts."

You go to the mall to buy a necklace that originally was $10. You see the necklace on sale at three different stores. You want to buy the necklace at the cheapest price. From which store will you buy it?

a. At JC Penny, the necklace is 2/5 off the original price.
b. At Belk, the necklace is $3.00 off the original price.
c. At Sears, the necklace is 20% off the original price.

Identify Objective   "We've been working with fractions, decimals and percents, but now we need to start working with all three of them. I want to find out how much you know about fractions, decimals and percents so that I can make sure my lessons are right on target with what you need to know."

Provide Rationale   "It's important that you can use all three of these and understand how they are related so you can understand how to compare to determine value."

Describe/Model and Check for Understanding   Explain the three stations to the students and expected behavior during the activity:

"Before I teach you about how to compare fractions, decimals, and percents, I want to find out how much you already know, so, I have set up three stations that have a few tasks." [Then briefly explain the tasks at each station.]

"Each of you will be assigned to a group and will start with station A (abstract). You will have 8 minutes at each station. When you have 1 minute left, I will give you a warning. I understand that some of the tasks may be more difficult than others. I do not expect you to know everything at every station, but I do expect you to try your best! While you are waiting to go to the stations or when you are finished and waiting for the other groups, you can choose three review activities." [Explain the review choices.]

Closure   After all of the students have completed the station, review your observations of effort and group cooperation and reinforce that there were some aspects of each station that were more difficult than others.

CONCRETE-LEVEL MATH LESSON PLAN
NUMBER AND NUMBER SENSE: LESSON 1

PHASE 1: Initial Acquisition of Skill

✏️ Teach Skill within Authentic Context

Description: A problem context of going shopping for sales

🏠 Build Meaningful Student Connections

Purpose: To help students make meaningful connections between what they have experienced with fractions, decimals, and percents in relation to bargain shopping.

Learning objective: Use concrete objects to solve problems using comparisons of fractions, decimals, and percents with 90% accuracy.

Materials: Rectangular shapes, dollar bills

Description:

1. Link to students' previous knowledge of fractions, decimals, and percents. Review the necklace problem:

   "You go to the mall to buy a necklace that originally was $10. You see the necklace on sale at three different stores. You want to buy the necklace at the cheapest price. From which store will you buy it?"

   a. At JC Penny, the necklace is 2/5 off the original price.
   b. At Belk, the necklace is $3.00 off the original price.
   c. At Sears, the necklace is 20% off the original price.

   Have the students identify the fraction, the percent and/or the decimal in each number sentence of the problem.

2. Identify the skill that students will learn.

   "Today we will be learning to compare fractions, decimal values, and percents.

3. Provide rationale/meaning for learning this skill:

   "Like in the shopping problem, there are times when you will be presented with all three forms of representation (fraction, decimal, and percents) and will have to compare to determine value."

🖼️ Provide Explicit Teacher Modeling

Purpose: To provide students a clear teacher model of how to compare fractions, decimals, and percents using concrete materials.

Learning objective: Use concrete objects to compare fractions, decimals, and percents.

Steps for learning objective:

1. Identify equal parts of the whole.

2. Identify fractional, decimal, and percentage representations.

3. Compare representations (fractions, decimals, and percents).

Materials: Rectangle shapes (see below)

Description: Show 20% of $10 using a rectangular model, such as a rectangle cut from card stock. It will be important to connect back to the definition of percent (i.e., per 100). The rectangle represents 100%, or the total $10. Work with the students to find ways to split the 100% or $10 into even amounts. The following is an example:

"Look at the rectangular model. Your goal is to try splitting the rectangle into 10 equal parts because 10 × 10 = 100." [Students may initially want to split the 100% into 100 parts. Validate this as a possible way to split the rectangle, but encourage them to look for bigger chunks to use and ask them to think of the ways to factor 100. Let them generate all of these factors and then refer back to the initial problem: "You are looking for 20%." Ask them to consider this information in selecting how to split up the rectangle.]

Guide the students' understandings by asking 1) what each part would equal in terms of percent (100% divided into 10 equal parts means each part is worth 10%), and 2) what each part would equal in terms of dollars ($10 divided into 10 equal parts means each part is worth $1).

Finally, summarize the model, emphasizing that each part would be worth 10% and is also worth $1. We are looking for 20% of the 100%, or $10. Two parts would be worth 20%, or $2. (See figure.)

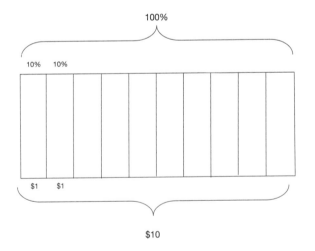

After describing and modeling this procedure, use this same model to help students compare 2/5 of $10 with 20% of $10. Have students refer back to the symbol 2/5 and ask students what each number in the fraction means.

"What does the bottom number, or denominator, tell you (how many equal pieces the whole is split into)? What does the top number, or numerator, tell you (how many pieces you are interested in)? So, 2/5 means that our whole is split into five equal parts."

Start with another rectangle and have students attempt to split the rectangle into five equal parts (use a pencil). Ask students what the whole rectangle represents ($10, 100%, 5/5)? How much is each part worth in terms of dollars ($10 divided into five equal groups is $2)? How much is each part worth in terms of fractions (1 whole divided into 5 equal parts means that each part is ⅕)? If you are interested in 2 of these parts, then you have $4, and each part is ⅕).

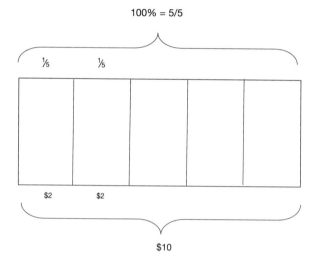

Write sets of three fractions, decimals, and percents on the overhead projector. Each representation will be used at least once in each set to order the values. Use manipulatives to model these sets. Compare these values before putting them in order. Use think-alouds to put each number within the set to order from least to greatest. Have three sets of values represented with concrete materials set up in advance, and determine whether the sets are in the right order. If not, then you will have to decide how to re-order them using think-alouds so that they are ordered from least to greatest. If they are in the correct order, then you will have to use think-alouds to give the reasoning for how you knew that they were ordered correctly. By doing so, you model examples and nonexamples of correctly ordering fractions, decimals, and percents.

Scaffold Instruction

Purpose: To provide students an opportunity to build their initial understanding of fractions, decimals, and percents

Materials:

Teacher: Rectangular model

Students: Rectangular representation pieces

Description: Scaffold using a high level of teacher direction/support. Show examples and have students model the representations using their materials to compare values. Fractions, decimals, and percents will be written on the board. Students will have to pick two values (not the same representations) and will have to model those values, using the materials, to you and/or and their peers to explain which is larger and explain their reasoning.

PHASE 2: Practice Strategies

☺ Receptive/Recognition Level

Purpose: To provide students with multiple practice opportunities to recognize and compare relationships between values in fractions, decimals, and percents.

Activity: Bingo

Materials: 3 × 3 bingo card with free space in the middle, overhead rectangualar models

Description: Students will fill in the nine spaces on their bingo card using three > (greater than) signs, three < (less than) signs, and three = (equals) signs. For example, a student's card could look like the following:

=	<	>
<	>	=
>	=	<

Show two models chosen from fractions, decimals, or percents. The students will have to fill in the correct space on their bingo card. The following is an example:

2/4 = 50%	<	>
<	.80 > 1/4	=
>	=	1/3 < 60%

✎ Expressive Level

Purpose: To provide students with multiple practice opportunities to make and compare given values of fractions, decimals and percents.

Activity: Show ME!

Materials: Rectangular model for each group of students, overhead models, deck of cards with fractions, percents or decimals, spinner or dice, timer

Description: Organize students as partners or in small groups. Pull two cards from the deck. Students will be given 4 minutes to use their rectangular models to show the two numbers on the cards. When time is called, spin or throw the dice to determine which group gets to come up and use the overhead models to SHOW the solution. If the team is correct, they get 2 points, if incorrect, spin again and give another team a chance to show their solution. If they are correct, they get 1 point. Continue the game until a team reaches 10 points.

PHASE 3: Evaluation

Continuously Monitor and Chart Student Performance

Materials: Rectangular models; paper for students to write responses

Description: Give students a mix of problems. For example, for some problems, students will have to convert between fractions, decimals, and percents. For other problems, students will have to compare and determine the greater value. Students must complete this activity with at least 90% accuracy.

Assessment: Flexible Math Interview

Description: For students who seem to have trouble with demonstrating their understanding, conduct individual flexible math interviews.

Phase 4: Maintenance

Purpose: To provide periodic review of the skill after students have mastered it.

Problem of the Day:

Miss Bailey and Mr. Stewart both have 20 students in their classrooms. Miss Bailey's class is 50% girls. Mr. Stewart's class is ¾ girls. How many girls are in each class, and which class has the most girls? Explain your reasoning.

(The problem will change daily but will provide the same type of practice in converting fractions, decimals, and percents and representing and comparing those values.)

Materials: Student cut-out manipulatives that represent the classes of 20 students, if needed

Description: Students will be given problems such as the one described here at the beginning of class. All students should complete the problem during independent work times throughout the day. Review the solutions at the end of the day.

Learning centers: Students will be given problems such as the shopping problem and will work in pairs at the centers to complete given problems using manipulatives to represent and compare fractions, decimals, and percents.

Algebraic Functions

(Positive and Negative Integers)

CRA ASSESSMENT

The following chart and accompanying outline describes how to conduct a CRA assessment. Notice that the chart allows assessment of students at all three levels of mathematical understanding (concrete, representational, and abstract) and provides tasks at both the receptive and the expressive levels.

Authentic context: Measuring heights/distances and comparing them

Standard: Solve one-step linear equations and inequalities in one variable with strategies that involve inverse operations and integers, using concrete materials, pictorial representations, and paper and pencil

Big ideas: The inverse operation for addition is subtraction, and the inverse operation for multiplication is division. A one-step equation is defined as an equation that requires the use of one operation to solve.

Key problem: Measuring and comparing heights and distances. For example: A mole is trying to crawl out of its burrow that is 12 inches below ground. The mole crawls up 6 inches and then slides down 2 inches. What integer represents the mole's location in relation to the surface?

Target objective: Solve 10/10 problems with adding and subtracting positive and negative integers.

Lesson Outline for Using the CRA Assessment

Introduce the Assessment   Open the lesson by explaining to the students that they will be working at centers and that the activities they are going to do will help guide their learning about negative integers. It is important to emphasize that you expect that the students will know how to do some

Sample CRA Chart

	Concrete	Representational	Abstract
Receptive			
Task 1	Students will look at integers mat with red and blue counter pieces on it. Students will circle on a worksheet which integers are represented.	Students will be given a number line that has integers shown on it. Students will match the integers on the worksheet to the timeline representations.	Students will examine a problem worked out by two different "students" and determine which student worked out the problem correctly.
Task 2	n/a	Students will look at a thermometer and match the temperatures shown with given integers.	Circle the equations where x = –2.
Expressive			
Task 1	Students will use pretend dollars to think about money and purchasing a desired CD. Students will have to determine whether they have enough money to buy a CD.	Students will represent on number line how to solve a problem using subtraction of integers.	Students will answer a word problem using subtraction of integers in linear equations.
Task 2	Student will use two different-colored counters and an integer mat to demonstrate subtraction of two integers.	Students will label different temperatures on a thermometer.	n/a

of the tasks but not all of them. Then go around and model every task at each table. The following are examples:

Abstract   "At this center, I want you to look at how two students solved this problem and circle the answer that is correct. For the second task in this problem, I am telling you what x equals. Look at the equations given and circle as many problems as you see in which x = –2. For the third task, look at/solve the problems."

Representational   "For the first task, look at this worksheet. Each item has 3 number lines. You need to choose which number line shows the integer(s). For the next task, match the temperatures with those shown on the thermometer. For the third task, look at the equation that I have given you and solve it using the number line. Be sure to show where the value of x might fall on the number line. For the last activity at this center, use the thermometer to show different temperatures.

Concrete   "For the first task, look at each set of counting pieces and choose which integer is shown by the counters. Remember that red pieces will always represent negative integers and that the blue ones will always be positive. Let's repeat that together. For the second activity of this center, we will see an envelope of money and a CD case with a price on it. Choose the envelope with your name and determine whether or not you have enough money to buy the CD, and if you don't, how much you are short. Write your answers in the blanks on the outside of the envelope. Finally, show how you would use the counting pieces to solve these five problems. Make sure you raise your hand so I can come see your work before you leave this station."

Maintenance Activity   Challenge students to create their own problems that address subtracting integers in linear equations. These problems can then be reviewed and, if needed, edited to be used for Problems of the Day.

Closure   For closure, have students fill out a survey about which centers they liked best and why and which centers gave them difficulty. Then use these surveys as well as students' answers to determine the students' level of understanding and how they like to learn.

Dynamic Math Assessment Center Activities: Directions for Setting Up Centers

Concrete Center

Activity 1 Receptive
Objective: Students will look at an integer mat with varied numbers of red and blue counter pieces on it and determine whether the solution of the chips would be negative or positive.
   Materials: Integer mat, red and blue counter pieces, paper, pencil/eraser
   Instructions: Students will examine blue and red counter pieces on an integer mat. Red counters will represent negative integers and blue counters will represent positive integers. If there were 6 red pieces and 5 blue pieces, then the answer would be = –1. Students would write this on a piece of paper with their name on it.

Activity 1 Expressive
Objective: Students will use pretend dollar bills to think about money and purchasing a desired CD. Students will have to determine whether they have enough money to buy a CD using subtraction of integers in a linear equation (expressive).
   Materials: Pretend dollar bills, a CD case, envelopes and pencil/eraser
   Instructions: Give students dollar bills in envelopes to represent allowance, and tell them they will have to give a portion to the store when they go to buy a new CD. The following is an example of a problem:

Charlie wants to get a CD that costs $13, and he gets an allowance of $10 a week. Will Charlie be able to buy the CD with 1 week's worth of allowance? If not, then how many more dollars will he need? Represent (expressive) this problem using dollar bills, and write your answer on the back of the envelope.

Activity 2
Objective: Students will use two different-colored counters and an integer mat to demonstrate subtraction of two integers (expressive).

Materials: Integer mat, red and blue counter pieces

Instructions: Give students a problem to solve using counters. Again, red counters will represent negative integers and blue ones will represent positive integers. Students will evaluate an equation; for example: –9 + 6 = x. For this example, a student would put 9 red counters and 6 blue counters on the mat. Then, students would remove 1 red counter for every blue counter until they could not match any more sets. The answer would be the number of counters left on the mat, and it would be negative because there would still be 3 red counters for this example.

Representational Center

Activity 1 Receptive
Objective: Students will represent (expressive) on a number line how to solve a problem using subtraction of integers.

Materials: A worksheet with three number lines clearly displayed for each item, pencil/eraser

Instructions: Students will look at a problem written down on a piece of paper, for example –4 – 5. Students will indicate which number line shows the problem.

Activity 2 Receptive
Objective: Students will examine varying temperatures using a thermometer already labeled, and students will determine differences between varying temperatures

Materials: Labeled thermometer, pencil/paper

Instructions: Students will look at the different temperatures labeled on the thermometer and match them with the given integers.

Activity 1 Expressive
Objective: Students will use the number line to solve integer equations.

Material: Laminated number lines, markers, problem sheet

Instructions: Students will look at a problem written down on a piece of paper, for example –4 – 5. Students will solve the problem using the number line. For instance, the student might begin at (–4) and then draw a line from the starting point to the ending point once the student subtracts 5 more on the number line. The answer should be circled clearly.

Activity 2 Expressive
Objective: Students will use a thermometer to label different temperatures.

Materials: Thermometer answer sheet, problem sheet

Instructions: Students will be given a problem sheet with five to seven problems regarding temperature changes. They will use the thermometer answer sheet to solve the problem.

Abstract Center

Activity 1 Receptive
Objective: Students will examine a problem worked out by two different students and determine which student worked out the problem correctly
(receptive).

Materials: A piece of paper with a problem worked out two different ways,
pencil/eraser

Instructions: The text on the sheet of paper would look something like
this:

Brad	Anna
$-16 - (-19) =$	$-16 - (-19) =$
$-16 + (-19) =$	$-16 + 19 =$
-35	3

Instruct students to circle the correct answer. Each student at one table
would have a different problem, but it would be a problem that was set up in
the same manner.

Activity 1 Expressive
Objective: Students will answer word problems using subtraction of integers in linear equations (expressive).

Materials: Paper and pencil/eraser

Instructions: Students will be given problems such as the following:

Henry drives a tractor through his field to plow the soil. He drives 55 yards in
one direction and then turns around and plows 47 yards back toward where
he started. How many yards away is Henry from the point where he originally
started plowing?

CONCRETE-LEVEL MATH LESSON PLAN: POSITIVE AND NEGATIVE INTEGERS

PHASE 1: Initial Acquisition of Skill

✎ Teach Skill within Authentic Context

Description: A problem context of comparing the heights of students in the class.

⌂ Build Meaningful Student Connections

Purpose: To help students make meaningful connections between what they have experienced with measuring their height to what they are studying in math class.

Materials: A couple of height measurement posters taped to the wall, pencils/erasers, paper

Description: A problem context of working with student heights and measurement and how it relates to solving equations with negative and positive integers.

1. Link to students' previous knowledge. We previously looked at fractions, parts of whole numbers, in the past few weeks. Today we are going to start looking at whole numbers that are both greater than and less than zero. We are going to study some skills that are necessary to understand as you move on to learn about algebra.

2. Identify the skill that students will learn.

    "To start this unit, you will consider how the practical example of thinking about your height can be compared with the heights of your classmates. We are going to use this measuring device that I have here on the wall, and you are going to measure your heights to the closest inch. You will compare your height with that of at least two of your classmates: somebody who is taller than you and somebody who is shorter than you. When we compare heights we are going to be using positive and negative integers.

3. Provide rationale/meaning for measuring heights. "Using positive and negative numbers helps us to show differences in quantities like temperatures, distances or heights."

🖼 Provide Explicit Teacher Modeling

Purpose: To provide students a clear teacher model of how to understand the addition and subtraction of integers using concrete materials.

Learning objective: Use concrete objects to solve problems with positive and negative integers.

*   Each student will measure his or her own height.

*   Students will see at least one student in the class who is shorter and one who is taller and ask them for their height.

- Each student will have a piece of paper on which they record their height and the heights of the two classmates.

- Students will write out two equations to determine the difference between their height and that of their classmate (e.g., 55 inches − x = 50 inches; 55 inches + x = 62 inches).

- Students will represent a number as negative when the student with whom they are comparing their height is shorter (x inches shorter) and as positive when the student is taller (x inches taller).

Materials: Connecting blocks, laminated number lines, number lines/overhead number line sheet, measuring tape

Description:

"We have measured our heights and compared them with those of our classmates. Now we are going to examine some other practical implications for learning about adding and subtracting integers with algebraic equations. Looking here at the overhead, I have these two sets of 1-inch connecting blocks. By looking at both sets, you can see that one set has more blocks than the other set. We can represent this algebraically by looking at how one set relates to the other set. The first set has 5 blocks, and the second one has 3 blocks, so you can write 5 − x = 3 and solve for x. If you are comparing the set of 5 blocks with the set of 3 blocks, then you would say that the set of 3 blocks has 2 blocks fewer than the set of 5, therefore representing a negative number relationship. To make this more clear, let's look at a number line."

Show the relationships of different numbers both negative and positive on a number line and ask for student input.

Scaffold Instruction

Purpose: To provide students with an opportunity to build their initial understanding of negative and positive integers and beginning algebra.

Materials:

Teacher: Overhead number lines and markers, connecting blocks

Students: Height-measuring charts, connecting blocks, laminated number line sheets with overhead markers

Description:

1. *Scaffold using a high level of teacher direction/support.* Students will display on notebook paper the equations that they have created to demonstrate the relation of heights between them and their classmates. They also will use the blocks to represent algebraic equations and write the algebraic equation on their paper. Students will use laminated charts to chart points and write an equation to define the relationship between two points.

2. *Scaffold using a medium level of teacher direction/support.* Students will pick a card that will tell them how many blocks to fit together in each set for the problem that they will write out. They also will pick a card to show them which points to plot on the number line for which they will develop an appropriate equation.

3. *Scaffold using a low level of teacher direction/support.* Have each student
    pick an additional card to represent a height relationship that they will
    have to chart and write out on paper, a block problem, and a number line
    problem. Students who complete the task will help other students to com-
    plete the task. Some students will display their results for the class to see
    on the board or overhead.

PHASE 2: Practice Strategies

Receptive/Recognition Level

Purpose: To provide students multiple practice opportunities to use negative and positive integers and simple algebraic problems.

Learning objective: Use concrete objects to represent simple algebraic
equations and negative and positive integers.

Activity: Integer Bingo

Materials: Bingo sheets, list of positive and negative integers to fill in
bingo sheets, red and blue overhead integer blocks.

Description: Give the students the bingo sheets and a series of answers
(positive and negative integers) to fill in the boxes on their bingo sheets. Using
the overhead and red and blue overhead counters, display addition and subtraction problems on the overhead. Students need to find the correct answer on
their bingo sheet. Have students come up and show solutions to the problems
once BINGO has been called.

Expressive Level

Purpose: To provide students multiple practice opportunities to use negative and positive integers and simple algebraic equations.

Learning objective: Use concrete objects to represent simple algebraic
equations and negative and positive integers.

Activity: Integer Jeopardy

Materials: Jeopardy board with questions on cards, individual paper and
pencils/erasers for all students

Description: Students will express the answers to questions involving integers, number lines, connecting blocks, and word problems in the form of a
Jeopardy game.

PHASE 3: Evaluation

Continuously Monitor and Chart Student Performance

Purpose: To provide you with continuous data for evaluating student
learning and whether your instruction is effective. It also provides students
with a way to visualize their learning/progress.

Materials: Measuring tape, pencils/erasers, paper

Description: Students will answer questions using a measuring tape. Each
student will be given a card listing two measurements that the student will

need to identify for a peer. Students will use these measurements to create an algebraic equation to solve.

PHASE 4: Maintenance

Purpose: To provide periodic student practice activities and teacher-directed review of the skill after students have mastered it.

Problem of the Day

Sally and Bob are running a race. Sally got a 5-mile head start, so she is 5 miles in front of Bob. After 1 hour, Sally has run 3 additional miles and Bob has run 4 miles. Where is Bob in relation to Sally in the race?

Using a Velcro number line on a laminated piece of paper along with a race track/number line and two different colors (one for Bob and one for Sally), indicate their starting and ending points on the number line. Velcro pictures of Sally and Bob to their end point, and use the marker to show the progress from their starting points. Then, write an equation to represent where Bob is in relation to Sally in the race (use a negative number if he is behind her and a positive number if he is in front of her).

Materials: Velcro/laminated number line, two different-colored markers, paper, eraser, pencil

Description: Students will work in small groups to accomplish this activity (pick pairings strategically, and monitor individual participation). Each group will get a laminated Velcro racetrack to accompany the example. These materials can be used many times for similar activities related to understanding the number line. Students will place Sally and Bob on the number line at their ending point and use markers to draw their journey. The students will look at the products of other groups once they are complete to make sure that they and their classmates are correct.

Home–School Connection
Students will measure at least three family members' or neighbors' heights and show how they compare with their own height.

REPRESENTATIONAL LEVEL MATH LESSON PLAN: ONE-STEP LINEAR EQUATIONS (POSITIVE AND NEGATIVE INTEGERS)

Standards   The student will

1. Solve one-step linear equations and inequalities in one variable with strategies involving inverse operations and integers, using concrete materials, pictorial representations, and paper and pencil.

2. Solve practical problems that require the solution of a one-step linear equation.

Lesson Objectives

1. Students will identify where positive and negative numbers are located on a number line with 90% accuracy.

2. Students will identify a given number on a number line 3/3 times.

3. Students will identify which number of two negative numbers on a number line is larger with 85% accuracy.

4. Some students will define and identify the absolute value of a set of numbers with 90% accuracy.

PHASE 1: Initial Acquisition of Skill

Teach Skill within Authentic Context

Build Meaningful Student Connections

Purpose: To help students make meaningful connections between what they have experienced and what they are studying.

Materials: Giant Velcro number line in the shape of a thermometer, wipe boards and markers, smaller thermometer, number lines for students, pencils, worksheets

Description: A problem-solving context of working with temperatures to determine how different temperatures affect the ecosystem

1. Link to previous learning.

   Review concrete lessons that were done in the previous class periods.

   Some of our previous lessons included measuring each other's height to show positive and negative integers, using blocks to show simple algebraic equations, Integer Bingo, and Integer Jeopardy.

   Recently, all of us discussed the idea of *inverse* and some of us discussed the idea of absolute value.

2. Identify learning objectives. Today we are going to look at number lines to determine where numbers are located, which numbers are larger than others and how we find that out, and where the inverses of numbers are located. Some of us also are going to discuss absolute value on the number line. We are going to use thermometer number lines to help us determine which temperatures are colder and hotter and use that information in our study of ecosystems.

3. Provide meaning for learning skill. All of these activities are helping us better understand number lines and how they can be useful to us when solving math problems. They will also help us in our science projects.

Describe/model and check for understanding:

- Ask students to show where on the large number line the positive and negative numbers are located.

- Tell students that when you see a negative sign in front of the number, you always thinks to yourself, "Look to the left," because that is where the negative numbers are located.

- Turn the number line vertically so that the negative numbers are on the bottom. Overlay a thermometer on top of the number line that is turned vertically.

- Tell the students that when you have to think about which number is larger on a number line, you think about a thermometer and how the negative numbers mean that it is colder, or the temperature is less hot. The students can think about it this way, too, remembering that the farther left you go, the less the number is and vice versa.

- The teacher will explain that when he or she sees the word "inverse," he or she thinks of opposite, so the inverse of a number is its opposite.

- The absolute value is the distance a number is from zero, so the teacher should explain to students that positive or negative does not matter, just how far away it is from zero on the number line.

Scaffold Instruction

Purpose: To provide students with an opportunity to build their initial understanding of negative and positive integers at the representational level

Materials: As above

1. *Scaffold using a high level of teacher support:* Have a student give you a positive number. Show how to find it on the large thermometer number line using think alouds. Have students suggest to you how to find the inverse. (e.g., counting back, putting the opposite sign). Use several strategies and show how to find the inverse. Use a measuring tape and measure the distance from each number to zero. Show how the distance is the same, but the value of the number is different. Write negative numbers in blue, positive in red.

2. *Scaffold using a medium level of teacher support:* Student groups will choose a number and teach you, the teacher, how to find the number and its inverse. Classmates will help guide you as needed.

3. *Scaffold using a low level of teacher support:* Ask student volunteers to pick a number card from a grab bag and, working in pairs, to circle the number and its inverse on their thermometer number lines, using red for positive numbers and blue for negative numbers.

PHASE 2: Practice Strategies

Receptive/Recognition Level

Purpose: To provide students with multiple practice opportunities to recognize positive and negative numbers

Tic-Tac-Toe Game

Materials: White boards, blue and red markers, classroom number line
Description: Have students fill in their Tic-Tac-Toe boards by looking at the numbers you show on the number line. They will mark their boards with blue for negative numbers and red for positive

Expressive Level

Purpose: To provide students multiple practice opportunities to show positive and negative numbers and absolute values

Fly Swatter Game

Materials: 1 fly swatter for each team, large number cards (positive and negative), 2 classroom-size number lines posted on board.
Description: Students will work in teams. A member from each team will be in front of one of the number lines on the board. When a number card is shown, the team member must swat the INVERSE of the number. First correct swat gets 2 points. The team with the most points is the winner.

PHASE 3: Evaluation

Continuously Monitor and Chart Student Performance

Purpose: To provide you with continuous data for evaluating student learning and the effectiveness of your instruction. It also provides students with a way to visualize their learning.
Materials: Thermometers and problem worksheets.
Description: All students will be given a 10-problem worksheet with number lines and asked to identify positive and negative numbers, to order numbers, and to identify which given negative numbers are larger and which are smaller.

Some students will also be asked to write the absolute value for each answer.

Students will track the number of correct versus incorrect responses.

PHASE 4: Maintenance

Purpose: To provide periodic student practice activities and teacher-directed review of the skill.

Using Math

Description: As students work with the ecosystems, they will have to determine the following information for each ecosystem:

Average daily temperature
Average elevation
Average vegetation height
Average rainfall

In groups, students will compare and contrast their assigned ecosystems and develop 5 word problems using positive and negative integers and absolute value.

Home–school connection:

Students will watch the Weather Channel and chart highs and lows for five key places in the United States over 5 days.

Individual accommodations:

Some students will be given temperature number lines while doing problems.

Some students will be asked to develop word problem

Index

Page numbers followed by "*f*" indicate figures; those followed by "*t*" indicate tables.